Baseball Anecdotes

BASEBALL ANECDOTES

Daniel Okrent
and
Steve Wulf

PERENNIAL LIBRARY

Harper & Row, Publishers, New York
Grand Rapids, Philadelphia, St. Louis, San Francisco
London, Singapore, Sydney, Tokyo, Toronto

Baseball Anecdotes is available on audiocassette from Harper Audio, a division of Harper & Row, Publishers, Inc.

This book was originally published in hardcover in 1989 by Oxford University Press. It is here reprinted by permission of Oxford University Press.

First PERENNIAL LIBRARY edition published 1990.

Library of Congress Cataloging-in-Publication Data

Okrent, Daniel, 1948–
     Baseball anecdotes / Daniel Okrent and Steve Wulf.—First PERENNIAL
LIBRARY edition.
     p. cm.
     Reprint. Originally published: New York : Oxford University Press, 1989.
     ISBN 0-06-097299-8 (pbk.)
     1. Baseball—United States—Anecdotes. I. Wulf, Steve.   II. Title.
     [GV873.O57 1990]   89-45793
     796.357'0973—dc20

90 91 92 93 94 FG 10 9 8 7 6 5 4 3 2 1

*For Gizella Adler Okrent
and Lydia Adler Okrent
D.O.*

*For Bambi and Bo
S.W.*

*The whole history of baseball
has the quality of mythology.*
BERNARD MALAMUD

PREFACE

A baseball reporter once asked a coach of long and varied experience what were his fondest memories of a lifetime in the game. The coach was removing his uniform after a spring training workout, an aging man whose shrunken chest and loose-fitting skin made him seem—to anyone but an experienced denizen of baseball clubhouses—incredibly out-of-place in that world of speed and muscle and skill. Yet at the same time the entire history of baseball seemed to reside in the gray stubble on his face, the wrinkles in his neck, the dry flesh on his arms and legs.

"Which stories do you want?" he asked the reporter. "The true ones or the other ones?"

If the Bernard Malamud statement that we have chosen for the epigraph to this book is right—and we think it is—preparing a volume of baseball anecdotage is both an easy task and a hard one. It's easy because myth tells us what we wish to know; in a way, it's less important that Babe Ruth called his shot in Wrigley Field in 1932 than it is that millions believe he did. But because baseball's historical substance is made of the bricks of thousands upon thousands of anecdotes, selecting among them provokes responsibility: the very act of repeating a tale is part of the mythifying process.

Consequently, we have tried to be responsible about this; some stories included here may not be precisely true in all respects, but we have in every obvious case attempted to indicate what is reliably so and what is likely an embroidering on reality.

We have also sought to be careful in choosing whom to trust. As in any other field, historical sources are of varying degrees of reliability; in baseball, if a story is told in the work of Lee Allen, say, or Robert Creamer, one can bank on its accuracy, while if it originates with certain other writers one would do

as well to claim that Abner Doubleday really did invent baseball.

But if you don't show a willingness to hear at least *something* in the obvious tall-tale, you're missing out on the game's
very music. A version of what might remain (for the anec-
dotally tone-deaf) could have been encountered in a small
lunchroom in Bradenton, Florida, in the early 1980s. An ancient Edd Roush, the great National League outfielder of the
1920s, had visited the Pirates' spring training camp and found
himself surrounded by a clutch of scouts, functionaries, and
writers, all of them eager to hear what the old man remembered. Names of the greatest and most colorful players of
baseball's golden age were tossed out, and Roush would comment briefly on each. He was a taciturn man, but he was, as
Wilfrid Sheed once described Connie Mack, "a tree with initials on it from the Garden of Eden." Everyone listened, and
eventually someone asked Roush about Babe Ruth.

Roush nodded sagely. "Babe Ruth," he repeated. Every upper body leaned forward. "I knew Ruth." Every ear opened
wide. "Left-handed hitter," Roush said, as if he were impart-
ing the secret of the Pyramids. "Hit a lot of home runs. Used
to be a pitcher."

In researching this book, the writers have depended upon
countless clubhouse raconteurs more forthcoming than Roush
who have told us stories from their own experience, and upon
countless writers who have written down the words of other
tale-tellers. Tom Heitz and his staff at the National Baseball
Library in Cooperstown, New York, helped lead us through
the library's remarkable collection of oral and written history.
Sheldon Meyer of Oxford University Press displayed oceanic
patience. Both Sheldon and his associate, Leona Capeless,
helped us turn an utterly unruly stew of material into a somewhat ruly stew. Our wives and our children were preposterously tolerant as we squeezed hours and days away from our
familial responsibilities, and our colleagues at *New England
Monthly* and *Sports Illustrated* abided any number of bleary-
eyed mornings following anecdote-bedeviled nights. We are
grateful to them all.

October 1988   D.O., Worthington, Massachusetts
                                S.W., New York City

CONTENTS

ONE

THE BOOK OF GENESIS: FROM CARTWRIGHT'S CODE
TO DELAHANTY'S DEATH

◇1◇

TWO

THE EARLY MODERNS: FROM THE FOUNDING
OF THE AMERICAN LEAGUE TO THE CORRUPTION
OF THE BLACK SOX

◇39◇

THREE

THE YEARS OF BABE RUTH: FROM BABE'S RISE
TO DIMAGGIO'S STREAK

◇81◇

INTERLUDE:

WARTIME

◇163◇

FOUR

THE RETURN TO GLORY: FROM THE ARRIVAL
OF JACKIE ROBINSON TO CASEY STENGEL'S
LAST HURRAH

◇177◇

FIVE
MODERN TIMES: FROM GIBBY AND YAZ TO THE GROUNDER THAT ATE BILL BUCKNER

INDEX

Baseball Anecdotes

```
┌─────────┬──┬──┬──┬──┬──┬──┬──┬──┬──┬──┐
│  PART   │  │  │  │  │  │  │  │  │  │  │
├─────────┼──┼──┼──┼──┼──┼──┼──┼──┼──┼──┤
│   1     │  │  │  │  │  │  │  │  │  │  │
└─────────┴──┴──┴──┴──┴──┴──┴──┴──┴──┴──┘
```

THE BOOK OF GENESIS

From Cartwright's Code
to Delahanty's Death

ABNER DOUBLEDAY

This first story was passed down as the gospel truth by sports-caster Bill Stern, and though it has absolutely no basis in fact, it is irresistible:

Abraham Lincoln is lying near death following the shooting at Ford's Theatre. With his closest advisers gathered around him, he calls over Major General Abner Doubleday. "Abner," whispers Lincoln, "don't . . . let . . . baseball . . . die." And with those final words, Lincoln goes down swinging.

As writer Art Hill had it, if that story is true, Doubleday probably would have replied, "What's baseball?" For Double-day is not the man who invented baseball, but rather the man whom baseball invented. He was a remarkable man, to be sure, a West Point graduate who sighted the first gun fired at Fort Sumter. He died in 1893 before anyone got around to asking him if he was, indeed, the inventor of baseball. He certainly made no such claim.

The myth about his youthful inventiveness in Cooperstown, New York, wasn't actually concocted until 1907, when Albert Goodwill Spalding formed a commission to discover the game's true origins. The basis for the group's finding was, in the words of the official report, a circumstantial statement by a "reputable gentleman." The reputable gentleman, an octogenarian mining engineer from Denver named Abner Graves, said that when he was a lad in Cooperstown in 1839, Abner Doubleday once drew a diagram of a diamond for a game of "Town-Ball" in farmer Elihu Phinney's pasture. Commission Chairman Mills, an Otis Elevator executive and Civil War veteran who happened to have served under Doubleday, wrote: "I can well understand how the orderly mind of the embryo West Pointer would devise a scheme for limiting the contestants on each side and allotting them to field positions, each with a certain amount of territory."

Not exactly an iron-clad case, especially given the fact that Doubleday was actually attending West Point at the time he was supposed to be inventing baseball.

As for the true origins of baseball, there are two schools of thought, as there are for the origins of life itself: creation vs. evolution. Many scholars maintain that a bank clerk and volunteer fireman named Alexander Joy Cartwright invented baseball. Spalding himself referred to Henry Chadwick, the game's first great sportswriter, as "the father of baseball." But Chadwick knew the game was derived from cricket and rounders. As early as 1796, Jane Austen mentioned a game of "base ball" in *Northanger Abbey,* and this anonymous poem appeared in *A Little Pretty Pocket-Book* in 1744:

> B is for
> Base-ball
> The ball once struck off
> Away flies the boy
> To the next destined post
> And then home with joy.

ALEXANDER JOY CARTWRIGHT

Cartwright does get an assist. He and his friends used to play a version of Town Ball in a Manhattan field located near what is now 34th Street and Lexington Avenue. The story goes that one day Cartwright showed up with a diagram of a diamond, plotting the bases 42 paces (90 feet) apart. He was also credited with making the game nine innings and limiting the number of players to nine a side, but those claims are a little more dubious. Cartwright was certainly the prime mover in organizing his friends into the Knickerbocker Base Ball Club, which officially came into being on September 23, 1845. Their first official game, not played until the following summer—June 19, 1846, to be exact—took place across the Hudson River in New Jersey at the Elysian Fields in Hoboken. Against a team called the New York Nine, the Knickerbockers went down to a resounding 23-1 defeat, but there is some cause to believe that the Knickerbockers lost on purpose to encourage the other team to actively pursue this new sport. For one thing, Cartwright, one of their best players, only served as the umpire.

But even in that capacity, Cartwright, was a pioneer. During the game, he fined a player named James Whyte Davis half a york shilling for swearing.

In 1849 Cartwright, who looked like Father Christmas, headed west in search of gold. He was a sort of Johnny Appleseed, teaching baseball along the way to settlers and Indians alike. He didn't find gold, though, and decided to seek his fortune in China. This son of a sea captain got seasick on the first leg of his voyage and so settled in Hawaii, where he became a respected merchant and eventually a friend of the Royal Family. In 1892, Cartwright died a rich man, revered by Hawaiians but forgotten by baseball. The oversight was partially atoned for in 1939, one hundred years after Doubleday supposedly invented baseball, when Babe Ruth placed flower leis on Cartwright's grave in Nuannu Cemetery.

HENRY CHADWICK

If not exactly the birthplace of baseball, the Elysian Fields in Hoboken may be thought of as the nursery. While covering a cricket match there for the *Long Island Star* in 1856, Henry Chadwick became enthralled with a baseball game he saw on the outskirts of a cricket field. He soon became the game's foremost authority, writing the first rule book. In 1859, for a game between the Stars and Excelsiors in South Brooklyn, he introduced the first box score. For the next forty-five years, he wrote for the *Brooklyn Eagle,* championing and safeguarding his sport. He was inducted into the Hall of Fame in its first year.

Chadwick was a bit of a stiff, though. He woke up every morning at five, took a cold dip, ate a light breakfast, and began to write. Active into his eighties, Chadwick was a great advocate of Turkish baths. Typical of his lectures was this excerpt from his column in an 1887 issue of *Sporting Life:* "If this season teaches anything . . . it is the utter folly of expecting good play and thorough teamwork out of a party of players, the majority of whom take no care of themselves in keeping their bodies in a healthy condition for the exacting work of the diamond field. To suppose that a man can play ball properly who guzzles beer daily, or indulges in spiritous liquors, or who sets up nightly gambling or does worse by still more enervating habits at brothels is nonsense."

THE WRIGHT BROTHERS

Baseball has its own version of the Wright brothers. By the end of the Civil War, baseball's Wrights, Harry and George, sons of a famous British cricketer, could often be found on the Elysian Fields. In 1865, Harry left New York to take a $1,200-a-year job as an instructor at the Union Cricket Club in Cincinnati. The next year he formed the first professional baseball club, the Red Stockings, recruiting for his lineup some of the best players in the land, including his brother George, a shortstop. Here is the roster of the first professional team, together with the players's occupations and salaries:

P	Asa Brainard, insurance	$1,100
C	Doug Allison, marblecutter	800
1B	Charles Gould, bookkeeper	800
2B	Charles Sweasy, hatter	800

SS	George Wright, engraver	1,400
3B	Fred Waterman, insurance	1,000
LF	Andrew Leonard, hatter	800
CF	Harry Wright, jeweler	1,200
RF	Cal McVey, piano maker	800

Harry Wright was a pretty good player: He once hit seven home runs in a game, and as a pitcher he supposedly threw the first changeup. But his true genius was as an organizer and a manager of men. In 1869 he put the Red Stockings on the road, traveling 11,877 miles and drawing some 200,000 spectators. The team would go on to win 91 consecutive games, a string that was frayed only by a tie with a team from Troy, N.Y., and broken in Brooklyn in June of 1870.

Harry also had a flair for promotion. His players would ride out to the field in decorated carriages, singing:

> We are a band of baseball players
> From Cincinnati city.
> We come to toss the ball around
> And sing to you our ditty.
> And if you listen to the song
> We are about to sing,
> We'll tell you all about base ball
> And make the welkin ring.

Harry, borrowing an idea from the theatre, kept a "property bouquet" around, which he would present to any of his players who had performed especially well. The ceremony became so common, however, that his players started turning down his flowers.

Still and all, Harry Wright was much beloved, and as early as 1874, he was being called "the father of the game." He managed every year until 1893, when he retired to become the chief of umpires. He died at the age of sixty in 1895 and was given a huge funeral in Philadelphia. One of the floral arrangements spelled out "Safe At Home."

George Wright was the game's first great shortstop. In 1869 with the Red Stockings, he scored 339 runs in 57 games, with 49 homers and a .629 batting average. He was one of the dominant hitters in the National Association, the first professional league, but his skills began to diminish after the National League came into being in 1876. He managed only one season, in Providence in 1879, and beat his brother Harry's Boston club by five games to win the pennant. He remains the lone major league manager to have won a pennant in his only season.

In the 1890s, George Wright came away from a baseball game sneering, "Imagine, players wearing gloves. We didn't need them in our day." George, however, made a nice living by selling baseball gloves through his early sporting goods conglomerate, Wright & Ditson, until he was ninety. His last contribution to baseball was of a dubious nature, however. He was a member of the Mills Commission which credited Abner Doubleday with the invention of baseball. He should have known better, having trod the same turf as Cartwright. Unfortunately George never attended any of the commission meetings.

RED STOCKINGS VS. BROOKLYN

The game in which the Red Stockings' 91-game undefeated streak ended took place at the Capitoline grounds in Brooklyn against the Atlantics on June 14, 1870. As it turned out, it was baseball's first truly great game. While 12,000 fans tried to squeeze into a park built for 5,000, the Cincinnati club took a 2-0 lead in the first inning, justifying the pre-game odds of 5 to 1. But then a pitchers' duel between Brainard of the Red Stockings and George (The Charmer) Zettlein of the Atlantics developed, and at the end of nine innings the score was tied at 5-5 (a very low total for the era). Brooklyn considered this a moral victory. But, as the crowd spilled out onto the field and the Atlantics hugged each other, Harry Wright and the

Brooklyn captain, Bob Ferguson, called upon Henry Chadwick. "The game should be resumed and continued until one team scores sufficient runs to win the game," the great man intoned.

So the field was cleared of spectators, and the game resumed. The Red Stockings failed to score in the top of the tenth, and the Atlantics might have scored in their half of the inning but for some gamesmanship by George Wright. With runners on first and second and one out, the Atlantics batter hit a soft popup to the shortstop. Wright cupped his hands as if to catch the ball, but let it trickle through his hands to the ground. He then tossed to Waterman at third for the force, and Waterman threw to Sweasy at second for a double play. This trick later gave birth to the infield fly rule; but for the time being, the fans were furious with rage. According to one account, "George was the victim of every name on the rooter's calendar . . . but through the atmospheric blue streaks, his white teeth gleamed and glistened in provoking amiability." Cincinnati scored two runs in the top of the twelfth, and as the sun began to set, so did the hopes of Brooklyn. Fans began to leave to beat the rush.

Then Charlie Smith led off for the Atlantics with a single and went to third on a wild pitch. The next batter, Joe Start, hit a long ball to right field that landed on the fringes of the crowd. When McVey attempted to pick it up, a Brooklyn fan climbed on his back. By the time he threw the fan off his back and returned the ball to the infield, Smith had scored and Start was standing on third.

The next batter was out, and then Ferguson, a right-handed hitter, surprised the Red Stockings by taking a left-handed stance. The captain wanted to avoid hitting the ball toward George Wright, and thus became the first recorded switch-hitter. He ripped the ball through the right side of the infield to tie the score, and the crowd went wild. Bothered by either the crowd or the gathering dusk, first baseman Gould bobbled a grounder, threw wide of second in an attempt to get Ferguson, and watched in despair as the Atlantics captain came all the way around to score. Brooklyn won 8-7, and Cincinnati's 91-game unbeaten streak was over.

The Atlantics had a number of players of note in their lineup against Cincinnati. "Charmer" Zettlein, an ex-sailor who had served under Admiral Farragut, was the hardest thrower of his day. Despite his nickname, Zettlein was not able to talk his way out of a case of mistaken identity during the Chicago Fire of 1871, when a mob took him for a looter and beat him severely. He still went on to win 125 games in the five years of the National Association.

Brooklyn's shortstop was the diminutive, five-foot-three Dickey Pearce. Pearce, for one thing, invented the bunt. For another, he was the first shortstop actually to position himself between second and third; until Pearce came along, shortstops inhabited the shallow outfield.

The second baseman for the Atlantics was Lipman Pike, the first great Jewish ballplayer. Pike, in fact, appeared in his first boxscore in 1858, one week after his Bar Mitzvah. He and his brother Boaz played for the Atlantics after the Civil War, but in 1866 the Philadelphia Athletics offered him $20 a week to play third base. By 1870 he was back with Brooklyn, and he played and managed another seventeen years until he retired from baseball at forty-two to go into the haberdashery business. Pike once ran a race against a standardbred horse named Charlie for $200—and won. The 100-yard race went off on August 27, 1873: The horse was allowed to start 25 yards behind the line, and Pike took off when the horse reached him. They were neck-and-neck for most of the race, and when Pike began to pull away, the horse broke stride and began to gallop. Pike still won by four yards.

Bob Ferguson, the captain of the Atlantics, was known as "Death to Flying Things." He was also death to eardrums. Ferguson was a forceful man who talked incessantly and was given to rages. Sam Crane, a ballplayer in the nineteenth century and a sportswriter in the twentieth, once wrote of Ferguson, "Turmoil was his middle name, and if he wasn't mixed up prominently in a scrap of some kind nearly every day, he would imagine he had not been of any use to the baseball fraternity and the community in general." Various stories have Ferguson fighting off an angry crowd with a bat and, when he was an umpire, using that same implement to break an impudent player's arm.

THE NATIONAL ASSOCIATION

The first professional league was formed on St. Patrick's Day in 1871 in a meeting at Collier's Cafe at 13th Street and Broadway in New York. The official name of the new body was the National Association of Professional Base Ball Players; the teams included the Philadelphia Athletics, the Chicago White Stockings, the Boston Red Stockings, the Washington Olympics, the Troy Haymakers, the New York Mutuals, the Cleveland Forest Citys (who introduced the concept of season tickets), the Rockford (Ill.) Forest Citys, and the unforgettable Fort Wayne Kekiongas. The franchise fee was all of $10, and the money was used to purchase a pennant for the championship club. The NA teams played an irregular schedule of about thirty games, but they produced a pretty good race for the $90 pennant, as the Athletics beat the Red Stockings by a game and a half and the White Stockings by two games.

Among the players that first year were two future stars of the game, Rockford third baseman Adrian (Cap) Anson and Cleveland catcher James (Deacon) White; three future sporting-goods magnates, second baseman Alfred Reach of the Athletics, pitcher Albert Spalding of the Red Stockings, and George Wright; the splendidly named center-fielder of the Athletics, John Phillips Jenkins (Count) Sensendorfer; the first Latin ballplayer, Troy third baseman Esteban (The Cuban Sylph) Bellan; and Chicago second baseman Jimmy Wood, the man who invented spring training when he took the White Stockings down to New Orleans prior to the 1870 season.

The National Association years were the prime of William Arthur Cummings, the 120-pounder pitcher who's in the Hall of Fame on the dubious claim that he was the inventor of the curveball. "Candy" Cummings, who once won 35 games in a season, is said to have gotten the idea for the curve while throwing a clamshell as a youngster in Ware, Mass., then trying to duplicate its arc with a baseball. What Cummings really did invent was a coupling device for railroad cars that paid him a small royalty in his later years.

The National Association has been referred to as "Baseball's Dark Ages," but that seems a little strong in light of the players, such as Anson, and the standards, such as the five-ounce baseball with a circumference of nine inches, that it introduced. Still, gambling on games was rife, and the fixing of them was not unheard of. Many of the players were "lushers," as Spalding called them, and others were "revolvers," men who went from team to team in search of better salaries.

THE BEGINNINGS OF THE NATIONAL LEAGUE

The National Association was succeeded two seasons later by the National League which opened for business on April 22, 1876, with teams in Boston, Philadelphia, Chicago, Cincinnati, Hartford, Louisville, New York, and St. Louis.

One of the new league's first major stars was Deacon White, who still isn't in the Hall of Fame even though he was the first player to log twenty years in the majors, the first catcher to wear a mask and a balloon glove, and a .300 hitter in thirteen of his seasons. He was also the first man to challenge the reserve clause and the first to prove that a thrown ball can actually curve.

According to White, a group of Harvard professors had claimed that the curveball was merely an optical illusion. So after his Boston team won the pennant in 1877, White and his brother Will, an accomplished curveball pitcher, offered to demonstrate the pitch for the professors. They drove three stakes into the ground in a straight line, and as the skeptics watched, Will's pitches went out around the middle stake and curved back to Deacon.

Had White been a betting man, he could have made some money off curveball demonstrations. But he didn't bet, drink, or smoke—hence his nickname. (Deacon was luckier than a Detroit pitcher of similar temperament, Charles Busted Baldwin. He was such a clean liver that his teammates called him Lady.) White did have a singular peculiarity, though. He truly believed that the earth was flat, and he was able to persuade at least one teammate, shortstop Jack Rowe, to his view when he asked Rowe how it was that a fly ball hit straight up into the air could come back into your hands if the earth was moving.

Hartford owner Morgan Bulkeley, who would go on to represent Connecticut in the U.S. Senate, was the first National League president, and he is in the Hall of Fame because of it. But William Hulbert of Chicago, who is not in Cooperstown, was the real power of the league, and after the 1876 season became president. The season had gone reasonably well, although New York and Philadelphia refused to make their last western road trips. In the Association days they could have gotten away with that, but Hulbert organized their expulsion from the league.

His next major problem was a scandal in Louisville in the middle of the 1877 season that presaged the 1919 Black Sox. This one started when Louisville third baseman Bill Hague developed a painful boil in his left armpit. Outfielder George Hall recommended Al Nichols, a former New York Mutual, as a replacement. The Grays, who were in first place at the time, began losing in a suspicious fashion.

As it turned out, Hall was the ringleader and Nichols his willing accomplice. After offering star pitcher Jim Devlin $100 to throw one game, they blackmailed him into further capitulations. When owner Charles Chase got wind of the scheme, he elicited confessions from both Hall and Devlin. He also ordered every member of the team to sign a statement giving him permission to inspect all telegrams sent or received by them. The only player who didn't go along was shortstop Bill Craver, who said to Chase, "You can if you pay me the three months' salary you owe me." Owners being owners, the unimplicated Craver was banned from baseball for life, as were Hall, Nichols, and Devlin. Both Devlin, who was a pitcher of Hall of Fame caliber, and the unfortunate Craver annually petitioned the National League for reinstatement, and were annually denied. Yet both men became decorated policemen, Devlin in Philadelphia and Craver in Troy.

Hulbert brought Troy into the National League. That first season it was a truly awful club, once committing 27 errors in a single game. Left-fielder Thomas Mansell caught only two of every three balls hit to him, and first baseman Aaron Clapp made 25 errors in 36 games, in part because the other players didn't like him and intentionally made him handle bad throws in the dirt.

But manager Bob Ferguson brought in seventeen new players in 1880 and pulled the team up to respectability. Troy, in fact, had five future Hall of Famers play on its team that season: Dan Brouthers (who was released after three games), Mickey Welch, Tim Keefe, Roger Connor, and Buck Ewing. The club also had an odd assortment of characters. One catcher, Fatty Briody, later became a faith healer; another catcher, Joseph Straub, could speak only German; and yet another catcher, Dick Higham, would later turn to umpiring (at least until he was caught fixing a game). In the outfield were John P. Cassidy, a man whose love of ice cream caused one Troy paper to comment, "He covers a lot of ground without moving," and Lewis Pessano Dickerson, nicknamed Buttercup after the character in *H.M.S. Pinafore*. Once while playing in Chicago, Dickerson went chasing after a ball that rolled between the legs of William Hulbert's fierce Newfoundland. Rather than disturb the dog, Buttercup let the batter have his home run.

But probably the most notorious figure on that Troy team was Terry Larkin, one of the saddest characters ever to play major league ball. Although once a pretty fair pitcher, Larkin was in the process of losing both his stuff and his mind by the time he joined Troy. In 1883 he came home drunk one night, shot his wife Maggie in the mouth, shot a policeman in the cheek, and cut his own throat with a razor. While recovering in the hospital, Larkin again attempted suicide by diving head first into a steam register. His wife, who recovered, nursed him back to health, a kindness for which Terry later beat her up. The tormented Larkin finally succeeded in killing himself in 1897.

The first perfect game in National League history belongs to John Lee Richmond, who managed the feat for Worcester against Cleveland on June 12, 1880. What makes his accomplishment even more remarkable is the fact that Richmond achieved it in the middle of his graduation events at Brown University. A left-hander with a curveball, Richmond had shut out Cleveland in Worcester two days before, then returned to Providence and Brown on Friday. He stayed up all night Friday after the class supper, took part in a class baseball game which started at 4:50 a.m. (!), went to bed at 6:30 a.m., and caught the 11:30 a.m. train to Worcester to pitch that afternoon. The train was delayed, so Richmond had to take the field on an empty stomach.

Richmond had two close calls in his 1-0 victory. Cleveland's Bill Phillips hit a ball through the right side of the infield, but the Worcester right-fielder charged the ball and fired to first. It was a close play, but umpire Foghorn Bradley called Phillips out. In the eighth inning, a cloudburst hit, threatening to halt the game, but it lasted only a few minutes, and with a heap of sawdust at his feet, Richmond completed his perfect game.

Just five days later, John Montgomery Ward of Providence pitched a perfect game against Buffalo. But the next wait was a bit longer—there wouldn't be another perfect game in the National League until Jim Bunning of the Phillies threw one against the Mets in 1964.

Before he died at age forty-nine in 1882, William Hulbert provided baseball a lasting legacy: the reserve clause, that section of the standard player's contract which tied him to his club in perpetuity. The clause was first introduced in 1880 (to prevent teams from raiding each other), and each club was allowed to designate five players who were "reserved" and thus inviolate. Hulbert's friend Albert Spalding, who by now owned the White Stockings, immediately snapped up a Cincinnati catcher who had not been protected, Mike Kelly.

KING KELLY

There have been a few larger-than-life characters in baseball, but King Kelly was the first. A catcher, he hit .384 with 12 homers in his best season, in 1884, but numbers could never do justice to his talents. He invented the hit-and-run. He devised a primitive series of signs with pitcher Larry Corcoran, who would move his chew of tobacco from one cheek to another to indicate a fastball or curve. Kelly also started the catcher's practice of backing up first base.

But Kelly's greatest skill was his sliding, which inspired the popular song "Slide, Kelly, Slide." He could do the hook, the fadeaway, and the fallaway so expertly that his admirers said he could box with his feet. After one especially dazzling effort, he was called out by umpire Honest John Kelly. But then King reached under his body, picked out the ball, and asked: "John, if I'm out, what's this?"

Kelly was as cunning as he was skilled. Sometimes when the lone umpire wasn't looking, Kelly would take a short cut home from second base. He would trip up runners with his mask. While playing right field, in one game against Boston, with dusk gathering in the twelfth inning, Kelly leaped high in the air, grabbed the ball with two hands, and ran into the dugout. The game was called because of darkness with the score tied, and when his teammates asked him how deep was the ball hit, Kelly replied, "How the hell should I know? It went a mile over my head."

His most celebrated stunt, though, occurred when Kelly was managing and a foul pop drifted over by the bench, out of reach of his catcher. As the substitution rules were fairly liberal at the time, he yelled out, "Kelly now catching for Murphy" and caught the ball.

Off the field, Kelly was equally outrageous. In his heyday, one newspaper account described "his cane a-twirling as though he were the entire population, his Ascot held by a giant jewel, his patent leather shoes as sharply pointed as Italian dirks." He was sometimes accompanied by a black monkey and a Japanese valet.

Once asked if he drank while playing baseball, Kelly said, "It depends on the length of the game."

In 1887, Albert Spalding sold Kelly to Boston for the unprecedented sum of $10,000. While Chicagoans were crushed—

such personages as Clarence Darrow and Eugene Field wrote irate letters to the city's newspapers—Bostonians giddily gave Kelly a horse and carriage and a house in nearby Hingham. Such was the King's immense popularity that he can claim the dubious distinction of having written America's first sports autobiography.

As Cap Anson wrote in his own autobiography, "Mike Kelly had only one enemy—himself." In 1893, when Kelly's skills were drifting away, John Montgomery Ward brought him to New York to catch for the Giants, but only on the proviso that King take a Turkish bath before every game to purge himself of the night before. When Kelly didn't show up one day, electing instead to go to the race track, Ward fired him.

His career over, Kelly talked of opening a bar in Manhattan along with his friend Honest John Kelly—"The Two Kels," they would call it. But the saloon never materialized, and Kelly devoted himself to performing in burlesque shows, where he would recite the popular poem of the day, "Casey at the Bat."

It was while traveling to Boston for Mike Murphy's Burlesque Corps in the fall of 1894 that Kelly caught a cold that turned to pneumonia. He was taken to the hospital on a stretcher on November 5, and while some claimed he fell off the stretcher, and others said he was dropped while going up the stairs, there was no dispute as to his final words. "This is my last slide," he whispered; three days later he was gone.

THE '80s

In 1882 the National League came up with an idea whose time would never come: color-coded uniforms. While all players wore white pants, ties, and belts, they were assigned different color jerseys according to position. Pitchers wore light blue, catchers scarlet, first basemen scarlet and white, second basemen orange and black, shortstops maroon, third basemen gray and white, left-fielders white, center-fielders red and white, right-fielders gray, and substitutes either green or brown. The players, however, threatened a so-called "prism riot," and the plan was scotched.

Tony Mullane—"the Apollo of the Box," he was called—won 285 games in the majors, but distinguished himself as the most daring player on July 18, 1882, in the brand-new American Association. Pitching for Louisville at Baltimore, Mullane, a natural right-hander, resorted to throwing with his left hand in the fourth inning to combat a string of left-handed hitters. According to the *Baltimore American*, "This was a novelty in pitching and excited much interest. He was not, however, able to keep the left-hand delivery up for any length of time, but it was very effective while it lasted."

With the advent of competition from the American Association, the weaker sisters of the National League—Troy and Worcester—were politely asked to leave the fold after the 1882 season, and the two clubs were reassembled in New York and Philadelphia. As part of the conditions for their withdrawal from the league, Troy and Worcester were granted honorary NL memberships and promised four exhibition games a year with league teams if they could field representative teams. Those promises have never been rescinded, so Troy and Worcester are still technically members of the National League, with the league owing each city 428 exhibition games by 1988.

Although the first night game in major league history wasn't played until 1935, there was night baseball as early as 1880, just one year after Thomas Edison invented the incandescent lamp. It happened at Oceanside Park in Hull, Mass., as part of a demonstration by the Northern Electric Light Company, and the teams represented Boston's two leading department stores, Jordan Marsh and R. H. White. Before 300 spectators, the teams tied 16-16.

Fred Pfeffer of the White Stockings was, according to King Kelly, "the greatest second baseman of them all . . . he could lay on his stomach and throw a hundred yards." Pfeffer, who could speak German fluently and would open the first baseball instructional camp, also was something of a perfectionist, as illustrated by this contemporary account of an evening with

Pfeffer and his parrot, the Dutchman, at his off-season home in Louisville:

"There was a little quartette of young ladies in the Pfeffer parlor last Thursday, with Fred, as usual, the center of attention. 'I have taught the Dutchman a verse, and he says it as feelingly as though he really understood its meaning. Come Dutchy,' and Fred took the bird upon his left hand. 'I shall have to repeat the first few lines of it for him I guess,' added Fred, with which explanation he began:

'The heiress drives out with her carriage and team,
  While the working girl slaves for a penny;
The rich man and his sons wear pants of sealskin,
  While the poor working man has not any.'

" 'Oh! Oh!' cried the girls in a chorus, 'does the parrot say all that?'

" 'Just listen to him,' answered Fred, proudly. 'Come Dutchy. The heiress drives out . . .'

"The bird cocked its head upon one side, and after a squawk or two, began:

" 'The heiress drives out with her carriage and team,
  While the working girl slaves for a penny;
The rich man and his sons wear pants of sealskin,
  While the poor working girl has _____ ' "

Poor Dutchy. The remaining words of the verse died in a gargle in his throat under the pressure of Fred's desperate clutch, and the girls, with horror upon their faces, fled from the parlor to find consolation in Mrs. Pfeffer's bedroom, where they poured the tale of "that horrid man's vulgarity" into the good lady's ears.

OLD HOSS RADBOURN

Charles (Old Hoss) Radbourn had the greatest season a pitcher ever had in 1884. Radbourn won 60 games for Providence that year, losing twelve, completing every one of his 73 starts and registering an ERA of 0.99 over 630 innings. In one 30-day span, he won 18 straight games. Then in the first World Series ever, with the American Association champion New York Metropolitans, he won all three games by scores of 6-0, 3-1, and 12-2.

Old Hoss was never a happy man. He had to be cajoled by a friend into giving up life as a butcher in Bloomington, Ill., to pursue a pitching career. He began the '84 season as the number 2 Providence pitcher behind Charlie Sweeney. Sweeney and Radbourn hated each other, and every time Sweeney did well, Radbourn sulked. Sweeney struck out 19 batters in a June game against champion Boston, and when a one-armed pitcher named Hugh Daley duplicated the feat shortly thereafter in the outlaw Union Association, Radbourn could only say, "What you did, any one-armed pitcher could do."

For his part, Sweeney was a reprobate who, on days he wasn't scheduled to pitch, would show up drunk, usually with a girl on his arm. When manager Frank Bancroft once tried to ask Sweeney to leave the mound in the seventh inning of a game, Sweeney bolted the club to join the Union Association. Radbourn, who was on suspension at the time for purposely ignoring the catcher's signals, was immediately reinstated, and Bancroft offered him a small raise if he agreed to pitch every game the rest of the season. Radbourn accepted, but only on the condition that he be set free by Providence at the end of the season.

However much the rest was history, it was pain for Old Hoss. In a 1912 interview, Bancroft described Radbourn's 1884 daily anguish: "The Old Hoss pitched his arm so sore he couldn't raise it high enough to lift his hat or comb his hair. Somebody had to help him dress every day." Though Radbourn remained with Providence and won a total of 306 games in the majors, he would never again get more than 28 wins in a season.

Upon his retirement, he opened a billiards parlor in Bloomington. He lost an eye in a hunting accident, and morose over his appearance he stayed in the back room of the pool hall and drank himself to death at forty-three.

Only a few of teams have ever finished a season with a winning percentage of better than .750, and two of them, the White Stockings and the Giants, accomplished the feat in the same year, 1885, with Chicago winning the pennant by two games. But the post-season championship series with the American Association champion St. Louis Browns was a disaster. The first game ended in a tie, the second in a forfeit for Chicago when Browns player-manager Charles Comiskey pulled his team off the field in protest of umpire Dan Sullivan. In the seventh and final game, the Browns tied the series with a 13-4 victory in a game that featured 17 errors by Chicago and 10 by St. Louis. Undaunted, both teams declared themselves world champions.

THE COLOR LINE

Chicago's manager and star player, Cap Anson, ran his club—and played for it—until 1897, when he was forty-five. When he finally retired, he continued for ten years to oil and dust every one of the 400 bats he kept in his basement, just in case some team should call in need of his services. He was one of the era's titanic figures, at once a brilliant businessman, a great player, and an imposing figure in the game's inner circles. But Anson also was responsible for one of the saddest events in the history of baseball, an occurrence that would retard the game's progress for more than half a century.

Moses Fleetwood Walker, the son of a physician, had been an outstanding athlete at Oberlin College, and while there he attracted the attention of the Toledo team in the Northwestern League, which signed him in 1883. The very next year Toledo was invited to join the American Association, and Walker was one of the few players the club retained. A catcher for Tony Mullane, he batted .263 in 152 at bats and was quite popular both in Toledo and in such road cities as Baltimore and Washington. His brother, Welday Wilberforce Walker, also played in five games for Toledo that season as an outfielder, going 4-for-18.

But when the White Stockings came to Toledo for an exhibition that year, Anson threatened to pull his team off the field if Fleet Walker played, Charley Morton, the Toledo manager, refused to comply with the demand. "The joke of the affair," according to one account, "was that up to the time Anson made his 'bluff,' the Toledo people had no intention of catching Walker, who was laid up with a sore hand, but when Anson said he wouldn't play with Walker, the Toledo people made up their minds that Walker would catch or there wouldn't be any game."

Anson's position soon took root. On July 14, 1887, the International League instituted an unofficial color line, and on that same day Anson succeeded in getting the Newark "Little Giants" to remove their black battery of pitcher George Stovey and Fleet Walker from an exhibition game with the White Stockings. Later in the year, all but two of the St. Louis Browns refused to take the field against the Cuban Giants. "Dear Sir," read their letter to club owner Chris Von der Ahe, "We the undersigned members of the St. Louis Base Ball Club do not agree to play against negroes tomorrow. We will cheerfully play against white people at any time, and think by refusing to play, we are only doing what is right." Von der Ahe informed the New York crowd of 7,000 that his team was too crippled to play, and in a way, he was right.

The Giants who won pennants in '88 and '89 could boast of the greatest pitching tandem in baseball history. Between them, Mickey Welch and Tim Keefe won 660 major league games, 558 of them while they were teammates in Troy and in New York. By all accounts, they were both hard-working gentlemen. Smiling Mickey earned his nickname during two late summer weeks in 1884 when he 1) took a shot in the hip off the bat of Dan Brouthers, 2) was knocked unconscious by a pitch from Cleveland rookie John Harkins, and 3) took another line drive, this time off Anson's bat. (The distance from the mound to home plate was only 50 feet at the time). In the middle of this barrage, Welch became the first pitcher to strike out the first nine batters he faced.

"CASEY AT THE BAT"

"The outlook wasn't brilliant for the Mudville nine that day . . ." So began "Casey at the Bat, A Ballad of the Republic, Sung in the Year 1888," a poem that appeared in the fourth column of page 4 of the Sunday, June 3, 1888, *San Francisco Examiner*. The poem that would become the most famous American verse ever written was bylined "Phin" and sandwiched inconspicuously between editorials on the left and Ambrose Bierce's weekly column on the right.

Ernest Lawrence Thayer, or "Phinney," as such classmates as William Randolph Hearst and George Santayana called him, had been the editor of the *Harvard Lampoon*. After Hearst was kicked out of Harvard for sending personalized chamber pots to several professors, his father gave him the *Examiner* to run, and the errant heir soon asked Thayer if he would write a humor column for the paper.

It took Thayer half a day to write "Casey." The piece might have been forgotten altogether had not a novelist named Archibald Clavering Gunter clipped it and given it to his actor friend William DeWolf Hopper, who was performing a comic opera entitled *Prince Methusalem* at New York's Wallack Theatre on August 14, 1888. The Giants and White Stockings had been invited to the show, and Hopper thought the new piece particularly appropriate. Before beginning, though, he congratulated Tim Keefe, who was in attendance, on his feat of 19 straight victories.

Hopper, whose fifth wife was gossip columnist Hedda Hopper (their son Paul Hopper played Paul Drake in the Perry Mason television series), later described his first reading of the poem in his autobiography, *Once a Clown, Always a Clown:* "When I dropped my voice to B flat, below low C, at 'the multitude was awed,' I remember seeing Buck Ewing's gallant mustachios give a single nervous twitch. And as the house, after a moment of startled silence, grasped the anticlimactic denouement, it shouted its glee."

Had Casey hit the ball out of the park, we might never have heard of Thayer or Hopper or been subjected to the countless parodies of "Casey at the Bat." Hooper hit upon its appeal when he wrote, "There is no more completely satisfactory drama in literature than the fall of Humpty Dumpty." He would go on to recite the poem more than 10,000 times, each time in five minutes, 40 seconds. "When my name is called upon the resurrection morning, I shall, very probably, unless some friend is there to pull the sleeve of my ascension robes, arise, clear my throat and begin: 'The outlook wasn't brilliant for the Mudville nine that day.'"

While Hopper rode the poem to fame, Thayer shied away from it, content after leaving the *Examiner* to manage the family's mill in Lawrence, Mass. "Its persistent vogue is simply unaccountable," he wrote, "and it would be hard to say, all things considered, if it has given me more pleasure than annoyance." But much as a player who softens to his own accomplishments, Thayer was genuinely touched by a banner at his fiftieth Harvard reunion in 1935 which read, "An '85 Man Wrote Casey."

Hopper and Thayer did meet, about a year after the poem made its debut. The actor gave a performance of Casey in Worcester, Mass., and afterwards he received a note inviting him to meet the author at a nearby club. The members of the club persuaded Thayer to perform the poem that night, and in the words of Hopper, "It was the worst delivery of the poem I had ever heard."

THREE OWNERS

After the 1888 season Albert Spalding sent his White Stockings and an "All-America Team" on a world tour. The party sailed for Australia on November 17, and the players received an enthusiastic welcome in their three weeks Down Under. Their reception spurred them further westward, but then came a three-week journey across the Indian Ocean in weather so hot that it left them "panting in the sun like so many lizards," according to Spalding. Their arrival in Ceylon went all but unnoticed, and a five-inning exhibition there was attended by people who "looked at us as though we were so many escaped inmates."

Cairo was the next stop, and a game at the Pyramids was arranged. After the exhibition, the players mounted the Sphinx, "to the horror of the native worshippers of Cheops and the dead Pharoahs," wrote Spalding. He was unsuccessful in his attempts to get up a game in Rome's Coliseum and to arrange an audience with the Pope. After games in Florence and Paris, Spalding took the group to England, where he hoped to get a better reception than the chilly one he had received there during an earlier trip in 1874. The British, though, remained unimpressed, and one commentator said that baseball was as out of place in England as "a nursery frolic in the House of Commons."

The tour lasted nearly six months, and even after touching home, Spalding kept the players going another two weeks in a series of welcome-home exhibitions. They were greeted as heroes—Henry Chadwick called the tour "the greatest event in the modern history of athletic sports." At a magnificent banquet "served in nine innings" at Delmonico's in New York, Mark Twain toasted the entourage, thanking them for revealing the mystery of the equator. They had made the imaginary line visible, Twain said, by "stealing bases on their bellies" and "leaving a nice deep trench along the way."

Baseball owes Christian Frederick Wilhelm Von der Ahe for two things: He introduced the hot dog to the ballpark, and when he referred in his thick Teutonic accent to the "fanatics" who peopled his park, the term "fan" was born.

Otherwise, the rotund beer baron who owned the St. Louis club in the American Association was a boor and a clown.

According to one contemporary account, he had a "face like
the full moon and a nose like a bunch of strawberries. It's a
wonder he didn't go cross-eyed to see around it."

With the help of St. Louis sportswriter Al Spink, who begat
The Sporting News, Von der Ahe assembled a formidable team
which won four straight championships, but his pomposity was
such that he used to have his players march single-file behind
him on the way to railroad stations.

The Louisville team of 1889 was one of the sorriest in history, finishing with a record of 27 wins and 111 defeats. In
midseason, six of its best players went on strike over fines
levied by owner Mordecai Davidson. They were in the middle
of a horrendous road trip in which they lost all 21 games and
were reported missing because of the Johnstown flood. The
Louisville Commercial had this to say about the team:
"The Athletics failed to lower Louisville's average yesterday.
The game scheduled to be played at Philadelphia did not take
place because Wandering Jays are waterbound somewhere between Columbus and the Quaker City. There is not much
sympathy for them here. In fact, if the entire team had been
standing in front of the Johnstown reservoir when it broke
last Friday evening, the majority of the people of Louisville
would have viewed the calamity as just a visitation of Providence."

Walter Arlington Latham, who loved to tweak Von der Ahe,
was known as "The Freshest Man on Earth." He loved to clown
around, and persisted in shouting and gesticulating throughout every game he played. Unofficially, he was the father of
"chatter," that baseball tradition of non-stop encouragement.
A man once offered Latham a box of silk socks and underwear
if he could remain quiet a whole game, and Latham couldn't
do it. He was also an expert tumbler: In one game in Chicago
against the White Stockings, Latham laid a bunt down the
first-base line and somersaulted clear over Anson, landing with
both feet on the base.

JOHN MONTGOMERY WARD

John Montgomery Ward was one of the most remarkable men ever to play the game. He invented the pitcher's mound and the intentional walk. After pitching his perfect game in 1880, he became baseball's best shortstop and base-stealer. While in New York in the '80s, he helped to form the first players' union—The Brotherhood—and obtained his law degree from Columbia. He married Helen Dauvray, a leading actress of the day, and when his playing career ended he became a prominent attorney—he represented the National League and was nearly elected its president in 1909—and an owner of the Boston Braves. He was also one of the country's leading amateur golfers. He died in 1925 "with his boots on," as Grantland Rice wrote. At sixty-five, he had just played in the Masters and was hunting in the Georgia woods despite what he said was a slight cold, which turned out to be pneumonia.

But Ward's boldest act occurred during the 1889 season, when the owners adopted a salary classification plan, under which every player would be "graded" and assigned a grade-related salary between $1,500 and $2,500 a year. On July 14, 1889, Ward urged a meeting of players to do the unthinkable—to form their own teams.

In some ways, The Brotherhood, or Players' League, was a success. It lured almost all of the game's top stars, outdrew the National League, and produced a strong champion in King Kelly's Boston club; Ward's own Brooklyn team finished second. Such was the loyalty of the players that when Spalding came to Boston to lure Kelly with a $10,000 offer (the classification plan had quickly come apart), the catcher simply said, "I can't go back on the boys." Spalding was so impressed that he asked him if he needed a loan anyway. "A thousand would be nice," Kelly admitted.

But the Brotherhood also lost a lot of money, and the backers Ward and others had recruited were hesitant to try it for another year. The players asked the owners for a truce. Spalding, on a bluff, demanded unconditional surrender, and the players agreed for nothing more than general amnesty. But had the Brotherhood known the National League's own tenuous financial condition, it might have put the established league out of business forever.

BILLY SUNDAY

If Ward had a rival as the fastest baserunner in the '80s, it was William A. Sunday, who would become better known as evangelist Billy Sunday. Anson, who had discovered him at a firemen's tournament in Ames, Iowa, wrote in his autobiography, "He was, in my opinion, the fastest man . . . on his feet in the profession, and one who could run the bases like a scared deer." Anson stayed with Sunday even after he struck out the first 13 times he stepped to the plate in the majors. He never became a great hitter, and he was only a parttime player for the White Stockings from '83 to '87, after which he was traded to Pittsburgh.

One Sunday afternoon in '86, Sunday was walking with some of the White Stockings down State Street in Chicago. "We entered a saloon and drank," he wrote in his autobiography, "and then walked to the corner of State and Van Buren streets." As they came to the corner, they stopped to hear a Gospel wagon, and Sunday was so moved by the hymns he used to hear his mother sing that he turned to his teammates and said, "Boys, I bid the old life good-by." According to Sunday, "Some laughed, some smiled, some shrugged their shoulders, and some looked with mingled expressions of admiration and disgust." Oddly, it was King Kelly who was most sincere in giving his best wishes to Sunday.

Sunday continued to play, of course. He didn't get his first preaching invitation until 1896 in Garner, Iowa, but his athletic, dramatic style soon made him the most popular preacher of his time, some say of all time. He is said to have converted 250,000 people—68,000 one 1917 night in New York City. Among his routines, he would wind up like a pitcher and slam a fist into his other hand to demonstrate a "fastball to the devil." And to illustrate a sinner coming home for salvation,

Sunday would slide headfirst on the stage and grope with his hand for home plate.

PETE BROWNING

Even though the American Association was considered an inferior league to the National, the leading hitter in the Brotherhood, with a .391 average, was Pete Browning, an Association product and the original Louisville slugger. In 1884, Browning was playing for his hometown Louisville Eclipse and in dire need of a new bat since his was broken. John Andrew Hillerich had gone to the game, playing hookey from his father's woodworking shop, and he took Browning back to the shop for a new bat. Browning watched as Hillerich selected a block of white ash and molded it on a lathe to Pete's specifications. The next day Browning went three-for-three, and soon the Hillerich family was out of the butter churn business.

Browning, called "The Old Gladiator," loved his bats, sometimes to the point of absurdity. He thought that a bat had only a certain number of hits in it, and he kept hundreds of them in his mother's basement, giving each one a name. On one tour of the cellar, Browning said to a visitor, "Now that stick over yonder, that's Hezekiah, and he did pretty well. Next to him, there, is Lazarus. Lazarus was a ten-hit bat, but I used him only in the tight places, when we needed a hit to win, and he delivered, every time."

But this same sentimentalist suffered the image of a clownish, illiterate drunk, and everyone knew stories of his stupidity and beer-drinking. When he was told that James A. Garfield had been assassinated, Browning was said to have replied, "Yeah? What league was he in?" He was also quoted as saying, "I can't hit the ball until I hit the bottle." In Kansas City, Browning once took advantage of a flash flood by sitting in a chair outside his hotel, fishing in the gutter. When he finally gave up, he told his manager, "No luck, they ain't running very well today."

The truth was that Browning suffered from a painful condition called mastoiditis, a disease that left him virtually deaf. It made him appear dumber than he actually was, and also made him drink to mask the pain. Eventually, it led to his unnecessary incarceration in an insane asylum and to his premature death at the age of forty-four.

But the disease never robbed him of his batting eyes, his "lamps" or "peeps" as he alternately called them. And he certainly never showed his rumored stupidity on the field. Baltimore's canny third baseman John McGraw liked to hook his hand inside the belts of runners tagging up at third base, often causing them to be thrown out at home, or out of the game for starting a brawl. But in one game, Browning surreptitiously unbuckled his belt, and when McGraw grabbed it, the third baseman was left standing with the belt while Browning dashed home holding his pants up.

1890s PITCHERS

When the American Association died, the National League took in the St. Louis, Baltimore, Washington, and Louisville franchises and devised a split season for 1892. Boston, the defending NL champion, won the first half, and Cleveland, with the youthful Cy Young, took the second half. Boston didn't want to get involved in a post-season series, but the league insisted on it, and so a nine-game contest was agreed upon. The first game was a magnificent pitching duel between Young and Jack Stivetts that ended in a 0-0 tie after 11 innings. But the Beaneaters swept the Spiders the next five games.

The split season was a financial and artistic disaster. This was also the last year the pitcher stood 50 feet away from the plate. Pitchers were clearly getting the upper hand: in '92 Anson batted only .272 and King Kelly .189.

The three dominant pitchers of the time were Young, Amos Rusie of the Giants, and Kid Nichols of the Beaneaters, as the

Boston team was called. Denton True Young had been picked up by Cleveland in 1890; his minor league team in Canton, Ohio, had folded, so his manager George Moreland sold him to Cleveland for a $300 commission and a new suit of clothes. The nickname Cy is short for either Cyclone or Cyrus, a name given to rubes back then. When Young first arrived in Cleveland, his appearance was so comical—trousers stopped well above his ankles, sleeves riding up his arms, a derby too small for his head—that club secretary David Hawley took him to a barber and a haberdasher before presenting him to his teammates.

In his first game, Young held Anson's White Stockings to just three hits. Afterwards, Anson struck up a conversation with Hawley. "Funny about that big rube of yours beating us today," said Anson. "He's too green to do your club much good, but I believe if I taught him what I know, I might make a pitcher out of him in a couple of years. He's not worth it now, but I am willing to give you $1,000 for him." Hawley's polite reply was, "Cap, you keep your thousand, and we'll keep the rube." The rube went on to win 509 more major league games.

From 1890 to 1892, Amos Rusie struck out 969 batters. He was the one pitcher most responsible for the lengthening of the distance from mound to plate, but even after it was moved back he won 32, 33, and 36 games from '93 to '95. He sat out the 1896 season in a salary dispute with Andrew Freedman, the Giants' exceptionally parsimonious owner, but so desperate was the league to get him back that the other owners chipped in the $5,000 salary he missed in '96.

His nickname, "Hoosier Thunderbolt," described his nature as well as his fastball. Rusie actively disliked sportswriters because he thought they portrayed him as a carouser. He sat out 1899 because of another salary dispute and 1900 because of a marital dispute. But Cincinnati still wanted the thirty-year-old Rusie and offered the Giants one of their rookie pitchers for him—a young man from Pennsylvania named Christy Mathewson.

THE ORIGINAL ORIOLES

In 1892 brewer Harry Vonderhorst, the owner of the Baltimore Orioles, was desperate. He relieved his first manager, outfielder George Van Haltren, after losing 14 of the first 15 games, and named one of his own beer salesmen, Jack Waltz, as an interim replacement until he could find a new manager. The new man turned out to be Ned Hanlon, a fine center-fielder with Detroit and Pittsburgh, but a decided bust as the Pittsburgh manager.

Hanlon had no immediate effect on the Orioles, but in time he began to assemble a formidable team. He already had the skinny third baseman John McGraw and catcher Wilbert Robinson. In the course of the next two years, he traded Van Haltren to Pittsburgh for left-fielder Joe Kelley, signed a rookie second baseman named Heinie Reitz, traded outfielder Voiceless Tim O'Rourke (as distinct from his contemporary Orator Jim O'Rourke) to Louisville for shortstop Hughie Jennings, bought center-fielder Walter Brodie (nicknamed Steve after the Steve Brodie who jumped off the Brooklyn Bridge) from St. Louis, and, in the winter of '93, traded infielder Bill Shindle (who once made a season-record 119 errors) and outfielder George Treadway to Brooklyn for the first baseman Dan Brouthers and 140-pound outfielder Wee Willie Keeler. Of the eight regulars usually on the field in 1894, only Reitz and Brodie would not make the Hall of Fame.

The Orioles would win back-to-back-to-back pennants, which one might have assumed would have made Vonderhorst very happy. Actually, the brewer was a little put out about the control his manager was assuming. Whenever Vonderhorst was asked a question about his club, he pointed to a button on his lapel which read "Ask Hanlon."

Hanlon's Orioles quickly became mythic. "Scrappy" would be the polite way to describe the way the Orioles played, but "dirty" would be more accurate. With McGraw showing the way, they would run into opposing first basemen, trip base-runners, and jostle the catcher when he was trying to make a throw. They even slipped their own fans dead balls to throw back out onto the field in place of the foul balls that were supposed to be returned to the umpire.

The Oriole style led to such characteristic scenes as this one, described by McGraw: "We were on the field and the other team had a runner on first who started to steal second, but first of all he spiked our first baseman on the foot. Our man retaliated by trying to trip him. He got away, but at second Heinie Reitz tried to block him off while Hughie . . . covered the bag to take the throw and tag him. The runner evaded Reitz and jumped feet first at Jennings to drive him away from the bag. Jennings dodged the flying spikes and threw himself bodily at the runner, knocking him flat. In the meantime the batter hit our catcher over the hands with his bat so he couldn't throw, and our catcher trod on the umpire's feet with his spikes and shoved his big mitt in his face so he couldn't see the play."

The umpire, Tim Hurst, recalled reacting the only way he could: "I punched Robbie"—Baltimore catcher Wilbert Robinson—"in the ribs, called it a foul, and sent the runner back."

The Orioles set the standard for the entire league. In 1898 the Philadelphia Phillies had a seldom-used catcher named Morgan Murphy. When he played, his real contribution was made while sitting in the center-field clubhouse, peering through a peephole with his binoculars to steal the opposing catcher's signs. He was only discovered after Cincinnati shortstop Tommy Corcoran tripped over what appeared to be a vine while rounding third. He pulled at the vine, which turned out to be a telegraph wire emanating from Murphy's perch. Murphy had been tapping the telegraph key once for fastball, twice for curve, three times for changeup. Phillies owner John I. Rogers actually thought the system was legal, but the National League overruled him.

Umpires did not have it easy in such an era. Stump Weidman, an ex-pitcher, was so intimidated, first by the Cleveland Spiders and then the Louisville Colonels, in an 1896 game, that he started a riot that led to the arrest of eight Spiders.

Another umpire, Tom Lynch, described a game he worked in Washington:

"The groundskeeper kept two large dogs chained to the clubhouse in deep center field. I think they were mastiffs; anyway, when they stood on their hind legs they were much taller than a man. Washington invariably had poor ball clubs, but in no city were the fans harder on the umpires. On this occasion I had to call several decisions against Washington . . . . At the end of the game there was a prolonged hiss. Someone then unleashed the big dogs in center field, and with canine intelligence they understood I was the object of the hisses. They came tearing across the field and leaped at my throat. It was the toughest spot I ever was in, and I don't know what might have happened if some friendly players hadn't driven off the big beasts with their bats."

1890s PLAYERS

Not all of the players of the period were so cheeky as the various McGraw clones. One antithetical sort was Emerson (Pink) Hawley, a right-hander who won 162 major league games despite a pronounced lack of confidence. Once, while pitching for St. Louis, Hawley motioned for catcher Heinie Peitz to come out to the mound for a conference. "Heinie," Hawley asked, "do you like to catch me?" When Reitz assured Pink that there was nothing he would rather do, the pitcher resumed the task at hand.

One day in the dead of winter, Hawley walked into the cigar store owned by National League catcher Chief Zimmer and asked, "Chief, will you forgive me?" Zimmer said he would although he had no idea what Hawley was talking about—he and Pink had never had so much as a cross word. During the following season, Zimmer came up to bat in the late innings of a game Hawley was winning 12-0, and Pink asked him his batting average. "Oh, about .214, I guess," said Zimmer. "Well, boost it a little," Hawley replied, whereupon he threw a nice fat pitch that Zimmer clobbered for a homer and his team's only run.

Charley Esper was an undistinguished left-handed pitcher with several teams in the 1890s, but he left a lasting legacy because his Baltimore teammates thought he ran like a lame horse—and every player with a cramp in his leg since Esper has suffered from a "charley horse."

Bill Lange, a splendid Chicago outfielder with the odd nickname of Little Eva, was such a boxing devotee that in 1897 he held out of spring training because he wanted to stay out west and see the Jim Corbett-Bob Fitzsimmons fight on March 17. He tried to buy time by demanding a $500 raise, but the club quickly granted it to him. Then he wired to Hot Springs, Ark., that he sprained his ankle but that it should be all right in a week. He reported in time to hit .340 with 73 stolen bases that season.

A big man (6'2", 200 lbs.) with surprising speed, Lange was rated over Tris Speaker as Albert Spalding's choice for the all-time best center-fielder. He quit the game cold at the age of twenty-eight to marry a young woman whose father took him into his real estate and insurance business. In later years, Lange became a scout and developed his nephew, George "High Pockets" Kelly, into a Hall of Famer.

Of all the great wastes of talent, few were more tragic than Louis Sockalexis, the Indian who gave Cleveland its nickname. In his first year in 1897, Sockalexis hit .331 and amazed the baseball world with his tremendous arm and equally impressive speed. The first time he faced Amos Rusie in New York he hit a towering home run. Said *The Sporting Life* in 1897, "There is no feature of the signing of Sockalexis more gratifying than the fact that his presence on the team will result in relegating to obscurity the title of 'Spiders,' by which the team has been handicapped for several seasons, to give place to the more significant name 'Indians.'"

The story has it that after a particularly thrilling victory over Baltimore, Cleveland fans rushed Sockalexis to a saloon where he had his first taste of alcohol, and Sockalexis rushed speedily down the road to ruin. So romantic a figure was Sockalexis that the most amazing stories began to spring up about him. Supposedly, his father, seeking to keep his son on the Penobscot reservation, paddled from Maine to Washington, D.C., to see President Cleveland and ask him to make Louis chief of the tribe.

The fact of the matter is that Sockalexis was well educated, having matriculated both at Holy Cross and Notre Dame. While in South Bend, he came to the attention of Cleveland manager Patsy Tebeau, a man who was not above chicanery. When Sockalexis told him he wanted to finish the year at Notre Dame, Tebeau fed him drink after drink until Sockalexis committed an act disgraceful enough to get him kicked out of Notre Dame.

And it was drink that did, in time, ruin Sockalexis. An ankle injury in July of '97, sustained when he jumped out of the second floor of a brothel, sidelined him for most of the rest of the season. While he was playing, he could hold his liquor, but on the bench he just got drunker and drunker.

He played parts of two more seasons for Cleveland, then stumbled into the minors. As for his demise, legend has it that he died drunk in an alley. In actuality, he returned to the Penobscot reservation after baseball and coached Indian youths while working as a wood cutter. He was forty-two when he died in the woods. His old newspaper clippings were found stuffed inside his shirt.

The Cleveland franchise was one of the best for most of the '90s, but before the '99 season the club's owners also bought Von der Ahe's St. Louis club and shipped all of Cleveland's best players west. Cleveland itself was left with a shell of a team that ended up winning 20 games and losing 134, a frightening percentage of .130, and to this day the worst season in major league history. Six times it lost 11 or more straight games, including a string of 24, and it finished 80 games behind Brooklyn.

Emblematic of the '99 Cleveland club was a thirty-year-old rookie named Harry Colliflower, who had a 1-11 record. By now the club was called the Exiles, the Wanderers, or the Forsakens because they played 113 of their 154 games on the road. Toward the end of the season, a few Cleveland players asked Eddie Kolb, the cigarstand clerk in their Cincinnati hotel, if he might like to pitch, and he did, losing 19-3.

After the last game, the players gathered in a hotel room for a little ceremony in which they presented traveling secretary George Muir with a diamond locket. "We are doing this for you," said a spokesman, "only because you deserve it. You are the only person in the world who had the misfortune to watch us in all our games."

As the century turned, the baseball firmament was filled with names that would resound for decades: Wagner, Lajoie, Young, Waddell, McGinnity. At the time the biggest of all might have been Delahanty—Ed Delahanty, that is, and not his brothers Frank, Jim, Joe, and Tom, all of whom also played in the majors. "We were given bats instead of rattles," said Ed of the brothers' upbringing in Cleveland.

From 1893 to 1899, Big Ed batted .370, .400, .399, .394, .377, .334, and .408 for the Phillies, and he hit the ball as hard as anyone before Babe Ruth. Turkey Mike Donlin once congratulated him on a tremendous homer he hit against St. Louis, saying, "That's one you can be proud of, Ed." Delahanty shook his head and said, "Hell, no. If I could have cut that hit into singles, I'd lead the whole damn league."

But, like so many of his contemporaries, Delahanty was a drinker. In 1903 he wanted to go to the Giants, but his Washington team would not release him, so Ed jumped the club. On the night of July 2, he bought a ticket at Detroit, bound for Buffalo aboard Michigan Central train No. 6. As the train arrived at Fort Erie, Ontario, on the Canadian side of the International Bridge, Delahanty, who had downed several whiskeys, was brandishing an open razor and terrifying the other passengers, according to the conductor who then put him off the train. After the train disappeared across the bridge, Delahanty began walking across the span, pushing aside a night watchman who tried to stop him. The bridge had opened up for a passing ship, and Delahanty plunged into the dark waters of the Niagara River. His body was found a week later below the Falls.

PART									
2									

THE EARLY MODERNS

From the Founding
of the American League
to the Corruption
of the Black Sox

THE MODERN OWNERS

In the nineteenth century, many ballclub owners were either players or managers; by the new century, only Connie Mack and Clark Griffith of the fledgling American League were moguls who had risen from uniformed ranks. What characterized the new owners was what would characterize owners ever after. This became clear to Pittsburgh owner Barney Dreyfuss when he arrived in Boston for the first game of the 1903 Series, and learned that Boston owner Henry J. Killilea was insisting that Dreyfuss pay his own way into the ballpark.

At the conclusion of that first Series, the two owners had conflicting reactions. Loser Dreyfuss, dismayed that his players hadn't made more money, gave over his entire owner's share to the player pool, and each Pirate took home more than each member of the winning Boston club. For his part, Boston owner Killilea, who had purchased the club a year earlier, promptly sold the team for a fast profit and left baseball altogether.

In 1904, when Charles Hercules Ebbets assumed full control of the Brooklyn franchise (he had been a minority shareholder until then), he raised his salary as club president from $4,000 to $10,000—and at the same time cut manager Ned Hanlon's salary from $11,500 to $7,500. Within a year, Hanlon quit.

Frustrated by local laws which forbade the playing of Sunday baseball games "at which admission was charged," Ebbets in early 1904 announced that his Brooklyn team would play Boston on Sunday, April 17, and that admission would be free. The Brooklyn owner was neither samaritan nor fool. He simply required that, once through the turnstiles, each spectator purchase a color-coded scorecard, the color determining whether the "free" seat was in the bleachers, the grandstand, or the box seats.

Ebbets proceeded to win the first round in court, and get in a few more Sunday games. But the blue law was upheld on appeal, and Sunday baseball did not return to New York until 1917.

If Ebbets represented the bean counters who would later reach their apotheosis in Walter O'Malley, then Garry Hermann, who presided over the Cincinnati club, represented the other primary model of owner—the Ted Turner type. At an exhibition game in Florida, Hermann was introduced to the crowd with all his titles—president of the Reds, chairman of the National Commission, and so on. And when the announcer finished, Hermann cupped his hands together and shouted to the crowd, "Yes, and I'm the champion beer drinker and sausage eater, too!" In historian Lee Allen's words, "Garry was a walking delicatessen. A connoisseur of sausage, he carried his own wherever he went. When he presided at a hotel suite or in a bar, his party sat around one or more tables that were piled high with roast chickens, boiled hams, cheeses of every description, Thuringian blood pudding, liver sausage, baked beans, radishes, cole slaw, potato salad, green onions, and every type of fermented drink that was known to Bacchus."

As Chairman of the National Commission, baseball's governing body before the advent of the commissioner, Hermann once required J. Cal Ewing, who owned the San Francisco team in the Pacific Coast League, to pay $2,500 for a second baseman the club had bought not knowing that the player was hospitalized with a broken leg. Hermann argued, as Allen wrote, that "Ewing should have provided himself with information concerning the condition of the player before making the deal."

Shortly thereafter, Hermann received a shipment of five barrels of sauerkraut from Ewing. He paid for the COD delivery and began to eat, too late to discover that the cabbage was rancid. Fulminating at Ewing, Hermann was stopped short when the San Francisco owner pointed out that he should have "provided himself with information concerning the condition of the sauerkraut before he paid for it."

Still, it was money and not sausage that motivated most of the era's owners. Thus did a cash-minded Bill Baker, owner of the Phillies, install temporary bleachers in center field during the 1915 Red Sox–Philadelphia World Series. But Boston's Harry Hooper, who had hit only two home runs all year long, proceeded to drop two more into Baker's extra seats in the final game, enabling the Sox to win the series.

RUBE WADDELL

More than anyone else, Rube Waddell carried the torch of dissolution into the twentieth century, as if passed directly to him by Ed Delahanty and Louis Sockalexis. After the twenty-four-year-old Waddell's drinking, carousing, and generally impossible behavior led Pittsburgh to give him his release in 1901—even though he had won the league ERA championship the year before—Connie Mack decided to sign the left-hander for his Milwaukee club. Waddell, living in Punxsatawney, Pa., wasn't especially interested and ignored Mack's blandishments. Finally, after a two-week series of letters and telegrams from Mack, Waddell responded with a terse wire: "Come and get me."

Mack traveled to Punxsatawney, and as he took Waddell to the train station the pitcher insisted on making a series of stops. At virtually every store in town, he would drag Mack inside and command his new employer to pay off Waddell's debts.

By the time they reached the station, Mack related, the cash in his pocket was virtually gone, and he and Waddell were approached by a group of seven men. The men formed a circle around Mack, and he regarded them apprehensively. Then one of the group stepped forward and informed Mack that they wished to thank him for taking Waddell out of town.

Not long before his sixty-six-year career as player, manager, and owner concluded in the early 1950s, Mack said, "I have seen all of the best left-handers since the late nineties, but none was greater than Waddell." He liked him so much, in fact, that when he bought the Athletics, Mack immediately went after his old employee, and sent two Pinkertons to California to ensure the pitcher's safe arrival in Philadelphia.

During his time with Philadelphia, Waddell would periodically disappear from the club to join a minstrel show, to wrestle alligators, to chase fires. At one point, Mack paid the pitcher's entire $2,200 salary in one-dollar bills, hoping this might make it last longer.

After Waddell got into a fight in a saloon, in 1907, Mack concocted a scheme to get the pitcher to behave. He paid the man who had fought Waddell to swath himself in impressive bandages, and then he took both Waddell and his victim to court, where a judge who was Mack's friend was presiding. The judge told Waddell that if he had so much as a single drink in the next months, he'd be slapped into jail forthwith. Chastened, the pitcher began to behave. And, said Mack, whenever he worried Waddell was about to stray, he'd point to somebody in the stands and say, "He looks like a detective to me." It worked only for that season, though, and the next year Waddell was sold to the Browns, where he lasted ten games into the 1910 season.

The greatest of all Waddell stories is probably apocryphal, but by its very attribution to the unlikely pitcher it does go a way toward defining both Waddell and the era he played in. As the story goes, a drunken Waddell asserted to his teammates that he could fly. Stepping out of his hotel window with his arms flapping, he found himself the next day waking up in a hospital. When he asked one of his pals what he had done, Waddell was indignant. "I coulda been killed!", he shouted. "Why didn't you stop me?" "What?" came the reply. "And lose the hundred I had bet on you?"

After he burned himself out in the majors, Waddell concluded his career in Minneapolis, in the American Association. Before a crucial July series against Toledo, manager Joe Cantillon told him, "You've gotta lay off the liquor for the next four days. You'll be pitching against Earl Yingling"— Toledo's ace—"at least once and maybe twice. I want you to be at your best."

When the series began on a Monday afternoon neither Waddell nor Yingling appeared at the ballpark. Nor did either pitcher show up for any of the following games. Finally, that Friday, after Toledo left town, Waddell appeared at the ballpark carrying a string of fish, which he gave to Cantillon. He had taken care of Yingling, he explained, by asking the Toledo pitcher to accompany him on a four-day fishing trip to Lake Minnetonka. A week later, Cantillon got a bill from a local market—a bill for some fish picked up on Friday by Rube Waddell.

McGRAW AND THE GIANTS

One of the feeblest managerial tenures in baseball history was that of Horace Fogel, who took over the New York Giants in 1902. He is perhaps best remembered for a player redeployment he attempted to engineer: trying to convert Christy Mathewson into a first baseman. By the end of June, Fogel was fired.

A month later, a manager who would last a bit longer than Fogel or his predecessors (there had been twelve New York managers in the preceding nine years) arrived at the Polo Grounds: John McGraw.

"His very walk across the field in a hostile town," wrote

Grantland Rice, "was a challenge to the multitude." George Bernard Shaw said, "In Mr. McGraw I at last discovered the real and most authentic Most Remarkable Man in America." At the time he took over the Giants in 1902—and then made them an instant contender by raiding his old Baltimore club— McGraw was twenty-nine; soon, he would become baseball's universally acknowledged genius, its strongest personality, the winner of ten National League pennants. His ferocity on the field and the extreme combativeness to which he drove his players made McGraw and his Giants a target of hostility wherever they went. The manager himself abetted the rancor by wiring ahead to the chief of police in every city they played, asking for "protection." Newspapers would publish news of the telegram, and the crowds would be suitably inflamed. In Cincinnati, he offered to fight everyone in the ballpark, which led one of his favorite ballplayers, outfielder Mike Donlin, to say, "He's a wonder. He can start more fights, and win fewer, than anybody I ever saw."

"Everything he did was calculated to draw people into the park," the long-time Giants secretary Eddie Brannick told Joseph Durso. "He would make a statement insulting someone in St. Louis when the team was in Cincinnati. Or he would insult an owner like Barney Dreyfuss in Pittsburgh. Or Ban Johnson and the American League. Even when he went on the stage"—McGraw made his off-season money on the vaudeville circuit, like many players of his time—"he would do a stand-up monologue and answer questions from the audience, and he would always be baiting them and stirring them up."

The great theorist could also be foiled by his own stratagems. In 1904, wrote Christy Mathewson, McGraw signaled batters to hit away by blowing his nose into his pocket handkerchief. In one particular game, he was suffering from a head cold but wanted to play a bunting game. If one can believe Mathewson (or his ghost writer), McGraw virtually suffocated before game's end.

McGraw's influence extended far beyond the Giants' own dugout. Near the end of his career, in 1925, Pittsburgh took the pennant, thereby putting an end to New York's four-year grip on the National League championship. When the Pirates found themselves trailing Washington three games to one in the Series, McGraw stormed into their clubhouse and persuaded manager Bill McKechnie to bench twenty-five-year-old first baseman George Grantham and replace him with aging Stuffy McInnis, who had only 155 at bats all season.

McKechnie obliged, and McInnis finished the Series with a batting average more than double Grantham's as the Pirates came back to win three in a row.

Without question, McGraw's favorite was Christy Mathewson. Mordecai Brown remembered Mathewson's "lordly entrance. He'd always wait until about ten minutes before game time, then he'd come from the clubhouse across the field in a long linen duster like auto drivers wore in those days, and at every step the crowd would yell louder and louder." Johnny Evers said, "He could throw a ball into a tin cup at pitching range." In 4,781 innings over 635 games—he won 373 of them, and had a lifetime ERA of 2.13—he was never thrown out of a game by an umpire. He was without question the most beloved player of his time, and one of the best. Wrote John Kieran, "He was the greatest pitcher I ever saw. He was the greatest anybody ever saw. Let them name all the others. I don't care how good they were. Matty was better."

One who might have been a good foil for Mathewson but declined the opportunity was a Texas boy named Henry Schmidt. On opening day at the Polo Grounds in 1903, the two men were the starting pitchers—and for Schmidt, pitching for Brooklyn, it was his very first major league appearance. Astonishingly, Schmidt prevailed, and as the season progressed, he pitched three straight shutouts and won a total of 21 games.

The following winter, Brooklyn owner Charles Ebbets sent his young star a contract for 1904. It came back unsigned, with a brief note attached: "I do not like living in the East," Schmidt wrote, "and will not report." He never appeared in the majors again.

Arthur "Bugs" Raymond didn't last nearly as long as Rube Waddell, but he was clearly cut from the same cloth, and created for John McGraw the same headaches Waddell brought to Connie Mack.

Raymond got his liquor during games by tossing baseballs out of the park over the bullpen fence, in exchange for pints that his admirers on the outside would hustle up for him. McGraw put an end to the practice by stationing guards outside the park, but when Raymond found a way around that ploy, McGraw began sending the pitcher's paycheck—as well as the proceeds from fines he regularly levied on Raymond—straight to Raymond's wife. With that, Raymond told McGraw, "If my wife gets the money, let *her* pitch." On occasion, McGraw would have Raymond's family travel with the team, hoping that would keep him in line. Once, when McGraw sent Raymond to the bullpen, the pitcher took the ball instead and kept walking right out of the Polo Grounds and over to Eighth Avenue, where he strode into a bar and traded the ball for a few shots of whiskey.

By 1910, the Giants had sent Raymond to a drying-out sanitarium in Illinois. When that, too, failed, McGraw gave up, and in 1911 Raymond was released. The following season, he wrote to McGraw requesting a last chance, and the manager wired back, "I have my own troubles."

Raymond died later that year, age thirty, from a cerebral hemorrhage precipitated by a fight in which he had been kicked in the head.

Frank Graham reported that when Larry Doyle, McGraw's second baseman, reached the big leagues in 1907 he found himself in this colloquy with Brooklyn catcher Bill Bergen in his first at bat against the Dodgers:

"What's your name?" Bergen asked.

"Doyle, sir," the youngster replied.

"Doyle, eh? Do you like it up here in the big leagues?"

"Yes, sir."

"And what do you like to hit?"

"A fast ball," Doyle said.

"On the outside?"

"No, sir. On the inside."

"High?"

"No, sir. Not too high."

The punch line to Graham's tale was obvious: Doyle saw nothing but high curves on the outside corner that day, and never hit the ball out of the infield. In time, though, he caught on, and became celebrated for the statement, "It's great to be young and a Giant."

McGraw's sense of charity and sentiment only manifested itself outside of baseball combat; when he traded Doyle to the Cubs, the second baseman's desperate entreaties went unheard. But after his retirement, Doyle was one of many ex-Giants McGraw put to work at the Polo Grounds, taking tickets or raking the infield or performing any of the tasks that the manager seemed to reserve for his old troops.

Just before his death in 1951, umpire Bill Klem wrote, "John McGraw off the field was a man in every old-fashioned sense of the word. He helped his friends; he fought for his rightful due with words, fists or whatever came readily to hand; his charity knew neither restraint nor publicity."

For seven years, one of McGraw's best pitchers was right-hander Jeff Tesreau. But the sort of combat McGraw himself perfected eventually cost Tesreau dearly. Bedeviled by Tesreau's spitball, Otto Knabe and Mike Doolan of the Phillies once clandestinely rubbed up a game ball with capsicum salve, a tissue irritant trainers used to carry in their medical kits. After three innings, Tesreau was forced to depart the game, his lips severely swollen.

There were few men who loved playing baseball quite so much as O'Rourke, known as "Orator Jim." His major league career in the nineteenth century encompassed 1,773 games over 18 seasons. At various times he played every position, although he was primarily an outfielder; he also spent five years as a manager.

After his retirement in 1893, O'Rourke found his way back

to his hometown of Bridgeport, and organized the Connecticut League. He immediately became owner, manager, and catcher for the Bridgeport franchise, and in time the league's secretary-treasurer as well.

By 1904, when he was fifty-two, O'Rourke was still his team's catcher. That year, as the New York Giants ran away with the National League pennant, he traveled down to New York to make an unlikely suggestion to McGraw. He wanted, he told the Giants manager, to play once again in the majors— for one inning. McGraw, who was more than twenty years younger than O'Rourke and had only appeared in five games himself that season, was adamant at first but finally relented.

With Joe McGinnity pitching for the pennant against Cincinnati, O'Rourke became the oldest catcher in major league history. The first inning went flawlessly, and McGraw let him remain in the game. When he came to bat in the third, he lined a pitch to left field, dashed ahead when the fielder bobbled the ball, and ended up on third when the throw to second came in wild. He eventually scored a run, and stayed in to catch a complete game.

After that one game, Jim O'Rourke went back to Bridgeport, clearly renewed. He remained his own team's regular catcher for another five seasons, not retiring from active play until he was fifty-seven.

THE GAME ON THE FIELD

The 1904 American League season was dignified by a spectacular pennant race between New York and Boston, and especially the stunning pitching of New York's Jack Chesbro, who won 41 games—nearly 45 percent of his team's total.

The season concluded in New York on October 10, a Monday, with the two teams facing each other in a doubleheader. New York needed to win to capture the pennant.

The first game was tied in the ninth inning, with two out and a Boston runner on third. Chesbro, of course, was pitching, with shortstop Freddy Parent at bat. The stocky right-hander wound up, reared back, and released a wild pitch that soared over the head of catcher Red Kleinow. The pennant was lost.

After Chesbro's death in 1931, his widow spent the rest of her own life vainly trying to get the official scorer's ruling changed from wild pitch to passed ball.

While McGraw's Giants were establishing themselves as the paladins of the Polo Grounds, their woeful rivals in Brooklyn floundered hopelessly. Then, in 1906, arrived pitcher George Rucker, immediately nicknamed Napoleon by Grantland Rice. He was Brooklyn's answer to Mathewson, an outstanding left-hander who labored in vain on a weak team for ten years.

Rucker himself never complained about his incompetent teammates, but New York writer Sid Mercer aptly summed up the pitcher's plight. Asked what team gave Rucker the most trouble, Mercer replied, "Brooklyn, unquestionably."

Ed Walsh, once described as a "man who could strut while standing still," arrived in Chicago in 1904 to begin an outstanding career in which he would win 195 games for the White Sox, primarily on the strength of one of baseball's most adept spitballs. Tall, strong, good-looking, he reveled in attention. In the words of one White Sox executive, "on the point of delivery he sometimes would stand for a minute or more, with arms poised on high, shoulders thrown back, one foot a step in front of the other and all the time never move a muscle."

None of this endeared Walsh to his employer, Charles Comiskey. Accosting Walsh after he came off the mound one day, Comiskey told him, "That's a great pose you got, Ed, but I don't think you keep it long enough. When you get your arms above your head hold the position until they get the cameras ready."

The celebrated Tinker-Evers-Chance combination owed their notoriety more to the meter requirements of Franklin P. Adams's famous verse than to their prowess at the double play. In fact, research by sportswriter Charlie Segar, years afterward, determined that from 1906 to 1909, at the height of their renown, the three men combined for only 56 double plays scored 4-6-3 or 6-4-3. They were together as a combination for eight full seasons, and only Tinker ever led the league in double plays at his position, and he managed that only once.

What marked them even more was the enmity that coursed between them, especially Johnny Evers and Joe Tinker. The two men disliked each other intensely, and played two full years as double-play partners without speaking to each other. Nor was the rancor suppressed by club management. Holding out for a $1,000 raise in 1909, Tinker was called in to see Charles Webb Murphy, the club's owner. He listened to the player's argument, and then said, "I grant you that everything you've said is true, but let me ask you one question: where would you be without Evers?"

If nothing else, Tinker would have been a happier man without Evers at his side. As Bill Wambsganss once said, Evers was "a maniac on the field. You hear a lot about Cobb being like that, but Evers was worse." In 1911, Evers, called "The Human Crab," suffered a nervous breakdown and missed more than 100 games.

EARLY UMPIRES

Back in the days when only one umpire worked a game, players would, in Sam Crawford's phrase, "run with one eye on the ball and the other on the umpire"—if the ump was following the action at second base, for instance, a baserunner coming around third would cut fifteen feet out of his path and not bother with touching the base at all.

In Cincinnati at the turn of the century, Crawford told Lawrence Ritter, the great National League first baseman Jake Beckley attempted this subterfuge and came around to score without a play even being made on him. Umpire Tim Hurst, whose attention had been directed elsewhere, nonetheless called the runner out: "You got here *too* quick," Hurst told Beckley.

Crowd behavior in the first decade of the century often matched player behavior; roughness on the field seemed to elicit the same from the stands. As a rookie umpire in April 1907, Billy Evans was working a game in Chicago with the redoubtable Hurst; as an aroused citizenry was showering the field with bottles and other forms of refuse, Evans looked toward Hurst for help.

Hurst carried on boldly through the end of the ninth, and in their dressing room afterward admonished his young partner. "You needn't worry about those boys in April or May," Hurst told Evans. "They got no control. When the weather warms up, watch out—they're deadly at a hundred yards."

As it happened, only five months later, Evans would take a bottle on the back of the head in St. Louis. It fractured his skull, and he was a long time recovering. Evans eventually went on to umpire another twenty-two years, and then to work in front offices with Cleveland, the Red Sox, and the Tigers.

Evans was much loved in baseball, but in his umpiring career he did manage to run afoul of Ty Cobb. The two men once agreed to fight after a game in Washington and went at each other underneath the grandstand until both were exhausted. "Players who broke it up scored it as a draw," Red Smith wrote.

Before the fight, it had been agreed by both combatants that it wouldn't be reported to league offices. In time, though, American League president Ban Johnson heard about it and, with uncharacteristic humor, said only that he was sorry he had missed it.

And then there was Bill Klem. In 1905, the very first time he encountered John McGraw, the young man who would become baseball's most famous umpire ejected the Giants manager. On getting the thumb, McGraw snapped, "I'm going to get your job, you busher!"

Klem replied, "Mr. Manager, if it's possible for you to get my job away from me, I don't want it."

For thirty-six more years Klem presided over baseball games as an unreconstructed oligarch, brooking neither criticism nor debate, always certain of both his authority and his judgment. This dauntless self-confidence—arrogance, some would have it—made itself felt to Frank Frisch when Frisch broke in with the Giants in 1919. Unhappy with a called strike, Frisch turned and looked at Klem. The umpire, as Frisch later told the story, responded immediately: "Don't ever do that again, young man. Don't look back when I call a strike. Just you concentrate on your hitting and you'll get the greatest job from the greatest umpire that ever lived."

His legendary rectitude notwithstanding, Klem nonetheless spent his last working years under something of a cloud. After the 1934 Series was over, the umpire accosted Detroit's Goose Goslin to lecture him on proper on-field conduct. Klem was fined $50 by Commissioner K. M. Landis "for using abusive language to a ballplayer," and he never again received a World Series assignment.

TY COBB

Whether Ty Cobb—he of the .367 career average, the twelve batting championships, the eight slugging championships— was the greatest player the game has ever known is exceedingly debatable; that he was its most singular and, in many ways, most horrifying figure is not. Cobb was beset, said Detroit teammate Sam Crawford, by "a persecution complex." Davy Jones, another teammate, said "he has such a rotten disposition that it was damn hard to be his friend." With uncharacteristic understatement, late in life Cobb described his youthful self as "a snarling wildcat."

Whatever the diagnosis, everything that Cobb did on or off the field during his extraordinary playing career was freighted by a bundle of neuroses that have not known their match in baseball history; chief among was a snarling, unabated racism. At various times in his career, Cobb slapped a black elevator operator in a Cleveland hotel, attempted to choke the wife of a black groundskeeper with whom he had quarreled in Detroit, pistol-whipped a black butcher's assistant in Washington, and punched a black groundskeeper in Philadelphia. But his rages were not strictly racial in nature: during a barnstorming tour in the 1912–13 offseason, Cobb found himself engaged in a quarrel with a student coach from Wofford College in South Carolina, and after the game beat the student in his room while three of Cobb's teammates held him down.

Cobb, said his contemporary, Rube Bressler, "did everything except steal first base—and I think he did that in the dead of night." He was the dominant hitter of his era, the dominant base-stealer, and unquestionably the dominant competitor.

During the 1909 season, Cobb—as he would acknowledge in his own autobiography—decided to scare off Boston pitcher Cy Morgan, who had, Cobb insisted, been throwing at his head. Standing on second base when Morgan threw a wild pitch, Cobb determined to charge all the way home, anticipating a collision with Morgan as the pitcher covered the plate.

Cobb was barely three steps past third when Morgan was ready at the plate with the ball, but still he charged forward. "As I came down the line and went whipping at him with my steel showing," Cobb wrote, "Morgan . . . turned and actually ran away from the plate. I scored, and Morgan was released by Boston that night."

At the close of the 1910 season, Cobb was locked in a tight battle for the batting championship—and for the new automobile that went with it—with Cleveland's Napoleon Lajoie. As the season came down to its last weekend, Cobb held a lead over Lajoie, and he left the team with two games still to be played. On Sunday, October 9, Cleveland was in St. Louis to play a doubleheader, and Lajoie needed a nearly perfect day to capture the championship from Cobb. So detested was Cobb by the league's players that St. Louis manager Jack O'Connor was able to hand the championship to Lajoie: he instructed his third baseman to play on the outfield grass all day, and all day Lajoie bunted to the left side of the infield. He came away with eight hits (the first was an out-and-out triple, before he caught on to O'Connor's gift) in nine at bats. The next day, eight players joined to send Lajoie a telegram of congratulations—all eight of them, Cobb's own teammates. Characteristically, Cobb's bitterness toward Lajoie never subsided. In 1945, in a letter to E. J. Lanigan, Cobb denigrated his great competitor by writing, "Lajoie could not go out, nor come in, and did not cover too much ground to his right or left."

On a trip to Chicago to play the White Sox, the Tigers were booked into a hotel that overlooked a train yard. Cobb, who had a room facing the yard, complained unavailingly to the desk clerk about the noise, and then called his manager, Hughie Jennings. He said he couldn't sleep and wouldn't be able to hit for the lack of sleep, and then he insisted Jennings find him another room. It was the middle of the night, and Jennings offered to make the appropriate arrangements the next day. But Cobb didn't give him the chance—infuriated, he returned to Detroit that morning, missing two games of the Chicago series.

The most widely reported incident of Cobb's career took place in New York, on May 15, 1912, when he became engaged in a verbal battle with a crippled heckler who had often insulted him in games at Hilltop Field. When the heckler, Claude Lueker, called the player a "half-nigger," Cobb vaulted the fence, dashed into the stands, and proceeded to knock Lueker down and then kick and stomp him viciously. When a bystander shouted that the fallen man had no hands, Cobb snarled, "I don't care if he has no feet," and continued flailing at him with his spiked shoes.

Shortly, Cobb was suspended by American League president Ban Johnson. Astonishingly, though, his teammates stood by him. On Saturday, May 18, in Shibe Park, the entire Detroit team walked off the field before the game in sympathy with their suspended teammate. Prepared for the walkout, Detroit manager Jennings had enlisted, at $10 each, twelve local semipro and amateur ballplayers to become Tigers for the day. With a crowd of some 15,000 in attendance, the Athletics defeated the ragtag team by a score of 24-2. The next Philadelphia-Detroit game was canceled, and a negotiated settlement finally brought the Tigers back onto the field.

Cobb remained suspended for a full ten days, his only succor coming from a letter signed by all twelve members of the Congressional delegation from his native state. "As Georgians," the lawmakers wrote, "we commend your action in resisting an uncalled for insult."

His psychological gamesmanship was so finely tuned that Cobb could win a battle with the best of pitchers without even acknowledging the other man's presence. In a 1917 game against Chicago, Cobb entered the batter's box to face Eddie Cicotte, and immediately upon settling his feet he turned toward Sam Crawford, in the on-deck circle, and engaged him in conversation. Cicotte waited briefly, but then proceeded to pitch to Cobb, whose back remained turned—and four straight balls whizzed past while he continued his artfully distracting conversation with his teammate.

Over the length of his career, Cobb batted .335 against the great Walter Johnson. Always crowding the plate against the Washington pitcher, Cobb claimed that he knew Johnson would never pitch him tight because his knowledge of phrenology had enabled him to read Johnson's features, which showed the pitcher to be mild-mannered and gentle.

Grantland Rice related that Cobb's fires did not abate in retirement. Many years after his career was over, Cobb found himself in reminiscent conversation with the old Cleveland catcher Nig Clarke. Clarke was boasting about his hand-speed and how he'd often appeared to make a tag when he actually hadn't, and how Cobb himself had probably been called out a dozen times on plays at Clarke's plate when he'd actually been safe.

Enraged, Cobb grabbed for Clarke's throat and, wrote Rice, "it took three men to pull him off."

Still, Cobb himself knew the demons that gripped him. Long after his career was over, he encountered the Yankee scout Paul Krichell after a World Series game. In their brief conversation, according to Krichell, the aging Cobb (who had become fabulously wealthy from his early investment in the Coca-

Cola company) "told me that he would give up all his money and just about everything else he's got—if the fellows he played with and against would only accept him and talk to him today."

CY YOUNG

Of the man who won more games than any pitcher in history, Ogden Nash wrote this:

> Y is for Young
> The Magnificent Cy;
> People batted against him,
> But I never knew why.

He threw his first major league pitch in 1890, and his last 7,356 innings later, when he was 44. Pitching for the Boston Braves, Young lost 1-0 to a rookie with Philadelphia, Grover Cleveland Alexander. He decided to retire, he said, not because he could no longer pitch, but because he could no longer field his position: opposing batters were murdering him with bunts.

Later, he told Francis Powers, "During my 23 years in the big leagues I pitched 472 games in the National League and won 291, and then I went into the American League and won 220 there. All told I worked 879 games [the actual number was 906] and won 511, and far as I can see these modern pitchers aren't going to catch me."

WALTER JOHNSON

Johnson came out of a semi-pro league in Idaho, and over the next two decades he established himself as the greatest pitcher of his era. His 416 victories are second only to Cy Young; his career strikeout record stood for more than half a century.

There was nothing guileful about Walter Johnson; he simply threw a fastball like nothing anyone had ever seen before. New York outfielder Birdie Cree said the only way to hit Johnson was to swing as the pitcher's arm began its descent.

It was late in his second season that Johnson firmly established his dominance over the American League. On Friday, September 4, 1908, he shut out New York 3-0, on five hits. The next day, he pitched again and once more shut out the Highlanders, this time on three hits. As there was no Sunday baseball in New York at that time, the two teams were scheduled to meet again in a doubleheader on Monday. As he was playing catch with teammate Gabby Street before the first game, Johnson noticed he was the only Washington pitcher on the field. He looked into the dugout and saw his manager, Joe Cantillon, nod his head.

Returning to the bench, Johnson told Cantillon, "It's all right with me if it's all right with you." This time, he shut out New York on two hits. He then took three days off before beating the A's, 3-2; the day after that, he again beat the A's, this time by a score of 5-4. Two more days off, and Johnson pitched three innings of shut-out relief against the White Sox. Then, finally, on Friday, September 18, his two remarkable weeks of pitching came to an end. Johnson lost to Rube Waddell in St. Louis—2-1, in ten innings, the run that beat him scoring on a popped-up bunt that no one could field.

During the streak, he had pitched 58 innings, allowing eight runs, winning five games, and saving one. For his trouble, he was paid $2,700 for the entire season.

Billy Evans maintained that calling balls and strikes when Johnson was pitching was among his easiest responsibilities. Once when Evans called a Johnson pitch to Joe Gedeon a strike, the Yankee second baseman turned and asked, "What was it, a fast ball or a curve?"

Evans asked Gedeon why he wanted to know.

The batter grinned. "I never saw it, I had to close my eyes." It was an encounter that gave the umpire confidence. "I knew the ballplayers couldn't second-guess me," Evans said, "if they were closing their eyes, too."

In 1912, the American League was gripped by the parallel progress of Johnson and Joe Wood of the Red Sox, both men winning 16 straight games during the course of the season. Johnson once acknowledged Wood's prowess thus: "Can I throw harder than Joe Wood? Listen, my friend, there's no man alive can throw harder than Smokey Joe Wood."

Early in September, Johnson's streak finally came to an end around the time that Wood's had reached thirteen. Washington was scheduled to visit Boston, and Clark Griffith of the Senators persuaded Red Sox manager Jake Stahl to let the two men face each other—to let, as Griffith put it, "Walter defend his record."

With a man on second in the sixth inning and the score tied 0-0, Duffy Lewis reached Johnson for a pop fly down the right-field line. The Washington outfielder, Danny Moeller, tried in vain to get to it, and the game's only run came in, extending Wood's streak.

Afterward in the Washington clubhouse, Johnson found Moeller in tears. "Don't feel badly," the pitcher told him. "I should have struck him out."

When the new Federal League staged its raid on American and National League players in 1914, Johnson was one of its prime targets. Working at the time on a $7,000 a year, three-year contract for Washington, Johnson was offered a $10,000 signing bonus by the Chicago franchise in the new league. Before accepting it, he told Washington owner Clark Griffith he would stay with the Senators if Griffith would match the $10,000.

Griffith didn't have the money, but he knew where to find it. He went to Charles Comiskey of the White Sox and persuaded Comiskey what it might mean to the Sox if Johnson were pitching regularly for another Chicago club. Comiskey wrote out a check for the full amount, and Johnson stayed a Senator.

The particular cross that Johnson bore was the perpetual ineptitude of his teammates, the condition that led to the popular adage about Washington—"First in war, first in peace, and last in the American League." It wasn't until the great pitcher's eighteenth season that he appeared in the World Series, and when he did he suffered a case of rookie's nerves. "Walter was so nervous before the game I felt sorry for him," said Art Nehf, who was the New York pitcher for the opening game. "He knew that millions of people were pulling for him. When we shook hands for the photographers, his hand trembled."

Johnson, who would turn thirty-eight a month after the Series ended, lost the first game to Nehf and the fifth to Jack Bentley. Then, coming in to pitch relief in the seventh game, the fading titan held New York for four innings as the Senators won in the twelfth. It was the only World Series a Washington team would ever win.

MERKLE'S BONER

For fourteen years, Fred Merkle was a fine ballplayer, a mainstay of teams that won five pennants. But Merkle had the misfortune, before he had played his first full season in the major leagues, to be the key figure in what remains the most famous single play in baseball history. That occurred, of course, during the Cubs-Giants contest of Thursday, September 24, 1908, when Merkle's teammate Al Bridwell hit a single that scored Moose McCormick with what appeared to be the winning New York run. In the custom of the day, Merkle, who had been on first, left the baseline as McCormick scored, hurrying to the home team clubhouse as ecstatic Giant fans poured onto the field. Johnny Evers of the Cubs, noticing that Merkle hadn't bothered to touch second, got the ball and tagged the base. Umpire Hank O'Day declared Merkle out on the force play, ending the inning and negating the run that had come in from third. When the game was replayed on October 9, Chicago's victory gave them the pennant by one game over New York.

Those are the generally known events that determined the outcome of that 1908 National League season. But the detail was even more complex, and far more bizarre. Take, for instance, the means by which second baseman Evers got his hands on the ball—or, at least, *a* ball.

It began when Chicago outfielder Art Hofman fielded Bridwell's single and threw it into the infield. The ball rolled unmolested toward the third base coach's box, where Joe McGinnity was coaching for New York. McGinnity picked up the ball, while both Evers and Joe Tinker wrestled him for it; McGinnity broke loose and threw it into the seats, where what Evers recalled as "a tall, stringy middle-aged gent with a brown bowler hat on" caught it. Meanwhile, Christy Mathewson and other Giants were trying to retrieve Merkle from the clubhouse. The Cubs' Harry Steinfeldt and Floyd Kroh chased the man in the bowler; Kroh hit him, got the ball, and tossed it to Tinker, who in turn relayed it to Evers at second.

Umpire O'Day intoned, "The run does not count," and walked off the field as the crowd milled around.

O'Day was especially alert to the circumstances because of an event that was still fresh in his mind. As Johnny Evers told John Carmichael many years later, "It was 19 days earlier, at Pittsburgh, that we really won the game at New York. The Pirates' Warren Gill, playing what would be his only major league season, didn't touch second in an identical situation in the tenth." Evers complained to O'Day, who was umpiring that game too; although O'Day let the run stand, the seed of doubt was planted in his mind, ready to flower at the next comparable moment.

After the famous game and O'Day's shocking decision, when the Cubs finally made it to their clubhouse, their joy was somewhat mitigated. Most teams in those days assigned a player who was not likely to appear in action—usually a pitcher—to guard a bag in which the players placed their money and valuables. On this day, the designated watchman was Kroh—and when he raced toward the stands to get the ball from the man in the bowler hat, he had left the bag unattended. Evers recalled the players lost cash and jewelry worth $5,200.

O'Day's pivotal role in the pennant race didn't end with the Merkle call. In late September the third team in the National League race, the Pirates, was playing the Cubs. In the ninth inning, with Chicago ahead 2-0 and the visiting Pirates at bat with the bases loaded, second baseman Ed Abbaticchio hit a rocket down the right-field line. O'Day ruled it foul, the Cubs won the game, and went on to win the pennant by one game over the Pirates as well as taking the playoff from the Giants.

Several months later, though, a woman fan brought a lawsuit to court, alleging injury suffered when she was struck by Abbaticchio's smash, an occurrence attested to in sworn statements by various witnesses. But the court ended up ruling against her—not because her story wasn't believed, but because it was conclusively established that she had been sitting in fair territory at the time.

Had umpire O'Day come to the same conclusion, the Pirates would have led the disputed game at least 4-2 going into the bottom of the ninth. Had they won, they would have finished alone in first place, the Giants would never have met the Cubs in the fateful playoff, and Fred Merkle's hideous gaffe of September 24 would be remembered barely, if at all.

"He was a good umpire," Johnny Evers said about O'Day, "if you didn't tell him so too often."

Still, despite all the unanticipated twists and turns of the 1908 season, Merkle's dash from the baseline determined its shape. Outraged by O'Day's call, Christy Mathewson vainly threatened, "If this game goes to Chicago by any trick or argument, you can take it from me that if we lose the pennant thereby, I will never play professional baseball again."

But when the season was over, both the events and their results were accepted, however grudgingly, by the Giants. What they did not accept was the obloquy cast on Merkle. John McGraw said, "It is criminal to say that Merkle is stupid and to blame the loss of the pennant on him. In the first place, he is one of the smartest and best players on this club. In the second place, . . . we lost a dozen games we should have won. Besides," he concluded, "we were robbed of it, and you can't say Merkle did that." That winter, John T. Brush, owner of the Giants, had 28 medals struck for the members of his team. Each read: "The Real Champions, 1908."

Years later, New York outfielder Fred Snodgrass, who would enter Series infamy in 1912 for his own overplayed mistake, said to Lawrence Ritter, "How could you blame Merkle, when we lost the playoff game, and besides that we lost five other games after the Merkle incident?"

And Al Bridwell, who made the hit that scored the run that was obliterated when Merkle failed to touch second, said the most wrenching thing of all: "I wish I'd never gotten that hit . . . I wish I'd struck out instead. If I'd have done that, then it would have spared Fred a lot of unfair humiliation."

In fact, Merkle figured twice more in critical World Series decisions. In the 1911 series, the Giants—down three games to one when the action returned to the Polo Grounds from Philadelphia—trailed 3-1 in the bottom of the ninth, when they tied the score and the game went into extra innings.

With one out in the bottom of the tenth and Larry Doyle on third base, Merkle reached Eddie Plank of Philadelphia for a long fly to right field. Danny Murphy made the catch and then fired the ball in, where the tagged-up Doyle and his fallaway slide beat the ball to home plate.

Bill Klem, umpiring, stood by silently as the players left the field. Doyle had never touched the plate, but as none of the Athletics attempted to tag him before he was in the clubhouse, the winning run stood.

Merkle's final moment at center stage occurred the next year and as much as he was unjustly accused of costing the Giants the pennant in 1908, he somehow escaped blame for a far greater lapse that led to his team's loss of the 1912 Series.

This was the Series known for Fred Snodgrass's notorious "Muff," an uncharacteristic error the Giant outfielder committed on an easy fly ball in the tenth inning of the seventh game. New York had taken a 2-1 lead over the Red Sox in the top of the inning, then the events that caused them to lose 3-2 began when pinch-hitter Clyde Engle lofted the fly that popped out of Snodgrass's glove, allowing Engle—the tying run—to take second base with no one out.

But it was Snodgrass who made an outstanding catch on a hard drive by the next batter, and nearly doubled Engle off second on his throw to the infield. And it was Christy Mathewson, the greatest control pitcher of his era, who allowed the winning run to take first on a base on balls.

And then, with one out and two on, Tris Speaker hit a pop foul near first. Inexplicably glued to his position, first baseman Merkle watched the ball drop unmolested. Given new life, Speaker singled in one run, and after an intentional walk the winning run scored on Larry Gardner's sacrifice fly to right—what would have been the third out had Merkle escaped from his trance and caught Speaker's foul.

OTHER EARLY STARS

The great Mordecai "Three-Finger" Brown, whose 2.06 lifetime ERA is history's third best, was once asked whether missing a finger on his pitching hand made it any harder to pitch successfully. "I don't know," Brown replied, "I've never done it the other way."

Napoleon Lajoie was one of the few men to have a team named for him; in the years he dominated the Cleveland club, they were universally known as the Naps. He didn't lead them in every fashion, though; terrified by any body of water, Lajoie would abandon the team when they traveled by lake steamer to Detroit.

Nig Clarke, who once hit eight home runs in a single Texas League game, reached the majors in 1905 and put in nine years as a catcher. Late in August of 1908, a newlywed, he wanted to leave the team for a brief trip to see his wife. Lajoie, Cleveland's manager at the time, declined permission; the team was in a close pennant race with the Tigers.

Clarke sulked a bit and then went to catch some warm-up throws from the Cleveland ace Addie Joss. Sticking his index finger straight into one of Joss's deliveries, Clarke achieved what he wanted. Going back to the bench, he showed the shattered, bloody finger to Lajoie and said, "Well, I guess I can go home now, can't I?"

Clarke was out five weeks, and Cleveland lost the pennant to Detroit by half a game.

In 1910, while Lajoie and Cobb were locked in their disputed race for the batting championship, New York's Russ Ford chose to pitch around Lajoie. This was before catchers would leave their positions and stand several feet from the plate on the intentional walk; at the time, the common practice was for the pitcher simply to throw wide, where the catcher would reach out from his crouch.

Each of the first three times Lajoie came to bat that day, Ford pitched wide—and each time, Lajoie reached out with one hand and hit the ball safely to the opposite field. Finally, the last time Lajoie came to bat that day, Ford adjusted his procedure and threw four straight pitches behind Lajoie's back.

THE PURPLE AGE OF SPORTSWRITING

Before the era when sportswriters were reporters, chasing after stories in the clubhouse, they made reputations only with the color of their prose. This inevitably pushed the less talented to the purple end of the spectrum, as this example cited by Douglas Wallop demonstrates:

"With the third inning faded into the dim and forgotten past, the fourth spasm in the afternoon's matinee of Dementia Baseballitis hopped into the glare of the calcium glim. It was the Giants' turn to paddle the pellet, Murderous Michael Donlin taking his turn beside the glad gum. Mike biffed the bulb on the proboscis and sent it gleefully gliding to the distant shrubbery . . . Bresnahan managed to get next to the seamy side of a floater and the Toledo kid sent the denizens of Coogan's Bluff into Seventh Heaven of Gleefulness by starting the pulsating pill on a line for the extreme backward. But they reckoned without the mighty Wagner. The Carnegie Dutchman extended a monster paw, the near-two bagger was cleverly captured by a dainty dab of his lunch hook and before you could bat an eye he had whipped the globule over to Abby, who made an earnest effort to put Donlin down and out but missed by a fraction of an inch."

Or, as Wallop summarized: "In the New York half of the fourth inning, Mike Donlin singled and catcher Roger Bresnahan lined out to Wagner, who almost doubled up Donlin at first base."

ZACK WHEAT

When scout Larry Sutton signed a young minor-leaguer named Zack Wheat to a Brooklyn contract in 1909, Charles Ebbets asked him, "What did Wheat hit at Mobile?"

"Two forty-five," Sutton replied.

Ebbets, ever the owner, was flabbergasted. "What do you expect me to do with a player who hit for such a low average in a minor league?"

The scout was one beat ahead of his boss. "Put him in the outfield," he said. "That's where he plays."

Wheat would retire nineteen years later, a lifetime .317 hitter with more than 1,200 RBIs.

HONUS WAGNER

In 1895, while operating the Paterson franchise in the Atlantic League, Ed Barrow—who would later build the great Yankee teams of the 1920s and 30s—went to Mansfield, Pa., to sign Honus Wagner.

The twenty-one year-old shortstop was a physical specimen: 5'11", 200 pounds, hideously bow-legged, and with arms so long that Lefty Gomez once said, "He can tie his shoelaces without bending down."

In his autobiography, Barrow revealed that the timeless spirit of the club owner existed even in the low minors, even in the nineteenth century. "I had to have this fellow on my ball club," Barrow wrote. "We had a league limit of $100 a month for players, but I offered Wagner $125."

Two seasons later, Wagner reached the majors for the beginning of a 21-year career, during which he dominated the National League as much as Ty Cobb dominated the American. Between 1900 and 1912, he led the league in major offensive categories thirty-eight times, including eight batting championships, six slugging championships, and five stolen base titles.

But Wagner couldn't have been more different from Cobb. He was as gentle as Cobb was ferocious, as beloved by his fellow players as Cobb was despised, as humble as Cobb was arrogant.

Wagner himself considered one of the most important events in his career a moment when, in his third big league season, he told a Giant who had cracked a home run, "Nice hit." The player, operating by the code of the day, snarled in response, "Go to hell."

"I liked that remark," Wagner told Arthur Daley years later. "He was the first major leaguer ever to speak to me."

In 1916, Burleigh Grimes was called up from Birmingham to finish the season in the big leagues. In his very first game as a major leaguer, he was facing the Dodgers at Ebbets Field, the score tied 1-1 in the seventh, a man on first. Wagner, who was closing down his career at shortstop, came to the mound to calm down the young Grimes. "Make him hit to me, kid," he intoned.

In fact, the next batter did hit a grounder to short, a perfect double-play ball. Wagner kicked it into center, the runner scored, and the batter went to third. Wagner returned to the mound and told Grimes, "Those damn big feet have always been in my way."

After his career was over, Wagner retained his kindly nature, but the loss of his athletic gifts proved psychologically unbearable. While Cobb was clipping coupons from his investments, the beloved Wagner came apart. As a coach with the Pirates in the late 40s and early 50s, he was mostly a mascot, a friendly, garrulous alcoholic. His habit, recalled Ralph Kiner, who played for the Pirates in that era, was to walk into a saloon in Pittsburgh and slap a silver dollar on the bar. People would look over at the noise, and immediately he'd be recognized. Someone would buy him a beer, Wagner would thank him, and then go to the next bar down the street and repeat the routine.

ADDIE JOSS

The ethos of baseball early in the century was such that even the finest of players, like the Cleveland pitcher Addie Joss, felt the need to play no matter how disabled. After missing most of the 1910 season, Joss pushed himself in spring training the following year never once admitting to illness; when he was hospitalized after fainting in Chattanooga, where the Indians were scheduled to play an exhibition game, he apologized to his teammates for what he called his "baby trick."

Joss finally sought medical help when the team made a stop in Cincinnati, and he died a week later of tubercular meningitis.

BEFORE THE INSTANT REPLAY

In the third game of the 1912 Series, the Giants led the Red Sox 2-1 in the bottom of the ninth, with two out and runners on second and third. The Boston catcher, a rookie named Hick Cady, hit a long fly ball deep to right field. As it dropped in the late afternoon twilight, the Giants' Josh Devore made a dive for it, his glove landing in the general area of the ball. Without missing a beat, Devore rose from his outstretched position and dashed into the locker room, just as he would have had he not missed the ball.

The umpires ruled it a catch, and thus a New York victory. The next day, three different Red Six fans showed up bearing balls that each claimed was the one that had skidded under Devore's glove and into the crowd.

GEORGE STALLINGS

The man who brought Boston's "Miracle Braves" of 1914 from oblivion to World Champions was an uncharacteristic figure: a graduate of Virginia Military Institute, a medical student at the College of Physicians and Surgeons in Baltimore, a challenger of orthodoxy who was the first manager to play platoon baseball, using lefty/righty tandems in both left and right fields. He was also a monomaniac of staggering proportions; wrote Tom Meany, "No man, not even John McGraw or Leo Durocher, ever reached the heights of invective stormed by George. He could fly into a schizophrenic rage at the drop of a pop fly."

Stallings could be victimized by his single-mindedness. He would, from habit and superstition, maintain the physical position he was in whenever his team got a hit. A fanatic for tidiness, as for everything else, Stallings found himself picking up a peanut shell in the dugout during a game in the 1914 season, when the Braves were in the midst of the miraculous pennant drive. At that moment the batter got a hit and Stallings remained in his awkward stoop. The next batter hit as well, and the next, until the Braves had amassed a ten-hit rally.

When the inning ended two of Stallings's players had to carry their spasm-ridden manager to the clubhouse.

THE FEDERAL LEAGUE

The challenge to organized baseball wrought by the new Federal League in 1914 had extensive consequences: some of the best American and National League players, including Hal Chase, Ed Reulbach, and Eddie Plank, jumped their clubs; player salaries went up with the competition; and Judge Kenesaw Mountain Landis, in whose court the dispute with the Federals was heard, was elevated to baseball prominence. Still the Feds were dead by the end of the 1915 season when a truce was signed, including compensation to the owners of the defunct teams.

But one legalistically minded player did his part to keep the Federals alive. Fresh out of Notre Dame, first baseman Rupert Mills was signed to a two-year contract, for $3,000 a year, with the league's Newark club in 1915. When the league folded at season's end, he refused to accept reassignment, and also rejected Newark's settlement offer of $600.

Acting for club owner Harry Sinclair, who would later figure in the Teapot Dome Scandal, Newark president Pat Powers attempted to break Mills's will by ordering him to report to work for a non-existent team. The resolute player, determined to collect his contractual salary, proceeded to show up at the Newark ballpark every day at 8:55 in the morning, work out until lunch, and then resume his efforts from 2 p.m. to 6 p.m. He continued abiding by his part of the contract through early July of the 1916 season, until Sinclair offered a settlement he could accept.

LIFE AT THE BOTTOM

After winning in 1914 his fourth pennant in five years, Connie Mack sold off his best players rather than meet the challenge from the Federal League, and proceeded to watch benignly as his Philadelphia Athletics plummeted to the basement. In 1914 they had won 99 games; in 1915 they managed to win only 43; and in 1916, they bottomed out at a modern record, 37. Between them, pitchers Tom Sheehan and John Nabors—they were roommates—went 2-37 in 1916.

The A's had two other pitchers, Elmer Myers and Joe Bush, who lost 23 and 22 games respectively. Their shortstop, Whitey Witt, made 70 errors. Their best catcher batted .232, then in July was lost for the season to appendicitis. Among his replacements were players who batted .195 and .091. At one point, the A's lost 19 straight on the road.

The dreadful season reached its nadir during a doubleheader in Boston. In the first game, Sheehan gave up one hit and lost 1-0. In the second, Nabors was leading 1-0 in the ninth. An error by Witt, then a walk; next a single by Harry Hooper that tied the game when the throw from the outfield bounced out of the catcher's glove.

Finally, with a runner on third and only one out, Nabors threw the next pitch twenty feet over the batter's head, and the winning run trotted home. After the game, Sheehan asked his roommate what happened. "Look," Nabors said, "I knew those guys wouldn't get me another run, and if you think I'm going to throw nine more innings on a hot day like this, you're crazy."

It was in the middle of the 1915 pennant race, and the Cardinals were playing Brooklyn in St. Louis. Miller Huggins, who was gaining the training that would eventually lead him to manage the great Yankee teams of the twenties, was running the St. Louis club from the third-base coach's box. In the top of the seventh, with two out, the score tied, and a Cardinals runner on third, Huggins called out to Brooklyn pitcher Ed Appleton: "Hey, bub, let me see that ball!"

The 23-year-old rookie obligingly tossed the ball to Huggins—whereupon the St. Louis manager, who hadn't called time, stepped aside, let the ball roll past, and watched his base runner cross home with the winning run.

A weak-hitting shortstop who nonetheless suffered from the vanity that plagues most players, Ivy Olson hated the instructions of his Brooklyn manager, Wilbert Robinson. There was a concrete post in the Brooklyn dugout, and Robinson usually sat near it. When Olson was at the plate, Robinson would flash the bunt sign, a clenched fist, but Olson would change his position in the batter's box so that the post was between him and the manager. In Burleigh Grimes's recollection, "We'd watch Robbie move in one direction, Olson in the other . . . Here's Robbie sliding around on a bench with that fist clenched, looking like he wanted to punch somebody, and there's Olson up at the plate ducking around to keep the post between them. Finally, Robbie would say, 'Ah, the hell with it.' "

UNLIKELY BASE-RUNNERS

It was in the final game of the 1917 Series when Heinie Zimmerman, the New York Giants' third baseman, entered baseball legend. In the third inning, a two-base throwing error by Zimmerman, who Warren Brown said "played baseball by ear," led to three Chicago runs. Later in the game, Zimmerman fielded a grounder while Eddie Collins raced home from third. He looked for someone to throw to, but catcher Bill Rariden had gone to back up third base, and neither first baseman Walter Holke nor pitcher Rube Benton had come in to cover the plate. With no other options, Zimmerman began to chase the fleet Collins home, across the plate, and into Series history.

Later, Ring Lardner imagined Zimmerman's most reasonable response to those who would question his feeble dash with the ball: "What was I supposed to do? Throw it to Klem?"

In that same Series, the pitching star was Chicago's Red Faber, who won three games. But Faber distinguished himself in a different fashion in the second game, his first start.

In the fifth inning of what would be a 7-2 White Sox victory, Faber hit safely and in time found himself at second base, with his teammate Buck Weaver on third and two out. Inexplicably, as New York's Pol Perritt went into his windup, Faber broke for third. As he concluded his head-first slide, Weaver—still on third—asked him, "Where in hell do you think you're going?"

"Back to pitch," Faber replied.

Of course, Faber may have been emboldened by his base-running exploits of two seasons earlier. Against the Athletics on July 14, 1915, he tried intentionally to get picked off first base in an effort to hurry a rain-threatened game. Philadelphia, wishing to extend the game, ignored him, and Faber proceeded to steal second, third, and home in the same inning—43 percent of the bases he would steal in his entire twenty-year career. The rain never came, and the White Sox ended up winning by two runs.

THE DOUBLE NO-HITTER

The facts are well known: May 2, 1917; Chicago's Weeghman Park; a cold, blustery Wednesday, only 2,500 in attendance as the game began. It was Fred Toney pitching for Cincinnati, Hippo Vaughn for the Cubs. Toney walked Cy Williams in the second and the fifth, but no other Cubs reached base. Vaughn walked Heinie Groh twice; both times he was erased in a double play. Cincinnati's Greasy Neale reached on an error, but was caught stealing. Into the tenth it went, an unprecedented double no-hitter, until Jim Thorpe dribbled a hit off of Vaughn in the top of the tenth that brought in a run for Cincinnati.

Once before, in the minor leagues, Toney had been equally adept, when in 1909 he pitched a 17-inning no-hitter. But it was only two months after his epic battle with Vaughn that he most distinguished himself, beating Pittsburgh in both ends of a double-header, 4-1 and 5-1. Afterwards, he said that he could have pitched a third game had he been asked to.

THE BLACK SOX SCANDAL

Hal Chase was a notorious thrower of games, a constant gambler, a thoroughly corrupt man who was a key figure in the fixing of the 1919 World Series. But he was also one of the very finest first basemen in the game, an exceptionally agile fielder who on at least one occasion charged from first, flipped a fielded bunt to third, and raced back to first to make the closing putout on a remarkable 3-5-3 double play. In 1907, *Sporting Life* called him "perhaps the biggest drawing card in baseball."

Chase found his career winding down with the Reds in 1918, where his manager was the recently retired Christy Mathewson. As Mathewson went off to fight in Europe that summer with the AEF, he charged that Chase had consciously thrown games while playing for him. Several times before there had been whispers about Chase in his long career, but only Mathewson had uttered such charges publicly. With Mathewson overseas when a mandated hearing took place, the National League tribunal that investigated the case dismissed it for lack of evidence.

After the war, though, both men found themselves with McGraw's Giants—Matty as a coach, Chase as first baseman. On the very first day of training camp, Larry Doyle's bat slipped from his hands during batting practice and struck Mathewson, who was standing nearby. While Doyle and his teammates rushed to their coach's assistance, Chase waited immobile by the batting cage, his face inscrutable. At least, said one newsman standing by, "he had the grace not to laugh out loud."

By 1920, Chase was back in California where he had played college ball; in August of that year he was banned from Pacific Coast League parks for allegedly trying to bribe pitcher Sider Baum of Salt Lake City. That fall he was indicted by a Cook County Grand Jury for his role in what would become known as the Black Sox scandal, but as California refused extradition, he was never brought to trial. His wife soon sued

Chase for divorce, citing "dissipation and gambling." Twenty-six years later, in an interview just before his death, Chase denied nothing, saying only that he didn't really profit very much from his inside information on the 1919 Series.

But Chase's proper epitaph had been written while he was still active. Said *The Sporting News* in 1913, "That he can play first as it never was and perhaps never will be played is a well-known truth. That he will is a different matter."

It was October 1, 1919, in Cincinnati, the opening of the sixteenth World Series. The visiting Chicago White Sox had been retired in the top of the first inning, and now Reds second baseman Maurice Rath came to the plate. As the crowd focused its attention on Rath, White Sox pitcher Eddie Cicotte plunked him in the back with a pitch.

The mass smile that spread across the faces of various gamblers in New York and Chicago when the telegraph wires reported Rath's fate was knowing, and it was greedy. For with his intentionally errant pitch, Cicotte had sent the agreed-upon signal: the fix was on.

The Black Sox scandal that shook the game in 1919 began not with the importunings of gamblers, but with the dishonest initiative of Chicago first baseman Chick Gandil. Having approached a Boston bookmaker with a scheme to throw the Series to the Reds for $80,000, Gandil had an easy enough time soliciting the complicity of his key teammates. The least likely member of the cabal—at least from the point of necessity—was utility infielder Fred McMullin.

On the day that Gandil approached shortstop Swede Risberg, Gandil thought their meeting place, the Sox clubhouse, was empty. But McMullin happened to be resting on a bench behind a row of lockers. Confronting Gandil with his eavesdropped knowledge, McMullin insisted on being cut in for a full share of the money. A blackmailer fleecing a briber, McMullin only batted 170 times during the entire 1919 season, and would appear in the Series itself for only two trips to the plate—but there was no way of keeping him out of the scheme.

McMullin's shakedown cost Gandil and his co-conspirators several thousand dollars. But after the scandal became public and Commissioner Kenesaw Mountain Landis suspended the Black Sox after the 1920 season, it cost McMullin the rest of his career. At the time he was twenty-nine.

Whispers about baseball gambling were rife in the months leading up to the Black Sox scandal. When the pathetic Phillies arrived in Chicago for a late August game that summer of 1919, rumors flew to the effect that the scheduled Cubs pitcher had been reached by gamblers and was going to throw the game. Fred Mitchell, the Cubs manager, quickly changed his rotation and inserted Grover Cleveland Alexander. Still, the Phillies—who would finish 47½ games out of first that season—prevailed, 3-0.

When the Phillies returned east, talk of a reputed fix was everywhere. Bill Brandt of the Philadelphia *Bulletin* called Phillies manager Gavvy Cravath for comment, and Cravath said, "Sure I heard something about it, but I certainly don't know anything about it. I don't know why they gotta bring a thing like this up just because we win one. We're liable to win a game anytime."

That Chicago was able to win a pennant in 1919 was evidence of remarkable talent, given that the White Sox clubhouse was as faction-ridden as any in baseball's history. On one side were Gandil, Risberg, and various other "hard guys," in Nelson Algren's term. On the other was a rather nobler faction that included pitcher Dickie Kerr and was led by the great second baseman Eddie Collins. Collins had a weak Series, but the 5'7" Kerr ("Little pitchers have big years," it was said of him) won two games despite his teammates' corruption. Collins was a Columbia University graduate, by far the highest-paid player on the team, a relative aristocrat in the coarse, rough world of baseball. Teammate Buck Weaver, who was among the players who despised him, later recalled that Collins was the only member of the Sox who would never sharpen his spikes. "He figures they might come back at him and he'd get hurt playing there in the infield. He was a great guy to look out for himself. If there was a tough gent coming down to second, he'd yell for the shortstop to take the play." So deep were the divisions on the team that neither Gandil, the first baseman, nor Risberg, the shortstop, would even speak to Collins.

Collins's chief complaint about his teammates was that unless catcher Ray Schalk threw him the ball every so often, he never even got the chance to feel it.

Perhaps the most chilling aspect of the fixed Series was the blatancy with which it was thrown. Rumors about the fix had traveled through baseball circles during the days leading up to the Series, and by the time the Reds had won the first game, scores of knowledgeable observers were convinced of the conspiracy. At the very first game, Chicago sportswriter Hugh Fullerton asked Christy Mathewson, with whom he was sitting in the press box, to help him spot any "suspicious" plays—and they found several. During the second game, catcher Schalk, one of the honest Sox, became furious at conspirator Lefty Williams, whose intentionally flabby pitching gave the game to Cincinnati. When Schalk reported to Chicago manager Kid Gleason that Williams had three times ignored his sign for a curveball in the critical fourth inning, Gleason's rage broke out.

Eyeing a complacent and unperturbed Gandil in the clubhouse after the game, Gleason sardonically said, "Gandil, you sure had a good day today." The first baseman replied, "So did you, Kid." The manager exploded, leaping for and getting his hands on the player's throat. Only the interference of several other players could pull him away.

As Schalk himself left the park, he encountered Williams. Schalk pulled the pitcher under the grandstand and assaulted him with both fists. Again, other players had to separate them. And when it came Williams's turn to pitch again in the fifth game, a dispirited Gleason was asked whether he'd use him again. "No," the manager replied, "I think I'll go in myself."

On the train back to Chicago after Game 2, writer Ring Lardner stumbled drunkenly through the White Sox car. As he lurched, he sang, "I'm forever blowing ball games, Pretty ball games in the air . . . I'm forever blowing ball games, And the gamblers treat us fair." In the words of Eliot Asinof, whose *Eight Men Out* is the definitive history of the Black Sox, "Nobody even told him to shut up."

Arnold Rothstein, the mobster who would provide most of the money for the corrupt players, bet several hundred thousand on the Series. His only apparent regret was the relatively amateurish fashion in which the fix proceeded; had the Sox won the first game and *then* started their cave-in, he could have made his bets on Cincinnati with Chicago a 2-1 favorite. As it turned out, Cincinnati became the favorite after the first game, and Rothstein had to settle for less favorable odds.

Joe Jackson, the great hitter who was part of Gandil's cabal but nonetheless hit .375 in the Series, was a natural target for the conspirators. A virtual illiterate from South Carolina, he had developed a somewhat misanthropic shell from the hectoring he had been subject to since he came into the league. In Detroit, in 1909, while playing for the A's, he hit a tremendous triple. As Jackson stood on third base after the play, a spectator yelled to him, "Hey, Jackson, can you spell 'cat'?"

The ballplayer looked at the heckler malevolently and replied, "Hey, mister, can you spell 'shit'?"

What is most often neglected in the handed-down memories of the 1919 Series is that, because of some suspiciously disappearing evidence, all eight of the accused men were acquitted by a jury in Cook County Court. Consequently, Commissioner Landis's statement banning the Black Sox for life began, "Regardless of the verdicts of juries. . . ."

The one man who didn't seem to care about the lifetime ban announced by Landis after the 1920 season was Gandil. After the fixed Series was over, he retired from baseball, announcing he was opening a restaurant in San Francisco. He had no good name to protect, and no apparent need to proceed with his athletic career.

And Jackson, his teammate with the third highest lifetime batting average in history—which undoubtedly would have gone even higher in the hitting-happy twenties—is remembered only for the apocryphal words of an imagined child: "Say it ain't so, Joe."

THE LAST GASP OF THE EARLY YEARS

The celebrated 26-inning tie played in Boston between the Dodgers and Braves on Saturday, June 1, 1920, concluded with Ivy Olson begging umpire Barry McCormick to let the game go one more inning into the gathering dusk—so that it could be said that the two teams played the equivalent of three games in one day. McCormick declined, saying, "My feet are killing me and I'm having trouble seeing the ball." Olson replied, "You have trouble seeing the ball at high noon." Astonishingly, all 26 innings were played in three hours and fifty minutes.

But even with the game suspended, Brooklyn found itself beginning a streak that should have exhausted them. The next day, back in Brooklyn, they lost to Philadelphia 4-3 in 14 innings; returning then to Boston on Monday—the Phillies game was scheduled in the midst of the Braves series because Sunday baseball was forbidden in Boston—they lost to the Braves 2-1, this time in 19 innings. In three days, they had strung together 58 innings of baseball without a single victory to show for it. Still, Brooklyn won the pennant by seven games.

THE YEARS
OF BABE RUTH

From Babe's Rise
to DiMaggio's Streak

BABE RUTH

When Robert Creamer was writing *Babe,* his wonderful biography of George Herman Ruth (which happens to be the source for the most reliable of Ruthian anecdotes), he received a letter from Waite Hoyt, the Hall of Fame pitcher. "I am almost convinced," Ruth's long-time teammate wrote, "that you will never learn the truth on Ruth. I roomed with Joe Dugan. He was a good friend of Babe's. But he will see Ruth in a different light than I did. Dugan's own opinion will be one in which Dugan revels in Ruth's crudities, and so on. While I can easily recognize all of this and admit it freely, yet there was buried in Ruth humanitarianism beyond belief, an intelligence he was never given credit for, a childish desire to be over-virile, living up to credits given his home-run power—and yet a need for intimate affection and respect, and a feverish desire to play baseball, perform, act and live a life he didn't and couldn't take time to understand."

As Ruth himself once said to Arthur Daley, "I guess I could have written two books of my life—one for the adults and one for the kids." He might also have written one on pitching—2.28 ERA, winning percentage of .671—as well as one on hitting. Ruth's impact was so great that this story cannot be separated from the story of the entire period between the World Wars. There was Ruth in this period, and there was everyone else.

The minor league Baltimore Orioles with whom Ruth got his start were as close to major league as a team could get without the official designation. At least eight of Ruth's teammates had major league experience, and owner Jack Dunn had pitched for Ned Hanlon and John McGraw. Ruth was still just an overgrown kid when the Orioles traveled down to Fayetteville, N.C., for spring training in 1914. He had never been on a train before, and the other players told him the little hammock for clothes next to his berth was meant for a pitcher's arm, which he believed.

In his very first professional game, a sort of rag-tag intrasquad affair, Ruth hit a tremendous drive that caused the *Baltimore American* to proclaim the next day, "RUTH MAKES MIGHTY CLOUT." The other players thought of him as "Dunnie's baby," and by the third week of camp, newspaper reports back to Baltimore were referring to him as Babe Ruth.

Ruth was 14-6 in early July, and though he was hitting only around .200, he was swinging from the heels, to the delight of those few who saw him. Attendance, savaged by the presence of a Federal League team in Baltimore, was so bad that only 150 people saw the hometown Orioles win their thirteenth straight game. Dunn kept hoping to be incorporated into a third major league, but when that wish came to naught, he decided to conduct a fire sale of his best players. On July 19, 1914, he sold Ruth, fellow pitcher Ernie Shore, and catcher Ben Egan to the Boston Red Sox for $30,000.

Dunn first offered Ruth to Connie Mack, who turned him down. John McGraw did want Ruth, but Dunn neglected to contact him. Ten years later, when Dunn tried to interest McGraw in another pitching prospect, the Giants manager, still angry he didn't get Ruth, ignored him. The pitcher was Lefty Grove, and Dunn sold him to Mack.

If beginnings augur the future, Ruth's coming dominance of the major leagues was established in his very first inning. Sold to the Red Sox in 1914, he was given the starting assignment against Cleveland on his first day in uniform.

The first batter Ruth faced, Jack Graney, singled and pro-

ceeded to second base on a groundout. The next batter was
Joe Jackson, maybe the best hitter in the American League
at the time, and he singled up the middle. Playing behind
Ruth, center-fielder Tris Speaker fielded Jackson's hit and
threw toward home, and Graney headed back toward third.
When Ruth cut off Speaker's mighty throw at the pitcher's
mound and threw to second, Jackson retreated toward first.
When the next throw went to first base, Graney broke for home
and was tagged out on the final relay in the four-throw se-
quence, Jackson holding first.

"On a solid base hit with a man in scoring position," Robert
Creamer wrote, "the Red Sox picked up an out and traded the
runner at second for a runner at first."

And before the next hitter was disposed of, Ruth picked
Jackson off first and the inning was over.

Even though 19-year-old Ruth and his new bride, Helen
Woodford, set up housekeeping in an apartment in Boston, he
was free to wander on the road, and he did. Red Sox manager
Bill Carrigan did as good a job of keeping Ruth in line as any
manager ever would, but he had to resort to extraordinary
measures. He made sure his room was always next to the
Babe's, and he kept him on a strict allowance. "He'd buy anything and everything," said Carrigan, who later became a
banker. "So I would draw Babe's pay"—$3,500 for the sea-
son—"and give him a little every day to spend. That generally
lasted about five minutes. At the end of the season I had to
give him the rest of it. I calculated it wouldn't last too long,
but that was the best I could do."

By the middle of the 1916 season, Ruth had become the best
pitcher in baseball; he would win 23 games that year (nine by
shutouts), and beat Walter Johnson four times. Carrigan was
tempted to use Ruth as an everyday outfielder, but he couldn't
bring himself to disrupt his pitching. Ruth himself, though,
was simply having fun, off in his own world. One evening in
the Red Sox hotel in Philadelphia, he was approached by Stuffy
McInnis, the Athletics star first baseman. "Babe, that was a
hell of a fine game you pitched this afternoon," said McInnis,
who had by this point played on four pennant winners. "Thanks,

that's very nice of you," said Ruth. "Glad you were able to come out and watch us play."

Ruth won 24 games in 1917, despite a 10-game suspension for punching umpire Brick Owens—a punch that would set the stage for one of the most remarkable games in baseball history. It was in Boston, on June 23, and Ruth disputed Owens on the very first call of the game, a ball to the Senators' Ray Morgan. He groused after ball two. After ball three, Ruth shouted, "Open your eyes! Open your eyes!"

When Owens instructed him to resume pitching, Ruth stomped back to the mound and promptly threw ball four. After more angry words, Owens ejected Ruth, and the irate pitcher rushed the umpire. He missed with a right, but connected with a left to the back of the neck. A policeman led Ruth off the field.

With the first batter on base and no one out, Carrigan brought Ernie Shore into the game. On his first pitch, Morgan tried to steal, and catcher Chester Thomas threw him out. Shore went on to retire the next 26 batters in a row: the fourth perfect game ever.

Ed Barrow, who would later become Ruth's general manager in New York, was the Red Sox manager in 1918. Since Barrow's background was in the office, he relied heavily on the advice of outfielder Harry Hooper, and it was Hooper who suggested that Ruth be put in the lineup on a regular basis. So on May 6, 1918, against the Yankees in the Polo Grounds, Barrow started Ruth at first base, the first time the Babe appeared in a major league lineup as other than a pitcher or pinch-hitter. Inevitably, he hit a majestic homer.

The Babe Ruth story very nearly ended soon after. Pitching and playing brought on a cold and sore throat. On an off-day, when Ruth should have rested, he and Helen went to the beach, ate, drank, swam, and played in the sand. That night he had a fever of 104°. The next day the Red Sox trainer applied too much silver nitrate to his throat and Ruth choked and collapsed. He was admitted in serious condition to Massachusetts General for swelling of the larynx.

A week after he was discharged, Ruth pitched and hit a home run. In center field the next day, he hit another homer. And the next day. And the day after: four home runs in four days. That season, for the first of twelve times, he led the American League in home runs.

Players used to rib Ruth because of his somewhat disgusting habit after a shower of putting on the same underwear he had worn during the game. The Babe's answer to the taunting was not, however, clean underwear. He simply stopped wearing undergarments altogether, putting nothing between his skin and his silk shirts and expensive suits. Still, in anticipation of Jim Palmer, Ruth modeled a line of underwear later in his career.

At times, though, his crudeness had a certain charm to it. A society matron who was part of the family that owned the *New York Times* once asked one of the paper's sportswriters to persuade Ruth to attend a charity event she was sponsoring. The sportswriter warned that Ruth was notoriously unreliable, but she persisted. On the evening of the benefit, Ruth arrived on time, mixed with the admiring crowd, and thrilled his hostess. As the evening ended, she thanked him for his attendance, and Ruth replied, "Oh, shit, lady, I'd do it for anybody."

In 1919, when pitcher Carl Mays jumped the club—he was later sold to the Yankees—Ruth was asked to return to the mound, which he did until 21-year-old Waite Hoyt arrived on the scene. On July 31, Ruth tied the AL home-run record with his sixteenth. Still ahead, though, was the major league mark of 27 set in 1884 by Ned Williamson of the Chicago Colts. Ruth tied the record on a special Babe Ruth Day in Boston; he pitched into the sixth inning, then won the game in the ninth with a spectacularly long homer. He ended up with 29 for the year, at age twenty-four the greatest home-run hitter baseball had ever seen.

But Red Sox owner Harry Frazee needed money, and after lengthy negotiations he agreed to sell Ruth to the Yankees for $100,000 and a loan of $300,000. Ruth himself was placated with a two-year contract at $20,000 per year, along with a $1,000 signing bonus.

The sale, announced on January 5, naturally caused a great sensation. Boston fans were heartbroken, and Yankee fans ecstatic. Frazee attempted to justify the move by asserting that "Ruth had become simply impossible, and the Boston Club could no longer put up with his eccentricities. I think the Yankees are taking a gamble. While Ruth is undoubtedly the greatest hitter the game has ever seen, he is likewise one of the most selfish and inconsiderate men ever to put on a baseball uniform."

A more succinct reaction came from Ping Bodie, who was the Yankees' incumbent left-fielder. Said Bodie, who was working in a New Jersey shipyard in the offseason, "I suppose this means I'll be sent to China."

Bodie, whose real name was Francesco Pezzolo, actually stayed with the Yankees long enough to become one of Ruth's pals. Until Ruth's arrival in New York, Bodie had been the team's champion trencherman but relinquished his unofficial title by announcing, "Anybody who eats three pounds of steak and a bottle of chili sauce for a starter has got me." Bodie was also the first of Ruth's many roommates to say, "I don't room with him, I room with his suitcase."

The wholesale shipment of star players from Boston to New York that characterized Harry Frazee's ownership of the Red Sox included the transfers of Babe Ruth, Waite Hoyt, Herb Pennock, Joe Dugan, Wally Schang, Joe Bush, Everett Scott, and George Pipgras, all of whom would star for the Yankees. Ever in need of cash to bankroll his various Broadway productions, Frazee dismantled one of the finest teams of the age. Of the 24 Yankee players who won the franchise's first World Series in 1923, eleven had come from the Sox.

But it wasn't only in the area of player sales that Frazee displayed his insatiable cash hunger. In his last full year in Boston, Ruth was the recipient of a "Day" in his honor at Fenway Park. According to Ruth, "I had to buy my wife's ticket to the game. Fifteen thousand fans show up and all I got was a cigar."

SPITBALLS AND BEANBALLS

In the winter of 1919–20, a symbol of the first two decades of the modern era faced its demise: the spitball was about to be declared illegal. In preparation for the rule change, every major league club was asked to submit the names of current spitballers whose use of the pitch would still be allowed, a procedure that extended the careers of such notables as Burleigh Grimes and Red Faber.

But Harry Grabiner, the White Sox general manager, forgot to include on the list the name of Frank Shellenback, who had won 10 games with the Sox in 1918 and had been sent out to Minneapolis for seasoning in 1919. Thus excluded from the grandfather clause, Shellenback, who was twenty-one at the time, was condemned to a life in the minor leagues. The Pacific Coast League gave him the spitball privilege he was denied in the majors, and Shellenback won 295 PCL games over the next 19 years.

The last of the spitballers was Burleigh Grimes, who started his career by winning only five of his first 24 decisions, but went on to win 265 more games before retiring in 1932.

But the spitball had its hazards. After pitching a shutout in the second game of the 1920 series, Grimes was hit badly in his next start. The problem was that second baseman Pete Kilduff didn't want to handle a slippery ball if it were hit to him, so that each time Brooklyn catcher Otto Miller called for the spitter, Kilduff would reach for a handful of dirt and deposit it in his glove. Cleveland quickly caught on, and Grimes's best weapon was taken away.

Fortunately for Grimes, Kilduff was gone by the end of the next year, and the pitcher could continue his spitballing unimpeded. For the rest of his career the man who looked, wrote John Kieran, "like a man who was about to commit assault and battery when he threw the ball" was the master of a dying style.

Earlier in the same season in which he would be killed by a pitch thrown by Carl Mays, Cleveland's Ray Chapman was facing Walter Johnson. When the pitcher quickly brought the count to two strikes, Chapman left the batter's box for the dugout. Reminded by Umpire Billy Evans that he had one strike left, Chapman said, "You can have it. It wouldn't do me any good." Evans declared Chapman out.

The tragic game that led to the only on-field death in major league history occurred in August of 1920, in New York. Mays, a submarine pitcher, was a notoriously nasty competitor, but there's no evidence that he was throwing at Chapman. Chapman liked to crowd the plate, and Muddy Ruel, Mays's catcher, later pointed out that had the ball not hit Chapman, it would have been called a strike.

MORE RUTH

The Yankees' opponents in the '21 Series were their hometown rivals and Polo Grounds landlords, the New York Giants. Babe Ruth played with an assortment of injuries, the most significant of which was an infected elbow. He had scraped the elbow while stealing third in Game 2, and after reinjuring it in Game 3, the Yankees announced he would be unavailable for the rest of the Series. But he took his bandaged arm out to right field in Game 4, and later singled and homered. In Game 5, he caught the Giants by surprise with a bunt, and when he slid home with what proved to be the winning run, he got up, stumbled into the Yankee dugout and collapsed. Still, he made it out to his position for the next inning.

Ruth's melodramatics raised a few cynical eyebrows, and he nearly came to blows with a sportswriter who questioned the extent of his injuries. But his elbow was so badly infected that the team doctor warned him of possible amputation if he continued to play, and Ruth sat out the next two games. Although he dressed for the eighth game—from 1919 to 1921 it took five victories to win the Series—he was not in the starting lineup. Then, in the bottom of the ninth, with the Giants leading 1-0, Higgins called upon Ruth to pinch-hit with the bases loaded. He grounded out.

The assertion that Ruth was part-black was a constant source of irritation to him, exacerbated by the likes of Ty Cobb. One offseason, according to Fred Lieb, Cobb and Ruth were assigned the same cabin at a Georgia hunting lodge popular with baseball people. Cobb refused to stay in the cabin. "I've never bedded down with a nigger," he said, "and I'm not going to start now."

During the 1922 World Series, Ruth was jockeyed mercilessly by a number of the Giants, especially reserve infielder Johnny Rawlings. After going hitless in Game 3, Ruth stormed over to the Giants clubhouse.

"Where's Rawlings?" he demanded.

"Right here," said his tormentor.

"You little bastard, if you ever call me that again, I'll choke you to death."

A mild scuffle ensued, broken up by Giants catcher Earl Smith, reputed to be the toughest man in baseball. Smith calmly asked Ruth, "What did he call you, Babe?"

"He called me a nigger."

"That's nothing," Smith said and walked away.

Before leaving the clubhouse, Ruth told the Giants, "Don't get me wrong, fellows. I don't mind being called a prick or a cocksucker or things like that. I expect that. But lay off the personal stuff."

Early in the 1920s, Judge Landis ruled that barnstorming big leagues couldn't play under their team names—couldn't play, say, as the Cubs or Tigers, but had to call themselves "all stars" or some other generic name. Landis didn't want a black league team claiming they had beaten an actual major league team.

In the ninth inning of a Yankees rout of the White Sox in Comiskey Park in 1923, a puppy wandered into the outfield. Ruth got down on all fours to follow the pup around, then threw his glove at it. The dog took the glove in its teeth just as Paul Castner, the batter for Chicago, hit a fly ball out to left, where Ruth was playing at the time. Ruth proceeded to catch the ball bare-handed. As Paul Gallico wrote in the *New York Daily News,* "Four strong men were assisted from the park with hysterics."

HACK WILSON

In the heat of the 1924 pennant race, the two contending teams—the Giants and the Dodgers—met in Brooklyn, on September 24. Although Ebbets Field's seating capacity was only 25,000, an estimated 32,000 found their way in that day, a large number of them coming in on the heels of a gang that had used a telephone pole to batter a hole in the center-field gate. As was the custom of the time, the excess spectators were herded into the outfield beyond a rope that stretched from foul line to foul line.

In the eighth inning, Eddie Brown of the Dodgers hit a drive to deep center. Hack Wilson, playing the position for the Giants, went into the crowd, which parted for him as he raced back and soon closed around him. Wilson—though he weighed 190 pounds, he stood only 5′6″—was lost in the mob, invisible to the umpires and the other players. What they first saw emerging was his cap, then his glove, and finally his sun glasses. When the outfielder himself made it out into the sunlight, he swore he had caught the ball, which had then been grabbed by one of the fans. But the umpire ruled Brown's hit a double.

The most humiliating moment of Wilson's career came during the fourth game of the 1929 Series, with the Cubs leading the A's 8-0. In the seventh inning, Wilson lost two fly balls in the sun—one for a three-run, inside-the-park home run—and the Philadelphia team wasn't retired until they had gone ahead 10-8.

By the following spring, though, Wilson had found the way to live with the ignominy of the previous fall. Eating one day in the Cubs' hotel dining room on Catalina Island, he pulled down the shade and asked the headwaiter to dim the lights so he wouldn't misjudge his soup.

According to Clyde Sukeforth, Wilson didn't hit 56 home runs in his magnificent 1930 season: "Hack really hit 57. He hit one up in the Crosley Field seats so hard that it bounced right back. The umpires figured it must have hit the screen. I was in the Reds' bullpen, and we didn't say a word."

SAM RICE

Sam Rice was the right-fielder for the Washington Senators from 1916 to 1933, a fast runner and slashing hitter who was known as Man O' War, both for his speed and for his service in both the Navy and the Army. The many years he spent in Washington are in direct contrast to his early wanderings. Born in Morocco, Indiana, in 1890, he bottled whiskey in Louisville, worked in the wheatfields of the Dakotas and Minnesota, toiled as a railroad gang hand, drifted to Norfolk, Va., and enlisted in the Navy, served aboard the *U.S.S. New Hampshire* stationed in Cuba, and saw action in Vera Cruz, Mexico. In 1914, while on furlough in Petersburgh, Va., he tried out for the minor league baseball team as a pitcher and was so good that the owner, Heinie Busch, bought his release from the Navy. A year later, Busch used Rice to pay off an $800 debt he owed Clark Griffith of the Senators. Rice pitched some for the Senators without much success, but after he pinch-hit one day and stretched a single into a double, Griffith said, "I don't think this boy is a pitcher, but he's something or other, and I'm going to find out just what he is."

Rice was no longer a boy; he was twenty-seven. But he had enough left in him to amass 2,987 hits before he retired in

1934. At the time he had no idea how many he had; but when it was established he declined an offer from Griffith to come back for the last thirteen.

Rice was involved in one of the most controversial catches in World Series history. It happened in the '25 Series, late in the third game, when Rice chased after an Earl Smith drive and crashed into the temporary bleachers in right. He disappeared out of sight before anyone could determine if he had made the catch, but as the umpire approached the bleachers, Rice emerged with the ball firmly in his glove. When Judge Landis called Rice in to ask if he had caught the ball, he replied, "Judge, the umpire said I did."

Rice never talked about the catch in his lifetime, but in 1965 he gave the Hall of Fame a sealed letter to be opened upon his death, which occurred in 1974. The letter was a detailed description of the catch, and it concluded with the phrase, "At no time did I lose possession of the ball."

Herald Dominic "Muddy" Ruel was a Washington teammate of Rice's, and a very fine catcher. The legacy he left to baseball was his expression for a catcher's equipment: "the tools of ignorance." Ruel himself was anything but ignorant. He studied law and became a practicing attorney authorized to argue before the U.S. Supreme Court.

Ruel was also the unofficial commissioner of baseball for a time during the reign of Happy Chandler, Judge Landis's successor. Rather than fire Chandler in 1945, the owners appointed Ruel as his chief aide. Ruel's job was, in the words of Red Smith, to "keep Happy's big fat foot out of Happy's big fat mouth."

MOE BERG

"The tools of ignorance" also ill-fit another catcher, Moe Berg. He knew several languages, including Sanskrit, versed himself well in the arts and sciences, and could call a good game besides. There was only one thing he couldn't do: "Berg can speak 12 languages," the phrase went, "but he can't hit in any of them." Originally an infielder, he signed his first contract with the Brooklyn Dodgers in 1923, when just out of Princeton. He was then purchased by the White Sox, who had to wait until Berg finished Columbia Law School before he could play full-time for them. When the White Sox lost two catchers to injuries in 1927, Berg found his true niche. He helped develop Ted Lyons into a Hall of Fame pitcher and, as Lyons later said, "He made up for all the bores in the world."

Berg had a unique offseason pursuit, too: He was a spy. When a team of all-stars, including Ruth and Gehrig, was sent to tour Japan in 1934, Berg was a last-minute addition to the squad. He delivered the welcoming speech in Japanese and addressed the Japanese legislature as well. Feigning illness one day, he fulfilled his assigned role and took reconnaissance photographs of Tokyo on orders from the State Department. Berg's pictures were used in World War II in preparation for General Jimmy Doolittle's bombers.

Berg retired from baseball in 1939 with a .243 lifetime average and soon joined what became the Office of Strategic Services. One of his responsibilities was to find out how German scientists were progressing with nuclear weapons, which brought him into contact with Albert Einstein. When Berg offered to trade his knowledge of baseball for Einstein's knowledge of mathematics, Einstein said, "I'm sure you would learn mathematics faster."

Berg was immensely popular with the press, who relished the feature stories they could get from him—usually about medieval French, or perhaps his dissertation on Sanskrit—and equally well-liked by his fellow players. Teammates said he was always cooperative, never complained about his usual second- or third-string status, and was unfailingly good-natured. His byword was the phrase he'd always use after playing a full game: "I've got to rest the body, rest the body."

During the 1934 season, he hadn't played in nearly six weeks when injuries required Washington coach Al Schacht to call on Berg. (Schacht was filling in for manager Joe Cronin, who was on his honeymoon.) It was a ferociously hot Indian Summer day in Philadelphia, and Berg was not in the best of con-

dition. Earl Whitehill was pitching for the Senators when Doc
Cramer came to bat for the A's in the seventh inning. Cramer
would step into the batter's box and then get out again; when
he was finally set, Whitehill would step off the rubber and rub
the ball some more. Berg, meanwhile, got angrier and angrier, getting up every time either pitcher or batter stalled,
crouching down again when it appeared they might actually
be ready to pitch and hit.

As Schacht remembered it, Berg "looks like an elevator and
he's roaring mad . . . Suddenly he calls 'time.' Umpire Bill
McGowan [asks] what Berg wants. Now here's Berg showing
his anger. He takes off his chest protector, takes off his mask,
takes his shin guards off and piles everything on home plate.
. . . He turns to McGowan and says, 'I'll return when those
two guys decide to play baseball. Right now I'm going to take
a shower.' "

When he appeared as a panelist on the *Information Please*
radio show near the end of his career, Berg performed su-
perbly. It led to a Detroit baseball writer's attempt to stump
him with a series of academic questions that ranged from as-
tronomy to Greek mythology, all of which Berg was able to
answer. The story was picked up by hundreds of newspapers,
and his locker at Fenway Park, where he was playing, was
flooded with thousands of letters from people who either wished
to express their admiration or ask him yet more questions.

Berg quickly regretted cooperating with the writer, feeling
that he ran the risk of being regarded as a sideshow freak,
and the letters went unopened. And when he appeared on field
during this period, he would be hounded by derisive questions
from fans and opposing players: "Moe, recite the Book of Lev-
iticus!" "Hey Moe, what color bloomers did Martha Washington wear at George's inauguration?"

LEFTY O'DOUL

Lefty O'Doul didn't reach the majors to stay until he was thirty-
one, but before he was through six years later he would win

two NL batting championships, including one in a season in
which he made a record 254 hits. O'Doul stayed in baseball
virtually the rest of his long life, and he was much in demand
as a figure who could relate the essence of the baseball era in
which he had started out. In 1959 he was at a banquet in his
native San Francisco, speaking about the baseball that was
played in the teens and twenties. Someone in the audience
asked him, "What do you think Cobb would hit today?"

"Oh," he replied, "about the same as Willie Mays, maybe
.340, something like that."

His questioner was surprised; O'Doul had just finished
speaking about how much better were the ballplayers of his
era than those of modern times. How was it that the great
Cobb would only hit .340?

"Well," O'Doul said, "you have to take into consideration
the man is now 73 years old."

RUTH'S STOMACH ACHE

Babe Ruth's appetite got the best of him in spring training of
1925. His weight had ballooned up to 270, and he felt pro-
gressively worse as the spring went along. "He was going day
and night, broads and booze," said Joe Dugan, and even though
he was hitting .447, he was clearly headed for trouble, suffering from stomach cramps and running a fever. On April 7
Ruth collapsed on a train platform in Asheville, N.C., and it
was agreed that he be sent back to New York. On the train
to New York, he again fainted, cracking his head against a
washbasin. Upon arrival at Penn Station, he was taken by
ambulance to St. Vincent's Hospital.

Ruth's physician, Dr. Edward King, said he was in no serious danger, but that he was badly run down and had a touch
of the flu, as well as suffering an intestinal attack. A week
later, Dr. King announced that Ruth would have to undergo
surgery for an intestinal abscess.

By the time Ruth returned to the starting lineup, on June
1, the Yankees were in seventh place, and heading for the
same finish. It was a lost season, and Ruth should have rested

more. Through June and July, he hit only .250 and only a few homers. He looked so bad that many observers thought he was through. Manager Miller Huggins even put in a pinch-hitter for him in one game. Although Ruth had begun to hit by August, he and Huggins had a blowup on August 29, when Ruth showed up late for a game in St. Louis after missing a 1 a.m. curfew. Huggins suspended Ruth and fined him $5,000. Rather than return to New York immediately, as ordered, Ruth checked out of his hotel, canceled his train reservations, and spent the night at a St. Louis bordello. The next day he went to Chicago, told reporters he was through with the Yankees, then disappeared into the night. He left word at the hotel that he was not to be disturbed until ten the next morning, and so a group of reporters gathered outside his door.

At the appointed hour, one of them knocked. The door opened a crack, and out came a suit. "Here," said Ruth, "have this pressed, and be sure it's back in an hour."

CASEY STENGEL

Another career that would produce nearly as many reams of prose as Ruth's had begun around the same time, and would last three decades longer.

Long before he became celebrated as the manager of the Yankees from 1949 to 1960, Casey Stengel had made his mark in baseball. He was a solid outfielder in the National League for 14 years, batted .393 in three World Series, and early on cultivated his reputation as a clown, and as a notable philosopher-logician.

When his playing career ended, Stengel was named manager and president of the Braves farm club in Worcester. As his first season in Worcester came to an end, he was offered a managerial job with Toledo, in the American Association.

Stengel that day composed two letters. The first was addressed to "Mr. Casey Stengel, President, Worcester Baseball Club," and it offered the resignation of its signer, "Casey Stengel, Manager, Worcester Baseball Club."

The second letter was addressed to Judge Emil Fuchs, the president of the Braves: "Dear Judge," it read. "My manager has just resigned to accept a job in a league of higher classification. Since it is impossible for me to operate without him, kindly consider this my resignation as president of the Worcester club, effective immediately."

In 1912 in the Southern League, Stengel was playing left field for Montgomery in Pensacola. In the seventh inning, noticing a box containing water pipes imbedded beneath the level of the field, he removed the lid and crawled into it. When the third batter of the inning hit a fly to left, the crowd noticed there was no left-fielder—until Stengel popped out of the box to make the catch.

World Series 1923, Yankees against the Giants, first game: ninth inning, 4-4 tie. Joe Bush pitching for the Yankees, a thirty-three year-old Casey Stengel at bat for the Giants, 55,307 people in Yankee Stadium. Stengel slashes a line drive to left-center that somehow eludes both Whitey Witt and Bob Meusel and rolls toward the fence. The rest of the story is told by Damon Runyon:

"This is the way old Casey Stengel ran yesterday afternoon running his home run home.

This is the way old Casey Stengel ran running his home run home to a Giant victory by a score of 5 to 4 in the first game of the World Series of 1923.

"This is the way old Casey Stengel ran running his home run home when two were out in the ninth inning and the score was tied, and the ball still bounding inside the Yankee yard.

"This is the way—

"His mouth wide open.

"His warped old legs bending beneath him at every stride.

"His arms flying back and forth like those of a man swimming with a crawl stroke.

"His flanks heaving, his breath whistling, his head far back. Yankee infielders, passed by Old Casey Stengel as he was running his home run home, say Casey was muttering to himself, adjuring himself to greater speed as a jockey mutters to his horse in a race, saying, 'Go on, Casey, go on.'

"The warped old legs, twisted and bent by many a year of baseball campaigning, just barely held out under Casey until he reached the plate, running his home run home.

"Then they collapsed."

Stengel's own version? He only recalled saying to himself, "Go, legs, go; drive this boy round the bases." Several years later, Quentin Reynolds wrote, "That was the big moment in Casey's life and maybe he should have died then."

After he became a manager one of Stengel's habits when caught in a quarrel with an umpire was to lie down on the ground in a mock faint. However, he once tried this tactic when Beans Reardon was umpiring, and the veteran umpire knew how to deal with it. Said Stengel, "When I peeked out of one eye and saw Reardon on the ground, too, I knew I was licked."

Unable to get his Brooklyn players to master the "daylight play" that occasionally enables a pitcher to pick a runner off second, Stengel tried to institute a pick-off play at third. With a man on third and a right-handed hitter at the plate, the Brooklyn pitcher would occasionally be instructed to throw at the batter's head; Stengel figured that the runner would freeze at the sight of the batter going down, and the catcher, rising with the pitch, would be in a perfect position to make the pick-off throw.

After a few attempts, though, Stengel dropped the play "because the fellows I had playing third base for me used to freeze right along with the base runner, and our left-fielder was kept busy running down the ball in the bull pen."

GROVER CLEVELAND ALEXANDER

It was one of the most dramatic, not to say unlikely, moments in World Series history. Representing the American League, of course, were the Yankees of Ruth and Gehrig; for the National, it was a fine Cardinals team built around Rogers Hornsby and Jim Bottomley.

But when it came down to the last three innings of the seventh game, with St. Louis leading 3-2, the Cardinals' Horatio at the bridge was Grover Cleveland Alexander. A drunk, thirty-nine years old, made vulnerable by his epilepsy, the great Alexander had stopped New York on three hits the previous day. Thinking he was through for the year, he had gone on one of his benders the night before the seventh game.

Now, though, player-manager Hornsby brought him in to pitch. "I was out there [on the mound] when he came in," Hornsby related years later, "and I said, 'How are you, kid?' "

"Okay," Alexander replied, "but no warm-up pitches. That would be the giveaway." The bases were loaded, there were two out, and Tony Lazzeri was at bat. Exactly as Ronald Reagan did it in the movies when he played Alexander in *The Winning Team*, Alexander struck him out.

What is largely forgotten about that game is that in the ninth, with the score still 3-2 and two out, Alexander walked Ruth—who proceeded to get thrown out while attempting an inexplicable steal of second. Bob O'Farrell, who made the throw that caught Ruth, two years later found the opportunity to ask him why he had been running. Ruth simply said he thought Alexander had forgotten he was there, and that the way Alex was pitching the Yankees weren't going to be able to score him from first anyway.

After the game, a reporter asked Alexander how he felt after striking out Lazzeri, and the pitcher snapped, "Go ask Lazzeri how he felt."

Of Alexander, his teammate, Bill Hallahan, said, "He was a loner. He would go off by himself and do what he did, which I suppose was drink."

Hornsby, for his part, said, "Hell, I'd rather him pitch a crucial game for me drunk than anyone I've ever known sober. He was that good."

And when his career ended in 1930, after 373 victories in 20 years, there was little else Alexander could do but try to continue to pitch. For a while, he barnstormed the tank town circuit with the House of David team, then he made his living for a while as a freak in a flea circus, and after that he simply got by on the handouts of friends.

Foremost among the latter was Sam Breadon, the old owner of the Cardinals. The checks Alexander got came with National League of Professional Baseball Clubs imprinted in the upper corner, and Alexander thought it was an official pension. In fact, it was Breadon's money, passed through National League accounts so that the old pitcher wouldn't know it was charity.

LOU GEHRIG

The 1927 Yankees won 110 games and dominated the league as no team had before or has since—their nearest competitors, the Athletics, finished 19 games back. They have become the standard for all great teams, although, oddly enough, most sportswriters picked the Philadelphia Athletics to win the pennant that year. As a team, the Yankees batted .307. They never had better pitching, either, with Waite Hoyt going 22-7, Herb Pennock 19-8, Wilcy Moore 19-7, Urban Shocker 18-6, Dutch Ruether 13-6, and rookie George Pipgras 10-3.

It was, of course, the year that Ruth hit his record 60 home runs; he also batted .356, with 164 RBIs. But the most valuable player award went to someone else—Lou Gehrig, who hit .373 with 47 homers, and 175 runs batted in. Gehrig couldn't match Ruth in color, and the nicknames contemporary writers tried to place on him—the Prince of Punch, the Slambino—just didn't fit. All he did was play—2,130 straight games in which he'd produce 1990 RBIs, a .632 slugging average, and a .340 batting average.

Amateur baseball psychologists have tried to read an Oedipus complex into the relationship between Gehrig and his mother. "Mom" Gehrig, as she was called by the Yankees, often accompanied her son to spring training or on short road trips or to the World Series. Fred Lieb described coming home from a road trip with Gehrig and being met at the train by Lou's mother: "Mom and Louie kissed and hugged for fully ten minutes, as though they had been parted for years." Only his mother's pleadings got him to leave her bedside after she underwent surgery before the 1927 World Series. "My place is at Mom's side," Gehrig said before she—and Huggins—persuaded him otherwise. "She is worth more to me than any ball game, or any World Series that was ever invented."

Gehrig had one other odd character trait. He never wore an overcoat or hat, no matter the weather. At first, some attributed this quirk to thrift, which Gehrig did practice to a fault. He insisted, though, that he just never felt cold.

According to a 1928 profile in *The New Yorker*, "Gehrig does not drink, smoke or gamble. He has never had a girl." Yet anybody who hung around with Ruth as much as Gehrig did could not have been that straight an arrow. And Gehrig liked to roughhouse. The two men were good friends until a falling out in the early '30s over a silly family matter. They often went fishing, and in the offseason they barnstormed together. Though on the surface Ruth and Gehrig might have seemed an odd couple, their admiration for each other was genuine. They were always quick and sincere in their congratulations for one another as they dueled for the home-run title in '27. In August of that year, Ford Frick would later remember, Gehrig said, "There'll never be another guy like the Babe. I get more kick out of seeing him hit one than I do from hitting one myself." For his part, Ruth told Frick, "There's only one man who ever had a chance of breaking my record, and that's Lou Gehrig. He's a great kid."

They were also partners in the bridge games that occupied the Yankees. According to one version of their friendship: "They disagree on only one subject, when to take your partner out of a one-no-trump bid."

WAITE HOYT

One of Ruth's other close friends on the Yankees was the pitcher who was forever being referred to as the "Brooklyn schoolboy-mortician." The New York Giants signed Waite Hoyt right out of high school in Brooklyn when he was seventeen, but McGraw ignored him and Hoyt quit, electing to go to Officer Candidate School at Middlebury College in Vermont. The Red Sox acquired his rights in 1919, and though Hoyt went only 10-12 in his two years in Boston, he pitched well against the Yankees. They traded for him in 1921, the year after they got Ruth, and he went 19-13 as the Yankees won their first pennant. Hoyt made sure McGraw did not ignore him in the Series; he pitched 27 innings against the Giants without allowing an earned run.

The mortician part of Hoyt's tag came about because his father-in-law was a funeral home director, and he toyed with the idea of getting a mortician's license. There is a story about Hoyt's picking up a corpse near Yankee Stadium as a favor for his father-in-law, depositing the body in the trunk of his car, then going on to the Stadium. He proceeded to pitch a shutout, then afterward delivered the corpse to its appointed designation.

Hoyt's own father was a vaudevillian, and Waite inherited his fine singing voice. In fact, Hoyt earned $1,500 a week in the '28 and '29 offseasons, appearing at Broadway's Palace Theater. A versatile and well-spoken man, Hoyt also dabbled in oil painting and later became one of the first athletes to go into sports broadcasting.

He was one of Ruth's early drinking buddies as well, a pastime that once landed him in the hospital. When the newspapers reported that Hoyt had a "case of amnesia," Ruth sent him a telegram: READ ABOUT YOUR CASE OF AMNESIA. MUST BE A NEW BRAND.

In his 22 years of pitching, Hoyt suffered from a sore arm only once, and that was the result of an innocent trip to a street fair in Kennett Square, Pa., where Herb Pennock lived. Hoyt, Ruth, and Joe Dugan had been invited by their teammate to attend a celebration in his honor after a game against the A's. There was a parade, a big dinner, and afterwards a visit to the fair. In one of the booths was a pyramid of papier-mâché bottles, and there were prizes for those who could knock over the entire pyramid with three throws of a small, light baseball. Naturally, the ballplayers had an easy time of the game, and Pennock's wife Esther had her arms filled with gifts. The proprietor, fearing he would go broke, begged the players to back up, which they did. "Not content with merely throwing the ball," Hoyt wrote in his Introduction to G.H. Fleming's excellent book about the 1927 Yankees, *Murderers Row,* "we began curving it." Eventually, the players tired of the game and returned most of the prizes.

The next morning Hoyt woke with his elbow swollen to three times its normal size. Dugan, his roommate, correctly surmised, "The curves did it—and the lightweight balls." Hoyt lied to Huggins and told him he hurt his arm on the field.

1920s PLAYERS

One of the relatively unsung mainstays of the '27 Yankees was an unformidable, balding Oklahoma farmer named Wilcy Moore, whom Ed Barrow had signed after reading in *The Sporting News* that he had won 30 games in the Sally League in 1926. Moore said he was twenty-eight, but he was clearly older. He had just one pitch, a sinking fastball, but he made it work through great control and, as Frank Graham wrote, "nerves of steel—or no nerves at all." Moore used to beg Huggins to let him throw his curve, but the manager told him, "Your curve ball wouldn't go around a button on my vest." Still, Moore became the prototype of the modern relief pitcher, winning 19 and saving 15 of the 50 games in which he appeared.

Moore was also a dreadful hitter, and Ruth put up $300 to Moore's $100 that he wouldn't get three hits all season. Moore ended up with six hits, including a home run, and Ruth made good on his bet. After the season, Moore wrote to his benefactor: "The $300 came in handy. I used it to buy a fine pair of mules. I named one Babe and the other Ruth."

Dramatics of a different sort were the province of Rabbit Maranville, whose 23 good-field, no-hit years were all spent in the National League. In Boston in the '20s, a 6:30 curfew governed the end of all baseball games, with the final outcome determined by where the score stood at the end of the last full inning played. During the second game of a doubleheader against the Cubs one Sunday, the Braves had lost the lead to Chicago in the top of the eighth. In the home half of the inning, Maranville came to bat with two outs, several minutes before the automatic closing hour. In the words of Al Hirshberg, "He watched the clock with one eye and the Cubs pitcher with the other."

Maranville also stalled and fidgeted and wasted as much time as possible before stepping into the batter's box. There, he calmly and scientifically fouled off fourteen consecutive pitches until the clock read half past six. The Cubs' eighth was obliterated, and the Braves took the victory.

At five feet five he should have known better, but Maranville loved to fight—especially when he was drunk, which was often. Recalled Bill Veeck, who knew Maranville when Veeck's father was president of the Cubs, "He once staggered out of the team hotel and got in a fight with a cabbie. He lost. So he picked a fight with the next cabbie and lost. He fought three more of them, and they all beat the hell out of him. So I asked him what he was doing. He said, 'I'm trying to find one I can whip.'"

Dutch Leonard's greatest baseball achievement was his 1.01 earned run average in 1914 with the Red Sox, but equally rare was his care with a dollar. One of the players unloaded by cash-hungry Boston owner Harry Frazee to the Yankees, Leonard at first refused to sign a contract unless his entire salary was placed, in advance, in a savings account; outraged by the suggestion, Jacob Ruppert sold Leonard directly to Detroit. He later refused to report to the Tigers in 1922 and 1923 over a contract dispute, and instead repaired to Fresno, where he played with an independent minor league team and established a wine business.

After retiring following the 1925 season on the heels of another dispute with Detroit management, Leonard made his notorious accusation that Ty Cobb and Tris Speaker had conspired to fix a game during the 1919 season. Judge Landis eventually exonerated Speaker and Cobb, but Leonard seemed not to suffer from any backlash. He in time owned one of the largest grape growing, packing, and shipping businesses in California, a full 2,500 acres in San Joaquin Valley farmland, and a famous record collection consisting of over 150,000 disks. When he died in 1952, Leonard left behind an estate valued at more than $2,000,000.

The foundation of his fortune? Partly, Leonard had saved as much of his baseball salary as he was able and invested it in his nascent business. But it also turned out that when he made his accusation against Speaker and Cobb, he managed to talk American League president Ban Johnson into purchasing two letters that were important pieces of evidence against the players. The American League gave Leonard something between $15,000 and $25,000; he invested it in farmland, and then never looked back.

The great Cincinnati left-hander Eppa Rixey was something of a hothead, a temperamental Virginian famous for tearing apart locker rooms when he lost a game, or for picking fights at the smallest provocation. Late in his career, opposing players would whistle "Marching Through Georgia" to get his goat, and invariably succeeded.

Once, while throwing batting practice, he heard the tune emanating from the other team's bench, and fired his next pitch straight at the head of the transgressor. His teammate, Clyde Sukeforth, approached Rixey later and asked why the song made him so mad.

"The song doesn't make me mad," Rixey said. "The thing that makes me made is that they *think* that they're making me mad."

Ruth made a feature movie, *Babe Comes Home,* in 1927. He played Babe Dugan, a slugger for the Los Angeles Angels who is so sloppy with his chewing tobacco that the laundry girl who cleans his uniform rebels. Babe and the girl meet and fall in love. The Babe swears off tobacco, and a wedding date is set. Just before their wedding, though, the girl becomes incensed over a gift of beautiful hand-painted cuspidors and returns to the laundry, while Babe tries to help the Angels win the pennant. Because he isn't chewing, he falls into a dreadful slump. In the ninth inning of the big game, the girl leans over from her box seat and hands Babe a plug of tobacco. He wins the day, and they live happily, and presumably sloppily, ever after.

According to one Detroit critic, "There is no reason for John Barrymore or any other noted thespian to become agitated about the matter."

ROGERS HORNSBY

The best right-handed hitter of the 1920s was Rogers Hornsby, a supremely self-assured man who always spoke and acted with brutal frankness. His idiosyncrasies included a passion for the race track and a fear of movies—he was convinced that watching them would hurt his batting eye.

And quite an eye it was. He had a lifetime average of .358—second only to Cobb's—and more than 300 home runs. In his incredible 1924 season with the Cardinals, he batted .424 and also led the league in walks, which yielded an on-base percentage of .505 to go with a slugging average of .696.

Invariably, his nature and his skills commanded a certain amount of respect. In 1927, when he was with the Giants, Hornsby stood in against the Dodgers' Jim Eliott. Eliott and his catcher Hank DeBerry soon began to argue with umpire Cy Pfirman over every pitch he called a ball. Finally, at 3-2, Elliott threw a pitch over the middle that Hornsby hit into the right-field seats. As Hornsby made his way around the bases, Pfirman stepped out toward the mound and shouted at Elliott, "Mr. Hornsby will let you know when the ball is over the plate."

When Hornsby was traded from the Cardinals to the Giants before the 1927 season, the deal was held up because Hornsby, as part of his managerial contract with St. Louis owner Sam Breadon, owned 1,167 shares of Cardinal stock. Under league rules, as a St. Louis shareholder he couldn't sign a contract with New York.

But Breadon and Hornsby couldn't agree on the price to be paid for the stock, the owner offering $80,000 and Hornsby insisting on $140,000. Neither would budge, and the matter wasn't resolved until National League president John Heydler got the other clubs in the league to pony up the difference.

He didn't smoke, he didn't drink, he didn't stay up late, and the only thing he read in the newspaper was the box scores. "Baseball," Hornsby told Robert Lipsyte when he was batting coach for the Mets, "is my life, the only thing I know and can talk about, my only interest."

When Bill Veeck hired Hornsby to manage the Browns in the early '50s, he was the second in his family to try to tame the unbending old second baseman. In the early '30s, Hornsby had managed the Cubs for two seasons when Bill Veeck, Sr., was running that franchise for the Wrigley family.

On the day the younger Veeck signed Hornsby, his mother wrote to him, "What makes you think you're smarter than your daddy was?" And on the day Veeck fired the manager less than two months later, Mrs. Veeck wrote again: "What did I tell you?"

AND MORE RUTH

"What a fantastic ballplayer he was," said Joe Dugan of Babe Ruth, "the things he could do. But he wasn't human. He dropped out of a tree." His appetites certainly didn't seem human. Breakfast might be an 18-egg omelet with three slices of ham, a half-dozen slices of toast and two bottles of beer; and dinner could be an entire capon, potatoes, spinach, corn, peas, beans, bread and butter, pie, ice cream, and a small pitcher of coffee. He was so fond of the barbecued spareribs at

a restaurant in St. Louis that he would order hundreds of them
to take on the road with him, then set up shop in a washroom
on the train and sell them to his teammates at 50 cents a
portion; he provided free beer.

Ruth's girth, incidentally, is the reason the Yankees wear
pinstripes. Ruppert thought he would look slimmer that way.

The Babe was a great sexual athlete, of course, as well as a
loud one—"the noisiest fucker in North America," said a friend.
He wasn't particularly well-endowed, though, according to one
teammate, who did say, "My God, you wouldn't believe Home
Run Baker's." Once on a barnstorming tour, Ruth and Meusel
shared a hotel suite. Meusel was half asleep in his room when
Ruth came in with his girl. He would make love in his own
bedroom, come out into the living room, smoke a cigar, and
then go back in again. He did this all night long, and when
Meusel asked him in the morning, "How many times did you
lay that girl last night?", Ruth glanced at the ashtray and
said, "Count the cigars." There were seven.

Ruth was vulgar, but sometimes delightfully so. Once while
sitting around a table with several players and their wives,
Ruth got up and said, "Excuse me, I've got to take a piss."
The gentlemanly Pennock, a friend of Ruth, followed him into
the men's room and said, "Babe, you shouldn't say that in
front of the ladies."

"Say what?"

"Say piss like that. You should say, "Excuse me, I have to
go to the bathroom," or something like that.

"I'm sorry, Herb."

When they went back to the table, Ruth sat down and said,
"I'm sorry I said piss."

Ruth's affection for children was genuine and he made
countless visits to orphanages and hospitals. The legend of
Ruth visiting a dying young boy in the hospital, promising to
hit a home run for him, then delivering and thus inspiring
the boy to a miraculous recovery, has a basis in fact. Before
the 1926 World Series, eleven-year-old Johnny Sylvester, badly

injured in a fall from a horse, was given baseballs auto-graphed by the Yankees and Cardinals, as well as a home-run promise from Ruth. Ruth did hit four in the Series, and afterwards, he visited Johnny. The visit was noted by the du-tifully sentimental press.

The next spring, Ruth was sitting with some writers when a man stepped forward and identified himself as Johnny Sylvester's uncle. "Mr. Ruth," he said, "I just want to thank you again for what you did for him."

"Glad to do it," Ruth said. "How is Johnny?"

"He's fine. He's home and everything looks okay."

"That's good. Give him my regards."

When the man left, Ruth said to the writers, "Who the hell is Johnny Sylvester?"

Johnny Sylvester need not have felt insulted. Ruth didn't even know the names of some of his teammates. Tony Lazzeri once brought pitcher Myles Thomas over to Ruth at a train station, jokingly introducing him as a new pitcher who had just joined the Yankees. "Hi, Keed." said Ruth. "Glad to have you on the club." Thomas had, in fact, been with the Yankees for three years.

Waite Hoyt reported that when he was traded to Detroit in 1930 after spending eleven seasons as Ruth's teammate in Boston and New York, Ruth shook his hand and solemnly said, "Goodbye, Walter."

On April 3, 1931, the Yankees were in Tennessee for an exhibition against the Chattanooga Lookouts. Chattanooga owner Joe Engle—who once traded a player for a Thanks-giving turkey—had been having trouble luring people to his ballpark, so he signed a seventeen-year-old, 5'8" pitcher named Jackie Mitchell to a contract. Jackie, whose full name was Virne Beatrice Mitchell, happened to be female. "All I want is to stay in baseball long enough to get money to buy a road-ster," she told reporters.

She did not start the game; former major leaguer Clyde Barfoot did. But when Barfoot gave up a double to Earle Combs and an RBI single to Lyn Lary, Chattanooga manager Ben

Niehoff brought Mitchell into the game to face Ruth. Mitchell threw something akin to a sidearm sinker, and her first pitch was outside, ball one. Ruth swung and missed at her next two pitches. With his customary flair, he asked the umpire to inspect the ball. Ruth let the 1-2 pitch go by, and the umpire yelled, "Steee-rike." Ruth flung down his bat in disgust and stalked off as the crowd went wild. Some fifty-five years later, Jackie Mitchell Gilbert would recall, "He was really mad . . . and something to behold."

Gehrig was the next batter and, even more chivalrous than Ruth, he fanned on three straight pitches. Lazzeri followed, and after working Jackie to a full count, he walked. That was all for Mitchell, and Barfoot returned to the mound. While it was widely suspected that Ruth and Gehrig struck out for the sake of publicity, Jackie always believed she fanned them fair and square. "I had a drop pitch," she said, "and when I was throwing it right, you couldn't touch it." She might have continued pitching, but Judge Landis, a confirmed misogynist, voided her contract.

By 1932 the Yankees had regrouped, and they won the first of eight pennants under the leadership of Joe McCarthy. These Yankees had a pitcher named Walter Brown, called Jumbo—at 265 pounds, he was the largest player in baseball. For some reason, McCarthy only liked to start Brown against the Athletics in Philadelphia. When asked why, he once said, "It's the only way I know to fill Shibe Park."

One of the unlikeliest Yankees of the '30s was Johnny Broaca, a student-athlete from Yale. Against the Red Sox one day, Broaca had a 1-0 lead with two outs in the ninth, the tying run on first base, and Joe Cronin at the plate. Jimmy Foxx was on deck.

"Broaca starts pitching to Cronin," Joe McCarthy later told Donald Honig, "and he's not coming close to the plate. I couldn't believe it—he's walking Cronin to get to Foxx. I yelled out to Bill Dickey, 'What the hell's going on?' Bill just shrugged. There wasn't anything he could do about it. And Broaca was pitching such a good game I couldn't take him out.

"So Foxx comes up and now the tying run is on second. And Jimmy laid into one. He hit it into deep center field, as far as any ball I ever saw hit in Yankee Stadium that wasn't a home run. DiMaggio went out there and caught it. It didn't miss by much from going into the bleachers in dead center. DiMaggio caught it and the game was over.

" 'I was afraid of Cronin,' Broaca said, 'but I knew I could get Foxx.' "

BILL DICKEY

Bill Dickey of Little Rock, Arkansas, was the big rock of the Yankees from 1929 to 1943. A superb catcher, unusually tall, Dickey hit at least .300 in nine of his first ten seasons, with power just a notch below that of his friend Gehrig. He was the first in the line of great Yankees catchers. Dickey never played for another major league team, nor did he ever play so much as an inning at any other position. "A catcher must want to catch," Dickey once said. "He must make up his mind that it isn't the terrible job it is painted, and that he isn't going to say almost every day, 'Why, oh why, with so many other positions in baseball, did I take up this one?' "

Dickey had an equivalent respect for umpires. During the 1939 World Series, Monte Pearson threw a pitch right over the plate, and umpire Beans Reardon called it a ball. Dickey stayed in his crouch and did not turn around, but he asked, "What was wrong with it?"

"Nothin'," said Reardon.

"I thought it was right over the middle," said Dickey.

"It was," said Reardon.

"Why ain't it a strike then?" asked Dickey.

"Because I called it a ball," said Reardon.

"Oh," Dickey replied.

Conveniently, Pearson ended up with a two-hit shutout. After the game, Dickey told reporters, "I'd like to say that guy behind the plate worked one helluva game. Didn't miss a pitch."

LEFTY GOMEZ

Vernon "Lefty" Gomez isn't the best pitcher in the Hall of Fame, but he may be the funniest. A favorite of both Ruth and DiMaggio, El Goofy was an essential part of the great Yankees teams of the '30s. In three of his first four full seasons he won 20 games but general manager Ed Barrow still thought he was too skinny. After the 1934 season, Barrow told him, "Lefty, years ago the Yankees owned Jack Chesbro, the first pitcher to win 16 in a row. Put on 20 pounds, and you'll make the fans forget Chesbro." Gomez did as suggested and went 12-15. According to Lefty, "Barrow told me to put on 20 pounds and I'd make the fans forget Chesbro. I put on 23 and almost made them forget Gomez."

Gomez often made fun of his own failings, both as a pitcher and as a hitter. Batting against Cleveland's young fireballer Bob Feller late in a game, Gomez lit a match as he came to the plate. "What's the matter with you, Gomez?" asked plate umpire Bill Summers. "You know you can see Feller." Replied Lefty, "Oh, I can see him. I just want to make sure he sees me."

After Lefty's playing career was over, he managed the Yankees farm team in Binghamton in the Eastern League. During one game, he was coaching third base when, with runners on first and second, the batter singled to center. The lead runner rounded third, paused, and came sliding back into the base just as the other runner slid into third. As the third baseman applied tags all around, Gomez gave out a terrible yell and joined them with a slide from the coach's box.

CONNIE MACK

Cornelius McGillicuddy began his baseball career in 1883, abandoning his job as a cobbler's assistant to catch for Meriden of the Connecticut State League. Connie Mack didn't give up his career until after the 1950 season, when at eighty-eight he retired as the last owner-manager in baseball after leading the Philadelphia Athletics to nine pennants in fifty years. Red Smith, who traveled with him for ten of those years, had this to say about baseball's grand old man: "He could be as tough as rawhide and as gentle as a mother, reasonable and obstinate beyond reason, and courtly and benevolent and fierce. He was kindhearted and hardfisted, drove a close bargain and was suckered in a hundred deals. He was generous and thoughtful and autocratic and shy and independent and altogether lovable."

Mack's masterstroke as a strategist came before the 1929 World Series against the Chicago Cubs. He started journeyman junkballer Howard Ehmke in the first game, even though he had Lefty Grove, George Earnshaw, and Rube Walberg available. Ehmke struck out 13, a Series record, en route to a 3-1 victory.

The way Mack told it, though, he chose Ehmke strictly on a hunch. Just before the end of the season, Mack had called Ehmke into his office and said, "Howard, the time has come for us to part."

Ehmke beseeched Mack for one more chance. "I have always wanted to pitch in the World Series," the pitcher said as he lifted his right arm. "Mr. Mack, there is one great game left in this old arm."

"All right, Howard," said Mack. "When the Cubs come in to play the Phillies, you watch them. Learn all you can about their hitters. Say nothing to anybody. You are my opening pitcher for the World Series."

The game was, of course, Ehmke's last hurrah; he did start the fifth and deciding game of the Series, but he wasn't around long enough to get credit for the victory, and never pitched again. Years later, Ehmke was riding in a car with his wife, listening on the radio to the 1953 World Series game in which Carl Erskine of the Brooklyn Dodgers was pitching against the Yankees and threatening Ehmke's record for strikeouts. The old pitcher pulled over to the side of the road, cut the motor, and tuned in on the suspense. When his record evaporated as Erskine struck out his fourteenth Yankee, Ehmke allowed himself a smile. Then he tried to start the car. He couldn't; the radio had drained the battery.

Actually back in 1923, Ehmke won 20 games for the last-place Red Sox—and among them were two victories that might have made his name among the most memorable in baseball's history.

On September 7 that season, Ehmke no-hit the A's. Four days later, against the Yankees in New York, he gave up a ground ball to lead-off hitter Whitey Witt that squirmed its way to third baseman Howard Shanks, took a strange bounce, and ricocheted off Shanks's chest. Official scorer Fred Lieb called it a hit.

From that point on, Ehmke retired twenty-seven batters in a row. In the press box, his colleagues tried to prevail upon Lieb to change his call on Witt's bouncer, but the scorer wouldn't give. Eventually, a petition was carried to American League president Ban Johnson, supported in part by an affidavit by umpire Tommy Connolly that Shanks should have made the play. But Johnson, no sentimentalist, upheld Lieb's prerogative and, by extension, his decision. The world would have to wait fifteen years for Johnny Vander Meer.

Like Ruth, Mack had a hard time with names; he called his star pitcher Lefty Grove "Groves," and he referred to Lou Boudreau, player-manager of the Indians, as "Mr. Bordiere." He also had a hard time with money. No sooner would he assemble a championship team than he would break it up again to bring in some cash. When he hired Jimmy Dykes, a former player and his eventual successor, to be a coach in 1948, Mack told him, "Jimmy, I'm afraid we can't pay you enough money."

Dykes replied, "Do we have to start in where we left off 16 years ago?"

Dykes was actually a surprise choice to succeed Mack; most people assumed Connie would hand over the reins to his son Earle. But both Earle and another son, Roy, who was in the front office, were the subjects of constant derision. Jimmy Isaminger of the *Philadelphia Inquirer* once wrote, "Connie Mack's sons became senile before Connie did."

BOBO NEWSOM

Earle Mack once went out to the mound to take pitcher Bobo Newsom out of a game. "Daddy says you should leave now," Earle told Newsom.

"Well, you can just tell Daddy," said Newsom, "to go fuck hisself."

Louis Norman Newsom, for his part, was one of the more colorful characters of this or any other time in baseball. As John Lardner wrote, Newsom "called himself and everyone else Bobo." He was hired seventeen different times in his twenty big league seasons and is the only pitcher in baseball history to win 200 games and still be under .500. His rubber arm made him highly desired, but his antics wore out his welcomes quickly. Still, Clark Griffith signed him five different times for the Senators, in part because Bobo was his favorite pinochle partner. He got the opening day assignment for Washington in 1936 against the Yankees, a particular honor since President Franklin Roosevelt was in attendance. In the third inning of the game, Newsom was knocked off his feet when a throw by his own third baseman struck him on the side of the face. As he lay on the ground, he was asked if he wanted to leave.

"Listen," he said, "when the President of the United States comes to see old Bobo pitch, old Bobo ain't gonna let him down."

Newsom proceeded to pitch a four-hit, 1-0 shutout, and after the game he had his jaw, which had been broken in two places, wired together. For the next few days, he only talked half as much as usual; manager Bucky Harris, though, pointed out that this was still much more than necessary.

The opening day adventure was characteristic. Newsom once finished a game after a line drive fractured his knee cap. Another time a shot by Oscar Judd of the Red Sox caromed off his head and landed in center field, and Newsom still stayed in the game, although he later admitted he was hearing music in his head in the latter stages of the contest. It was after that particular misadventure that a sportswriter introduced his wife to Newsom. "A pleasure, madam," Newsom said. "Would you like to feel the bump on my head?"

When Newsom was pitching for the Red Sox, he kept a hutch of rabbits in his room just for company. But he forgot about them when he went on the road, and they ate their way through the hotel furnishings. Manager Joe Cronin was presented the bill, and soon thereafter Bobo was sent packing.

He even reduced Leo Durocher to tears, when the Lip was managing the Dodgers and Bobo was pitching for them. After Durocher suspended him indefinitely for insubordination, Bobo led a mutiny. Leo had to tearfully address his troops before a game with the Pirates to convince them to go out onto the field. Thus moved, they destroyed Pittsburgh 23-6.

Newsom's finest hour, though, came during a time of personal sadness. He won the first game of the 1940 World Series against Cincinnati 7-2, but his father, in town to see the game, died the next morning of a heart attack. Four days later, dedicating the game to his father, Bobo pitched a three-hit shutout. Two days later, he was called upon again for the seventh game, and as he oiled his glove before the game, a reporter approached him. "Will you try to win this one for your daddy, too?" asked the reporter.

"Why, no," Newsom said, "No, I think I'll win this one for Bobo." He lost, 2-1.

THE RABBIT BALL

As the power-hitting pioneered by Ruth became more and more popular, progressive hopping-up of the official baseball reached its pinnacle—or, perhaps, its nadir—in 1930, when the entire

National League batted .303, the American .288. Not only was the core of the ball juiced to increase resiliency, but the seams were sewn flush to the cowhide, so that pitchers could not grip it so readily. Joe Tinker said, "Pitchers are afraid to get off-balance for fear they'll get killed when the ball comes back at them."

According to William B. Mead, whose study of the 1930 season is the best account of the Era of the Too-Live Ball, John McGraw proposed deadening the ball and moving the pitcher's mound in a few feet. "Youngsters in the amateur ranks and on the sandlots no longer have ambitions to become pitchers," Mead quotes McGraw. "They want to play some other position in which they can get by without being discouraged."

But the best of all hitting seasons had a bizarre conclusion—in the Cardinals–A's World Series that fall, Philadelphia batters hit only .197, St. Louis .200.

THE FUTILE PHILLIES

The most notorious beneficiaries (if that's the word) of the rabbit ball were the 1930 Phillies. Wrote Mead, "For hitting, no team was the superior of the Phillies, except whomever they were playing. In the nightcap of a doubleheader on July 23, the Phils attacked the Pirates with 27 hits, including two home runs by Don Hurst. Not enough; the Pirates won 16-15." And on the next day, against the Cubs, the Phils lost again, this time 19-15.

For the season, exploiting the right-field wall in Baker Bowl (it was only 300 feet straight away, 280 down the line), the Phils had a team batting average of .315, and scored 6.13 runs per game. Still they finished last—40 games out of first, 7 out of seventh—as Philadelphia pitchers allowed opposing hitters to bat .350 at Baker Bowl.

The best player the Phils had in the '30s was their right-fielder, Chuck Klein. But his lot was a hapless one; it was rumored in Philadelphia during the Klein years that the local papers kept in standing type a headline that read, "KLEIN HITS TWO AS PHILS LOSE."

Used even more often than the Klein "headline" was the Baker Bowl public-address announcer's phrase, "Willoughby now pitching." That signified Claude "Weeping Willie" Willoughby, who in 1930 started 24 games, relieved in another 17, and concluded the season with a record of 4-17, abetted by his teammates' misplays and his own ERA of 7.59. Fresco Thompson, who was the team's captain, once took a line-up card to the umpire on which he had written in the pitcher's slot, "Willoughby—and others."

If anything, the Phillies at the other end of the decade were even worse. They were managed by James T. "Doc" Prothro, the second-best dental school alumnus (after Casey Stengel) to manage in the majors. Prothro presided over three straight last-place finishes from 1939 to 1941; in the best of those seasons, 1940, they won 50 and lost 103, and finished 50 games behind the pennant-winning Reds. In '41, the Dodgers beat them by 57 games.

Kirby Higbe, who played for Prothro, recalled the young pitcher who complained, "After pitching on this club for a couple of months, I'm not sure whether I'm in the big leagues or not."

Prothro told him, "Don't ever think you are not in the big leagues, son. We may not be a big-league club, but we are playing against big-league clubs."

One who simply couldn't take it any longer was pitcher Hugh Mulcahy, a decent right-hander who had lost 18 games for the Phillies in 1937, 20 in 1938, and 16 in 1939. When he peaked at 22 losses in 1940, he left baseball to become the first major leaguer to enter military service during World War II. Mulcahy had by then earned a nickname fully as descriptive as "Red" or "Lefty": he was called, simply enough, "Losing Pitcher."

Prothro's Phillies were so inept that in 1939, after ending an eight-game losing streak by beating the Giants in New

York, they were reprieved by a New York policeman who had apprehended them for throwing soft-drink bottles out of the windows of the Governor Clinton Hotel. When he learned who they were, the policeman told his partner, "Let them have their fun. They don't have much chance to celebrate."

FLINT RHEM

Rhem was a mediocre right-hander who managed an occasional good season every few years, almost as if by accident. One such seemed to be on its way when he was with the Cardinals in 1930 and won six in a row. But scheduled to face the Dodgers, Rhem simply disappeared, for two days. When he finally returned to the club, he told manager Gabby Street that he had been kidnapped by a group of men who took him to a hotel, locked him in a room, and forced him to drink huge amounts of liquor at the point of a gun. According to John Lardner, Rhem punctuated his tale by insisting to Street, "They wouldn't take no for an answer, boss. It was terrible."

Street declined to fine Rhem; he thought the story was too good for that.

1930s PLAYERS

The biggest thorn in the side of the Ruth-and-Gehrig Yankees was Mickey Cochrane, the preeminent catcher of the era. He helped the Philadelphia Athletics to their three straight pennants in 1929, 1930, and 1931, and after Connie Mack traded him to Detroit before the '34 season to become the Tigers player-manager, Cochrane led the Tigers to two American League pennants and the 1935 world championship. He hit .300 or more eight times in his eleven full seasons, ran the bases exceptionally well for a catcher, and had no peer behind the plate. Billy Evans called him "a shortstop with shin-guards and a chest protector."

In college, Cochrane had been a halfback and kicker, as well as a boxer and a saxophone player. Cochrane was as tough as he was versatile. His bench-jockeying of the Chicago Cubs during the '29 Series was so relentless that Judge Landis threatened him with suspension if he didn't stop. Not exactly chastened, Cochrane told one of the Cubs batters the next day, "Hello, sweetheart! We're gonna serve tea this afternoon."

In 1924, the old Philadelphia star Home Run Baker sent Mack a sixteen-year-old catcher named Jimmie Foxx. How the Maryland farmboy got the extra x in his name was something even he wasn't sure of. "I don't know where it came from," he said, "But that was the way my grandfather handed it down to us, so I guess it belongs there." As Cochrane flourished behind the plate, Mack moved Foxx to first base, and he became one of the most feared hitters in baseball. By the time The Beast called it quits—he had starred for Boston after he left Philadelphia—he had 534 homers, more than any right-handed hitter in history up to that point, and three MVP awards. He hit 58 homers in 1932 and might have broken Ruth's record if he hadn't hurt his wrist falling off a stepladder at home in September. He was nearly as versatile as Ruth, too. He filled in once at shortstop, and in his final season, 1945 with the Phillies, he pitched nine games—all this despite a sometimes debilitating sinus condition.

Red Smith wrote this about one of Foxx's legendary homers in Shibe Park: "It looked like a low line drive streaking over the infield, but it was still climbing when it clipped the very peak of the roofed upper deck in left and took off for the clouds. Three days later a small boy in Bustleton, on the northeast fringe of town, found a baseball with snow on it."

Lefty Gomez once said of Foxx, "He wasn't scouted—he was trapped." He also once said he gave up wearing glasses because of Foxx: "I had been having trouble with my eyes. One day my glasses fogged up while I was pitching, but when I cleaned them and looked at the plate and saw Foxx clearly, it frightened me so much I never wore them again." Gomez once had to face Foxx with two men on in the fifth, and the pitcher kept shaking Dickey off. The catcher called time, went out to the mound and asked, "What do you want to throw?"

"I want to throw nothing up there to that brute," said Gomez.

"Well, we can't stand here till everybody goes home to eat," said Dickey. "Let's try to buzz the fast one past him."

The fast one went even faster on the way out, breaking the upright portion of a seat in Yankee Stadium's left-field grandstand.

Robert Moses Grove—Lefty to most, Mose to some—was a late bloomer. The Martinsburg, Va., team he pitched for sold him to Jack Dunn's Baltimore team for $3,000, the cost of the outfield fence it needed, but Grove didn't get to the majors and the A's until he was twenty-five, and even then he was wild. By 1927, when he was twenty-seven, he had found his control, although he never quite got control of his temper. His motion was something to see—he would rock back until the knuckles of his left hand nearly brushed the earth, then come up and over. From 1927 to 1933 he won 20, 24, 20, 28, 31, 25, and 24 games, and in this era of the hitter his lifetime ERA was 3.06. In 1931, the year in which he finished 31-4 and won the first official Most Valuable Player award bestowed by the baseball writers, Grove was trying for his seventeenth straight victory against the Browns, a streak that would have broken the AL record held by Walter Johnson and Smokey Joe Wood. But rookie outfielder Jim Moore, who was playing in place of the ailing Al Simmons, dropped an easy fly ball that led Grove to lose 1-0. "After that game," said Grove, "I went in and tore the clubhouse up. Wrecked the place, tore those stall lockers off the wall and everything else. Threw everything I could get my hands on, giving Al Simmons hell all the while."

Grove despised idle conversation as much as he hated losing. When a writer asked him if he had any funny baseball stories, Grove said, "I never saw anything funny about the game." He finished out his career with the Red Sox, who had a fellow of like mind, Ted Williams. "He was a moody guy, a tantrum thrower like me," Williams said of Grove. "But when he punched a locker or something he always did it with his right hand. He was a careful tantrum thrower."

Another Hall of Famer on those great A's teams was Al Simmons, born Aloysius Harry Szymanski; he borrowed his last name from a billboard advertising a hardware company. Simmons grew up in Milwaukee, the son of Polish immigrants, and although he showed great hitting talent early on, he had an off-putting batting stance. A right-handed hitter, his left foot would be pointed toward third base, and he came to be known as Bucketfoot Al. But people got used to it, for Simmons batted at least .308 and drove in at least 102 runs in 12 of his first 13 seasons. "Pitchers!" he once exclaimed. "I wanted them dead."

In 1931, Simmons held out the entire spring, signing his contract only hours before the first game. On the first pitch he saw, he hit a homer. He went on to win his second straight batting title that season with a .390 average.

When he was coaching for Connie Mack in the 1940s, Simmons was told by the old man there would always be a place for him in the Philadelphia organization.

With as much delicacy as he could muster, Simmons thanked him, but allowed that Mack himself wasn't likely to be around much longer to guarantee it. Mack took it in stride. "I think my sons know how I feel about it," he said reassuringly. But Simmons wasn't content. "Maybe they do," he said, "but would you mind telling them?"

THE CALLED SHOT

The '32 Yankees were not far from the '27 Yankees; they won 107 games. The Babe did pretty well, with 41 homers and 137 RBIs, but Jimmie Foxx hit 58 homers that year with 163 RBIs. Ruth, at thirty-seven, would never again be the league's dominant player. But he still had one great moment left, in the World Series against the Cubs—the Series of the notorious "called shot."

There was no love lost between the Yankees and the Cubs. The National League team had, after all, fired McCarthy two years before. There was also the matter of the stinginess shown by the Cubs when they divided their World Series shares just before the first game. Rogers Hornsby, who had managed the team the first two-thirds of the season, received nothing. Worse still, Mark Koenig, the old Yankees shortstop who had been acquired by the Cubs in midseason, received only a half share even though he was a major factor in their pennant drive. Ruth fired the first volley in a World Series of bench-jockeying when he yelled to Koenig, "Hey, Mark, who are those cheapskates you're with?"

The Yankees won the first two games in New York 12-6 and 5-2, and it was an ugly crowd they faced in Chicago for the third game. The fans kept throwing lemons to Ruth, who just threw them back. He hit a three-run homer in the first and Gehrig a solo shot in the third, but the Cubs rallied to tie the score at 4-4 in the fourth. When Ruth stepped to the plate in the fifth with one out and none on, Wrigley Field was in an uproar. The Cubs were on the top of the dugout steps, yelling at Ruth. The pitcher, Charlie Root, threw the first pitch for a called strike. The din increased, but Ruth, grinning, looked over at the Cubs and raised one finger of his right hand—the gesture that triggered the "called shot" rumors. Root's next pitches were balls, but when Ruth looked at another called strike, the Cubs were so excited they ran out onto the field to razz Ruth. At that point, Ruth waved them back to their dugout and held up two fingers, more fuel for the legend. The Cubs catcher, Gabby Hartnett, thought he heard Ruth say, "'It only takes one to hit it." Root hollered something from the mound, and Ruth shouted back, "I'm going to knock the next pitch right down your goddamned throat."

The next pitch was a changeup curve, low and away. Ruth went down to get it, and hit a tremendous line-drive homer deep into the seats in center field, the longest home run ever hit in Wrigley Field. Gehrig followed Ruth with another blast, as the Yankees went on to a 7-5 victory and then a sweep of the Series after thrashing the Cubs 13-6 the next day.

Root went to his deathbed saying that Ruth didn't point to center field; all Ruth ever admitted was saying to himself, as he rounded the bases, "You lucky, lucky bum."

Ruth's numbers in 1933, his twentieth season, don't look so bad now: .301, 34 home runs, 103 RBIs. But he was fading, and so were the Yankees, who wouldn't win another pennant until '36. But on the last day of the season, he brought back the memory of a younger, different Ruth by pitching a complete game, a 6-5 victory over his old team, the Red Sox; it was only his second appearance as a pitcher in the preceding 12 years. The fans must have sensed this was his last hurrah, as thousands of them waited outside the Stadium after the game to applaud him as he made his way to his car.

PAUL WANER

Like a small-scale Ruth, Paul Waner, the elder of the two Hall of Fame Waner brothers, was nearly as celebrated a carouser as he was a hitter; he was also a widely liked, considerate, and introspective man known to read Seneca in his more sober hours.

But Waner's attachment to liquor became, as his career proceeded, his most distinguishing characteristic. He acknowledged he often played while drunk or hung over, and slyly admitted that there was a certain advantage to it: a pitched ball looked so blurry to him at times that there was "More of it to hit." Bill Veeck swore he once saw Waner play *in extremis*—and knew this was so not because of the double and the game-winning home run that Waner hit in the course of the game, but because of what he did after he hit the double: Veeck said he saw him "take a wide turn at second base and go sliding into the bullpen mound in the left-field foul ground . . . more than 60 feet away from his destination."

Roy Parmalee of the Giants maintained that the best way to pitch to Waner could be determined by talking to him before the game, to see if he'd been drinking. If Waner had had a drink, he'd pull the ball to right; if he'd made it to the afternoon sober, he'd go left. "So we'd pitch him just the opposite, depending on whether or not he had a drunk," Parmalee said. "Not that it made a great deal of difference."

Casey Stengel admired him, too. Waner "had to be a very graceful player," Stengel said, "because he could slide without breaking the bottle on his hip."

Waner entered the 1942 season, with the Braves, with 2,955 hits to his credit. He was thirty-nine, and it was his seventeenth year in the major leagues. By June 17, he had pulled himself up to 2,999. But he had already played 25 games in which he had gotten no hits at all.

With a man on first and the hit-and-run on, Cincinnati shortstop Eddie Joost dashed to cover second; Waner put the ball in the spot that the shortstop had just abandoned. Joost reversed his course, dove back, and got his glove on the ball, but it squirted away, and Waner was safe.

The official scorer gave the sign for a base hit, and umpire Beans Reardon came over to first to present it to him as the crowd applauded the milestone. But Waner refused to accept the ball, looked up at the press box, and shook his head vigorously—he wanted the "hit" call reversed. The scorer obliged, and Waner waited another two days for number three thousand.

RUTH'S LAST HURRAH

The Yankees no longer wanted Ruth; Judge Emil Fuchs, who owned the Boston Braves, did—not so much for his waning abilities as a player or his potential as a manager, but strictly for his proven abilities as a box-office attraction. So Fuchs lied to Ruth, or rather promised much more than he intended to deliver. He said he would make the Babe vice-president of the

Braves, as well as a player-coach until such time, probably the next year, as the Braves needed a new manager to replace Bill McKechnie. All this for $25,000 a year, plus a share of the profits.

The city of Boston was delighted finally to have Ruth back, even though he was forty-one, overweight, and immobile in the field. In his very first game as a Brave, Ruth hit a two-run homer off Carl Hubbell, drove in another run, and made a diving catch. The next day, he got two more hits. But Ruth's crumbling skills were soon exposed and attendance fell off. Exposed, too, was Fuchs, who had no apparent intention of actually naming Ruth manager; Ruth realized soon enough that he had been played a sucker.

But he still had one Ruthian game left in him. On Saturday, May 25, 1935, against Pittsburgh, Ruth went 4 for 4 with three home runs, two of them off Guy Bush, one of the Cubs who razzed him back in '32. The last home run went over the roof of Forbes Field. "I never saw a ball hit so hard before or since," said Bush. "It's probably still going." Someone estimated the ball traveled 600 feet.

His old teammate Duffy Lewis, then the Braves traveling secretary, and his wife Claire both tried to talk Ruth into quitting after that game, but Ruth said he had promised Fuchs he would complete the road trip, so he played a few more games.

But Fuchs, who chose to use Ruth as a scapegoat for his team's poor play, suddenly released him as a player and assistant coach and fired him from his "vice-presidency." Except for his brief brief stint a few years later as a coach with the Brooklyn Dodgers, baseball was done with Babe Ruth. When he asked the Yankees for opening day tickets in 1936, the club said sure, just send a check.

JUDGE FUCHS

Fuchs had earlier distinguished himself in 1929, when he appointed himself manager of the Braves. "The time has gone when a manager has to chew tobacco and talk from the side of his mouth," Fuchs said. "I don't think our club can do any worse with me as manager than it has done the last few years."

True enough; in 1928 Boston lost 103 games, while in '29 they dropped a mere 98. By and large, Fuchs let coach Johnny Evers run the team, but he did make the occasional decision. Most of the Boston players, who liked Fuchs, generally tolerated his tenancy of the manager's chair, but Joe Dugan—who had joined the team on waivers from the Yankees—offered no such goodwill. When Fuchs asked the old third baseman to go in at shortstop in one game, Dugan asked ingenuously, "Where is shortstop on this field?"

Fuchs stiffened and said, "Show Mr. Dugan where the clubhouse is and how to take off his uniform."

Most Fuchs stories revolve around his unfamiliarity with the game's subtler points, or his inattention to the action around him. He once told Ed Brandt, a left-handed hitter, to pinch-hit against Jumbo Elliott of the Phillies. Brandt demurred, pointing out Elliott himself was a lefty.

The Judge looked out at the mound and, after a brief hesitation, replied, "So he is."

By opening day in 1930, Bill McKechnie had taken over as manager.

THE DAFFINESS DODGERS

The Babe who grew up in Brooklyn was a very different sort from the one who flourished in the Bronx. The Dodgers' Babe Herman fit his surroundings; he was simply the strangest character among the collection of oddities who gathered in Ebbets Field.

Herman's celebrated doubling into a double play—not tripling into a double play, John Lardner wrote, "but the next best thing"—wasn't entirely his fault. For one thing, coaching third for Brooklyn in that 1926 game against the Braves—for the only time in his life—was back-up catcher Mickey O'Neil, who upon complaining that he never saw any action was invited into the coaching box by its usual occupant, Otto Miller. For another, one of the base runners ahead of Herman was Dazzy Vance.

Actually, there were three runners ahead of Herman. He had hit his immense one-out fly to center field with the bases loaded. After the ball hit the wall, Hank DeBerry scored. Chick Fewster was on his way from first to third. And Vance, who had begun the play perched on second, found himself hung up between third and home when O'Neil, spying Herman rounding second on Fewster's heels, screamed "Back! Back!"

Vance, unused as he was to so much running, thought O'Neil had been yelling at *him,* so the pitcher retreated to third. Fewster, standing on the base, suddenly found both Herman and Vance sliding into the bag, from opposite directions.

The Boston third baseman, Eddie Taylor, tagged Vance. Then he tagged Herman. Fewster, for some reason, he left unmolested; under the rules, Vance, as the lead runner, had the rights to the base. But Fewster thought both of his mates were out, and walked off the bag toward his defensive position at second, whereupon Boston's Doc Gautreau shouted for the ball. Fewster caught on immediately, and dashed out to right field before Gautreau apprehended him.

For some unimaginable reason, the world soon forgot that Herman's clout had enabled DeBerry to score the game's winning run. Instead, the incident led to a standing piece of Brooklyn humor. Whenever an announcer would say "the Dodgers have three men on base," the customary response was, "Which one?"

After the famous play had concluded and the inevitable argument had began, Vance, still on his back after his slide, lifted his head and said (according to Rube Bressler), "Mr. Umpire, fellow teammates, and members of the opposition. If you carefully peruse the rules of our national pastime you will find that there is one and only one protagonist in rightful occupancy of this hassock—namely yours truly, Arthur C. Vance."

Herman no doubt would have explained the odd base-running circumstance differently. As James T. Farrell wrote, Herman "did not run. He got to first base"—any base, he might have said—"by sheer will power."

Confronting a group of New York baseball writers who made their livings off of their embroidered stories of his exploits afield, Herman once tried to persuade them to stop. He had never, he said, been hit on the head by a fly ball, despite their constant stories to the contrary. "Let me tell you this," writer Tommy Holmes recalled him saying, "if a fly ever hits me on the head, I'll quit."

"How about the shoulder?" someone asked.

Replied Herman, "On the shoulders don't count."

Eight years after Herman left the majors, the Dodgers were desperate for wartime help, and Herman was brought back as a pinch-hitter, aged forty-one. In his first appearance at the plate, he singled to right, rounded first, and fell flat on his face.

Dazzy Vance, Herman's teammate, had one of the most miraculous of major league careers—he didn't win his first big league game until he was thirty-one, but he proceeded thereafter to win so many—197—he was elected to the Hall of Fame. But as late as he arrived in the majors, Vance just barely made it even then. Dodger scout Larry Sutton wanted to sign catcher Hank DeBerry off the New Orleans roster, but the New Orleans owner insisted on a package deal—$10,000 for DeBerry and Vance both.

DeBerry stayed with the Dodgers for nine years, but was utterly overshadowed by his prodigious battery mate, and forever referred to himself as "the tail of the comet."

Late in the 1930 season, Vance found himself pitching against the Cardinals, who were trailing the Dodgers by half a game in the pennant race. It was a game that eventually went into the tenth inning without a run scored, but only barely so. In the sixth, with Sparky Adams on third, Vance was pitching to Chick Hafey. As he went into his motion, Adams broke for the plate. Seeing that the Pittsburgh runner likely had home stolen, Vance made a slight alteration in his delivery and plunked Hafey.

With that the ball was dead, and Adams sent back to third.

Vance never pitched at tiny Baker Bowl, in Philadelphia, because it "might hurt my record." And manager Wilbert Robinson, by and large, let him have his way. But that was Robinson's style. Years earlier he had been John McGraw's drinking partner with the old Orioles, but by this point in his career he was a gentle and somewhat bumbling sort—who probably became such because there was no other way to contend with the peculiar personalities who seemed to flock to the Dodgers. As Harold Parrott said, Uncle Robbie was "more of habit than a manager."

One of the Dodgers' colorful fans in those days was a peddler named Abe Rettan, who always sat behind third base and cheered for the visiting team. At one point Robinson offered Rettan a season's pass if he would transfer his loyalties to Brooklyn. He accepted, but shortly came back to Robinson, pass in hand; he said he'd prefer to pay his way in and boo.

Brooklyn pitcher Clyde Day was called Pea Ridge, in honor of his hometown in Arkansas, and he celebrated any inning-ending strikeout by standing on the mound, flapping his arms, and emitting an ear-shattering hog call.

Eventually, in 1931, Robinson put an end to Day's triumphant bellows. "A man," the manager said, "has no right to be sillier than God intended him to be."

A brief interregnum separated Robinson's tenure in Brooklyn from that of a man equally suited to such a team. Imagine this scenario:

On the Brooklyn bench, new manager Casey Stengel; in right field, a declining Hack Wilson; pitching, Walter Beck, called "Boom-Boom" for the sound his pitches made as they caromed off outfield walls.

In Philadelphia one day, Stengel went to pull a struggling Beck; he begged for one more chance, Stengel relented, and the next batter hit a home run. When the manager again went out to pull his pitcher, Beck turned in rage and threw the ball against Baker Bowl's tin right-field wall.

Thereupon Wilson, gazing dumbly at the ground in the grip of what was presumed to be his usual afternoon hangover, heard the sound of ball on tin, raced to field the ricochet, then spun and threw to second base. "A hell of a play," his teammate, Tony Cuccinello, said.

As for Beck, he kicked over a bucket of ice water when he reached the dugout. Stengel admonished him. "Stop that," he said. "If you break a toe I won't be able to get anything for you."

Like Yogi Berra after him, Brooklyn outfielder Frenchy Bordagaray's exploits and statements took on an air of mythology; writers would attribute their own clever phrases to him (when he was fined $50 for spitting at an umpire, Bordagaray reputedly said, "That's more than I expectorated"), and fill sparse columns with characterizations of his unlikely personality.

But Bordagaray did come to spring training in 1936 wearing a mustache and a van dyke, which Stengel ordered him to shave; and once when his cap came off his head in his pursuit of a fly ball, he retrieved hat first, ball second.

According to his teammate, Buddy Hassett, Stengel was philosophic after the hat incident. "The cap wasn't going anywhere," Stengel said, "but the ball was."

McGRAW'S EXIT

By the second month of the 1932 season, John McGraw clearly was no longer the manager he'd once been. He was fifty-nine years old, and New York hadn't won a pennant in eight years. On June 1, he called first baseman Bill Terry into his office. The two men, feuding over Terry's salary, hadn't spoken in a year and a half. As Terry came to McGraw's office, he was prepared for the inevitable confrontation which had been building.

McGraw said, "Stand with your back to the door. I don't want to close it, and I don't want anybody to know what we're saying. I'm retiring from this job. If you want it, you can have it."

The most stunned member of the Giants, after perhaps Terry himself, was outfielder-third baseman Freddie Lindstrom. He had joined the Giants as an eighteen-year-old in 1924, had long been one of McGraw's favorites, and expected to succeed his mentor to the manager's chair. On hearing of Terry's appointment, he said he couldn't play for him and demanded a trade. The next opening day, Lindstrom was a Pirate.

Terry went on to win three pennants in the next five years, and gave to the world the famous apothegm, "Is Brooklyn still in the league?" Lindstrom, for his part, retired from baseball at thirty-one, and said many years later that demanding the trade was the worst mistake he'd ever made.

THE LAST OF GEHRIG

Eleanor Twitchell, the former debutante who married Lou Gehrig in 1933, had a strong influence on her husband. Before the marriage, he had parked his car a few blocks from Yankee Stadium, ducking in and out to avoid the public, but after 1933 he parked in front of the clubhouse entrance and freely signed autographs. Eleanor also attempted to cultivate his tastes in art, music, and literature. Gehrig used to cause amusement among his teammates by bringing the works of Socrates, Schopenhauer, and Kant into a clubhouse where *The Sporting News* was considered heavy reading.

Along with his prodigious hitting, Gehrig's great accomplishment was his phenomenal 2,130-game playing streak. It was a streak abetted by a sympathetic manager; McCarthy occasionally nursed him on the road by writing him into the lineup as the shortstop, then taking him out after he batted in the first inning. His luck was such that the one time he did suffer a serious injury while playing baseball was when his right hand was broken by a pitched ball—while on a Yankees tour of Japan in the 1931 off-season.

Gehrig was clearly not himself in 1938, although most players would have been proud to have 29 homers and 114 RBIs, not to mention a .295 average. Some observers attributed Gehrig's sub-par year to the Hollywood malady known as "Klieg eyes"—like Ruth before him, he starred in a B-movie during the winter—but Gehrig pointed out that most of the filming had been done outdoors. Others thought the strain of the consecutive-game streak had finally taken its toll. Ruth further ruptured their already strained relationship when he suggested in print that Gehrig had sacrificed several seasons of his career for the sake of his record. McCarthy became annoyed at all the "Whatever happened to Lou Gehrig?" stories, muttering, "I wish I had more players on this club that would be so off in their play that they could give me 200 runs." Besides, Gehrig had that year hit his twenty-third grand slam, a record that now seems as unapproachable as his playing streak.

The tipoff came in the World Series against the Cubs. Gehrig had thrived in Series play, but this time he hit only four singles without an RBI in the Yankees' sweep of the Cubs.

Gehrig, who was approaching thirty-six, thought he could stem the tide by getting in better shape, and he put himself through an exhausting regimen in spring training of 1939. He had been treated for a gall-bladder problem that offseason, but only Eleanor had any idea that something was seriously wrong. She had noticed that when he stepped off curbs while crossing streets, he stepped as a blind man would. He was, it turned out, in the early stages of a degenerative muscle disease, amyotrophic lateral sclerosis.

Gehrig gave false hope by hitting three home runs in a game against the Yankees' Norfolk farm club. But once the season started, he was a sad sight at first and at the plate. Several games were lost when balls went through his legs, and in the first eight games he had but four singles. On May 2, at the start of the Yankees' western trip in Detroit, Gehrig went to McCarthy and said, "You better put Babe [Dahlgren] on first today. I'm not doing the club any good out there." And so Gehrig's streak stopped at a mind-boggling 2,130 games.

A few weeks later, Gehrig said he actually came to his decision in the last game before the road trip. "Late in the game, I scooped up an ordinary ground ball and threw it over to the pitcher, covering first base. It was the same kind of play I had made several hundred times in my big league career, just a routine play. But Bill Dickey, Joe Gordon and the pitcher all got around me, slapped me on the back, and said, 'Great going, Lou,' and 'Nice stop, big boy.' They meant it to be kind, but it hurt worse than any bawling out I ever received in baseball. They were saying 'great stop' because I had fielded a grounder. I decided then and there, I would ask McCarthy to take me out of the lineup."

On July 4, 1939, the Yankees held a testimonial day for Gehrig. He remained in uniform with the Yankees for the rest of that season, cheering on the bench and rooming with his old friend Bill Dickey. A cruel rumor circulated that the disease was contagious, but Dickey stayed by Gehrig's side, helping him walk and get dressed. When the Yankees swept the Reds in the '39 Series, Gehrig participated in the celebration, then bid goodby to his teammates.

Mayor Fiorello La Guardia made Gehrig the New York City Parole Commissioner, and for the next year or so, Gehrig worked conscientiously at his job. He seldom attended a ballgame, preferring to stay at home with Eleanor, reading and playing bridge. He also corresponded with fellow victims of ALS to keep their spirits up. But in the spring of 1941, the illness (which would enter the language as "Lou Gehrig's Disease") worsened, and on June 2, 1941, Gehrig died almost eighteen years to the day after Miller Huggins installed him at first base. He was thirty-eight.

TWO TIGERS

Charlie Gehringer, the second baseman on the Detroit teams that won pennants in 1934 and 1935, was known as "The Mechanical Man." Said Doc Cramer, an outfielder and teammate, "All you have to do is wind him up on opening day, and he runs on and on, doing everything right all season." Yankees coach Art Fletcher, to put it another way, said, "Gehringer made two hits the first day of the season, and it should be a warning, for that is what he will do in every game all year."

Although he later became a front office executive with the Tigers, Gehringer was remarkably quiet as a player. The story goes that he and the equally laconic Elon Hogsett, a pitcher of Indian descent, were eating breakfast, and during the course of the meal Hogsett said to Gehringer, "Pass the salt." To which Gehringer replied, "You might have pointed."

Like Lou Gehrig, Hank Greenberg was a power-hitting first baseman who grew up in New York City as the son of European immigrants. He once recalled how his father came home from work one day to find a pile of sawdust on his lawn. Furious when he discovered his own son had put the sawdust there as a makeshift sliding pit, he made him remove it. But Hank, who could neither bear to lose his sliding pit nor dare defy his father, simply put the sawdust down every day, and cleaned it up before his father got home.

By the time he was eighteen, Greenberg was 6'4" and 210 pounds. Paul Krichell, who had signed Gehrig for the Yankees, wanted to sign him, as did the Senators and the Tigers; John McGraw thought him too clumsy for the Giants. Greenberg ended up with the Tigers only after they agreed to let him continue his education at New York University. He cracked the Detroit lineup in 1933, and the next year Mickey Cochrane inserted him in the cleanup spot, where he batted .336 with 26 homers, 139 RBIs, and a staggering 63 doubles.

Along the way to the pennant that season, a crucial game with Boston fell on the Jewish New Year. Greenberg, though not very religious, did not want to offend his parents or the Jewish community by playing, so he consulted local rabbis. One rabbi left the decision entirely up to Greenberg, which did not satisfy him. A second rabbi, though, consulted the Talmud and found a reference to ballplaying in the 900-year-old guide that indicated it would be all right to play on Rosh Hashanah. Greenberg did play and hit two homers in the Tigers' 2-1 victory. Eight days later, on Yom Kippur, the Day of Atonement, he absolutely refused to play, and though the Tigers lost, the poet Edgar Guest saluted him with this four-line verse:

> We shall miss him in the infield,
> And we shall miss him at the bat,
> But he's true to his religion,
> And I honor him for that.

In 1938, Greenberg—who was the American League MVP in the Tigers' World Series-winning 1935 campaign, and who drove in 183 runs in 1937—mounted an assault on Babe Ruth's home-run record. Upset that Joe McCarthy had not played him in the '37 All-Star Game, Greenberg refused to go to the '38 game, taking batting practice instead. He soon was hitting homers in bunches, and by September 1 he had 46. On September 23 he hit numbers 55 and 56 off Earl Whitehill, who had been one of Ruth's victims in 1927. Number 57 was an inside-the-park homer on what should have been a single; Greenberg himself thought he should have been called out at the plate, but the umpire signaled safe. He hit number 58 his next time up. Now, with five games to play, he needed two to tie, three to break the record. His mother was so excited she promised to make him 61 baseball-shaped portions of gefilte fish if he broke Ruth's record.

Greenberg could do nothing against the Browns the next two games, though he did hit a long shot that just carried foul. Still, that left him three games in Cleveland, two of them to be played in tiny League Park, which had a 290-foot right-field porch. But to take advantage of the publicity, the Indians decided to reschedule Friday's game as part of a Sunday doubleheader in cavernous, new Municipal Stadium. Greenberg went hitless on Saturday in League Park. In the first game on Sunday, against a nineteen-year-old Bob Feller, Greenberg doubled off the fence in left-center, 450 feet from home plate—a home run in almost any other park in the league. In the second game, as the shadows lengthened, he singled his first three times up. Then, when Umpire Cal Hubbard decided to call the game after seven because of darkness, he said, "I'm sorry, Hank, this is as far as I can go." Replied Greenberg, "That's all right, this is as far as I can go, too."

Greenberg encountered so many anti-Semitic comments in the early stages of his career that he almost never acknowledged razzing from the other team, even innocent razzing. In a game against the Red Sox, Greenberg was playing in particularly close at first, and Red Sox pitcher Jim Bagby, who suffered from a harelip, tried to warn him. "Hank, you had better get back!" Bagby shouted. "You don't know this guy, you better get back." Four or five times Bagby delivered the message, but Greenberg paid no attention. Finally, Bagby yelled, "All right, Hank, if you want to look like me and talk like me, stand right where you are."

In 1938 the Tigers gave Greenberg a $10,000 bonus just to move to left field to make room for Rudy York, who was described by Tom Meany as "part Indian and part first baseman." York was a powerful hitter, but he failed in attempts to make him an outfielder, a third baseman, and a catcher. He best position was first base, but that's not saying much. York had a disturbing habit of catching every ball thrown to him with his glove alone. Wrote Warren Brown, "He had a great pair of hand."

York, who hit 18 homers one August, was such a natural slugger that during one of the first All-Star games played at night, he fell away from an inside pitch and hit the ball into the right-field seats. According to Red Smith, "The scorer ruled self-defense."

JOE DiMAGGIO

In 1936 Joe DiMaggio arrived in New York. His grace in the outfield and at the plate would become so engraved on our collective consciousness that, thirty years later, Paul Simon would sing, "Where have you gone, Joe DiMaggio? Our nation turns it lonely eyes to you." Ernest Hemingway would pay tribute to him in *The Old Man and the Sea:* "I would like to take the great DiMaggio fishing," the old man said. "They say his father was a fisherman."

His father was indeed a fisherman in San Francisco, but Joe himself suffered from seasickness. And a good thing that was for the Yankees. Instead of working on the boats, Joe sold newspapers and played baseball. There were five sons, all of them good baseball players, and three of them—brothers Vince and Dom as well as Joe—would make the majors. But the best of all, according to Joe, was Tom. "He could hit a ball a mile," Joe said, "but as the oldest son he had to have a steady job."

After Joe dropped out of high school, his father didn't like the fact that his son was devoting so much time to a game, but Vince, three years older than Joe, helped clear the way by winning an outfield job with the San Francisco Seals in 1932. (Vince also had a beautiful voice, and the family actually considered sending him to Italy to study opera.) When the other San Francisco team, the Missions, offered Joe—he was then a seventeen-year-old shortstop—a job for $150 a month, the senior DiMaggio gave his consent.

Before Joe ever played a game with the Missions, though, the Seals entered the picture, offering him $225 a month if he signed with them. Joe had never played the outfield until Seals manager Ike Caveney sent him out to right after a pinch-hitting appearance early in the 1933 season, and he stayed in the outfield for the rest of his career.

DiMaggio suffered a freak knee injury in the middle of the '34 season—his left foot fell asleep while he was riding in a cab, and when he got out of the cab, he put all his weight on the foot and his knee buckled. The injury, torn cartilage in the knee, turned out to be a break for the Yankees. Before then, several clubs were interested in purchasing DiMaggio, and the bidding had gone as high as $75,000. After the injury, Yankee scout Bill Essick told Ed Barrow, "Don't back off because of the kid's knee. He'll be all right. And you can get him cheap." The Yankees bought him, along with five other players as well, for $25,000.

DiMaggio was horribly green when he reached New York. When a reporter asked him for a quote, he thought it was some sort of soft drink. He burned his sore left foot by keeping it in a diathermy machine too long during spring training and missed the first 16 games of the season. But in his first major league game, he had three hits, including a triple. During that first season, DiMaggio stayed close to his fellow San Francisco Italians, Tony Lazzeri and Frank Crosetti, and there may never have been a less loquacious threesome in Yankees history. One day newspaperman Jack Mahon sat in the lobby of the Chase Hotel in St. Louis near the three Yankees and noted that a full one hour and 20 minutes of total silence went by. Then DiMaggio cleared his throat.

"What did you say?" asked Crosetti.

"Shut up," said Lazzeri. "He didn't say nothing."

DiMaggio quickly learned, though, what mattered in baseball. In 1937, his second season, he batted .346, with 46 homers and 167 runs batted in. That winter of '38, he sought a $40,000 contract from the Yankees, up from $15,000. Barrow said, "Young man, do you realize that Lou Gehrig only makes $43,000 a year after thirteen years?" To which DiMaggio replied, "In that case Mr. Barrow, Mr. Gehrig is a very underpaid ballplayer."

CLOWNS

Robert "Fatty" Fothergill was a good-hitting, awful-fielding outfielder for several American League clubs in the '20s and '30s. While playing for the White Sox in an exhibition game in Roanoke, Va., he crashed into a fence chasing a fly ball, splintering the wooden barricade. This was in the days before public address systems, so an announcer with a megaphone rushed out onto the field and shouted, "Is there a doctor in the stands?"

Then, from the seats, came another call: "Is there an outfielder in the stands?"

Managers like ballplayers to have a little fight in them. But Art Shires, a first baseman for the White Sox, Senators, and Braves, had a little too much fight for his manager in Chicago, Lena Blackburne. Shires flattened Blackburne twice during the 1929 season. A playboy and braggart of the highest order—who called himself "Art the Great"—Shires felt he was entitled to a boxing career after that.

After decking a fighter named Dan Daly—who later admitted he went in the tank—Shires said, "Now get me Gene Tunney." This, of course, put Shires in great demand, and the Philadelphia sports writers invited him to their annual dinner.

Eddie Gottlieb, the Philadelphia sports impresario, was so impressed with the turnout at the dinner that he invited Shires, who also claimed to be a great basketball player, to play with his Sphas against the Renaissance Big Five, one of the great black teams of the time. But during practice Shires, who had a bathtub full of beer waiting back at his hotel, missed every shot by a foot or more. Gottlieb was thus reluctant to use him in the game, but once the fans began chanting, "We want Shires!" Gottlieb relented—at the same time instructing his other players not to give him the ball. Whereupon the fans chanted, "Give it to Shires!"

The Sphas wouldn't, but the Big Five did. The opposition simply handed the ball to Shires, who of course shot and missed. They handed it to him again and again until Gottlieb yanked him out of the game. At halftime Gottlieb, grateful for the big crowd that Shires had drawn, paid him off with $250—$50 more than promised.

That was the end of Art the Great's basketball career; his boxing career concluded a week later when Judge Landis notified Shires that if he continued to fight, he should consider himself permanently retired from baseball. He gave up the ring, but didn't last very long on the diamond, either—in 1932, his fourth season, he batted .238 and was gone.

Cletus Elwood "Boots" Poffenberger was from the same mold as Shires. A pitcher with a thirst, Boots lasted only three years in the majors. In his last go-round with the Dodgers, he pitched in just three games, but he still left a memorable impression. Once, while the Dodgers' train was waiting in the station, Boots rigged a dummy of himself, placed it in his berth, then snuck out to a nearby bar. Another time he decided to skip a game in Cincinnati, and gave teammate Dolf Camilli this message to take to the clubhouse: "Tell Durocher I am tired of the way he is keeping me, like a bird in a cage."

His finest moment, though, occurred when Poffenberger stumbled into the lobby of Philadelphia's Bellevue-Stratford late one night and was confronted by Dodgers owner Larry MacPhail. "You are two hours late!" MacPhail shouted. "Not by the time I go by, I ain't," said Boots, pointing in the direction of the out-of-town clocks over the front desk. "It's only 8 o'clock in Honolulu."

DIZZY DEAN

If ever there was a player who knew he was one-of-a-kind, it was Dizzy Dean. At nineteen, in 1930, he pitched one game, a three-hit shutout; within five years, he won another 120. He played to the press, he murdered the language, he had a hell of time. By the time an injury cut his career short at the end of the thirties, he knew his favorite characterization of himself was undeniable: "There'll never be another one like me."

It was hard to keep track of what was real about Dean. He'd tell contradictory stories to different reporters and justify the practice by saying, "Them ain't lies, them's scoops." But what happened to him in the 1934 Series against Detroit was unquestionably real. While running the bases in the fifth game,

Dean was beaned by a throw from Detroit shortstop Billy Rogell. He was taken to the hospital, and the famous headline
that ensued read, X-RAY OF DEAN'S HEAD SHOWS
NOTHING. Before, though, the pitcher had to be carried off
the field. One of the stretcher-bearers was his brother and
teammate Paul. After the game, writer Tom Meany asked the
younger Dean if Dizzy had been knocked unconscious.

"He wasn't unconscious at all," Paul said. "He talked all the
time we carried him off the field."

"What was he saying?"

"He wasn't *saying* anything. He was just *talking*."

That was the same Series that concluded with the Detroit
fans bombarding Cardinals left-fielder Joe Medwick with fruit,
vegetables, and bottles. Years later, Medwick said, "I know
why they threw it"—he had just crashed into Detroit third
baseman Marv Owen with a particularly vicious slide—"what
I could never figure out is why they brought it to the park in
the first place."

When Paul joined the Cardinals in the spring of 1934 Dean
announced that the pennant would belong to St. Louis: "Me
and Paul will win between forty-five and fifty games this year,"
he told the press. Asked how many he'd win on his own, Dean
answered, "Why, all the games that Paul don't." The brothers
achieved Dizzy's prediction: they won 49 games between them,
19 by Paul.

During that 1934 season, as the Dean brothers led the club
toward the pennant, their manager, Frank Frisch, fined them
both for missing a train. Dizzy led Paul in a walkout, initiat-
ing it in a dramatic confrontation with Frisch in which he
ripped his uniform into shreds as his manager watched.

When Judge Landis later held a hearing to investigate the
walkout, the fines, and the Deans' subsequent suspension by
the St. Louis front office, he first announced that the hearing
was closed to the press. Then, having entered the hearing room,
the Commissioner opened the transom vent, and the gathered

reporters were able to hear every word of the four-hour confrontation of the two pitchers, their manager, and St. Louis
owner Sam Breadon. During the hearing, it was revealed that
the Cardinals had added to Dizzy's fine a charge of $36 for
two destroyed uniforms: the one he had ripped apart in front
of Frisch, and the one he had shredded afterward, for the benefit
of the wire service photographers.

In May of 1937, peevish over a balk that had been called
against him several days earlier, Dean initiated something of
a protest strike on the mound. Asserting that "you can't commit a balk if you don't pitch," Dean stalled so egregiously that
it took him eleven minutes to throw three pitches.

His pitching career ended by injury when he was thirty (save
for a one-inning appearance six years later with the Browns),
Dean embarked on what would become the most remarkable
broadcasting career any ex-player has known. Keenly aware
of the listener appeal of his bizarre syntax and brutalized
grammar, he played the hick role to its fullest. "He slood safe
into second" was perhaps his best-known locution; his most
ornate might have been that "argyin' with an umparr is like
argyin' with a stump. Maybe you city folks don't know what
a stump is. Well, it's somethin' a tree has been cut off of." His
pronunciation of player names was equally loony, and Curt
Smith quotes him on his attempt to say the name of Cubs
pitcher Ed Hanyzewski: "I liked to have broken my jaw tryin'
to pronounce that one," Dean explained, "but I said his name
just by holdin' my nose and sneezin'."
It was when the St. Louis Board of Education, distressed by
the example Dean was setting, asked that he be removed from
the air that Dean uttered the most celebrated line of his career: "A lot of folks that ain't sayin' 'ain't,' " he intoned, " 'ain't
eatin.' "

Wrote Jack Clarke of the *Chicago Sun-Times* when the
Cardinals finally dropped Dean from their announcing team,
"When Dean did not have at his disposal a word suitable for
the occasion, he simply invented one." And when his broad-

cast career was over, he gave a lecture at Southern Methodist University entitled, "Radio Announcing I Have Did."

THE GASHOUSE GANG

One of the St. Louis "Gashouse Gang" (a team of clowns and characters distinguished from Brooklyn's because these had real talent), Pepper Martin was nearly a match for Dean. He was fond of childish pranks like throwing sneezing powder into the blades of hotel lobby ventilation fans, or sitting in his room and dropping water balloons on the heads of passers-by. But he also mastered a subtler form of humor, usually directed at Frank Frisch.

After one Cardinal loss, the manager called a team meeting to chew out his players. Players present later told St. Louis reporter Bob Broeg how the room was morgue-like when Martin interrupted.

"Frank, can I ask you a question?"

"Yeah," Frisch replied, "what?"

"Frank," he said, "I was just wondering whether I ought to paint my midget auto racer red with white wheels or white with red wheels." With that, the manager gave up and the meeting was over.

Martin had his black moments, too. Managing a Dodgers minor league team in 1949, he became so enraged by an umpire's call that he grabbed the man's neck and began choking him. Called on the carpet, Martin was asked by the league president, "Pepper, when you had your hands around that man's neck, what were you thinking?"

"I was thinking," Martin said, "that I'd choke the son of a bitch to death."

Few players were so unpopular as the hypercompetitive Leo Durocher, the Gashouse Gang ring-leader who was known for his fielding, his weak hitting, and his obnoxious on-field behavior. Once, when Durocher was nearly beaned by Hi Bithorn of the Cubs, John Lardner wrote that the pitcher "missed by a millimeter, to the profound regret of uncounted millions."

OTHER PLAYERS OF THE THIRTIES

At 6'3", 210 pounds, Dale Alexander was a prodigious hitter in a hitters' era, the early thirties. He came up with Detroit in 1929, purchased from Toronto of the International League for the stunning price of $100,000. He batted .343 his rookie year, with 25 home runs (only Jimmie Foxx, Babe Ruth, Lou Gehrig, and Al Simmons had more in the AL that year), and followed that with seasons of .326, .325, and in 1932 a league-championship .367 (the only AL batting championship, incidentally, won by a man who played parts of the championship year for two different teams; the Tigers had traded Alexander to Boston in May).

But on Memorial Day weekend the following season, the Red Sox playing at Philadelphia, Alexander twisted his knee. Diathermy treatment was administered in the clubhouse, and it fundamentally put an end to Alexander's career. "It was a new treatment and not too much was known about it," Alexander later remembered. "I noticed my leg felt awfully hot. Anyway, I ended up with third-degree burns and a gangrene infection and I almost lost my leg. I was finished in the majors."

Realistically appraising his talents, Alexander acknowledged that "I couldn't run and I couldn't field. And when I got hurt, that was the end."

Sportswriter Al Horwits was much like everyone else with Athletics' pitcher Rube Walberg—they didn't get along. Jimmy Dykes used to say that when Walberg was pitching and he started to smile, it was time for his fielders to back up. After writing something about Walberg that the player didn't like, Horwits once found himself with a hand around his throat on a train traveling from St. Louis to Boston. "I ought to strangle you for what you wrote about me," Walberg snarled.

According to Horwits, "I said, 'How about the things you've been saying about me?' "

" 'Yeah,' Walberg said, 'but when I say 'em, only three guys hear it. When you write it, thousands of people read it."

"I told him, 'Well, let that be a lesson to you.' And with that, he let go."

He was born Eugene Rudolph Mercantelli in Chicago, in 1906. Twenty-four years later, now called Gene Rye, he was playing for Waco in the Texas League and hit 26 home runs. On August 6 of that year, trailing Beaumont 6-2, he led off Waco's eighth.

On the second pitch, Rye hit a home run. His teammates suddenly came alive and batted around. With two on base when he next came to bat, Rye homered once more, and his teammates kept the astonishing rally going. Finally, with the bases loaded and two out, he came to bat once more and sent a pitch straight over the center-field wall: three at bats, three home runs, seven runs batted in—all in one inning.

The Red Sox proceeded to buy Rye's contract, and took him north in 1931. After thirty-nine at bats, with only seven singles to show for it, his major league career came to an end.

Cubs second baseman Billy Herman habitually changed his stance several times in the course of a game, or even during one at bat, depending on the situation. Casey Stengel said, "He's an unusual hitter. Sometimes he stands straight up, and sometimes his head is so close to the plate he looks like John the Baptist."

Carl Hubbell's successive strikeouts of Babe Ruth, Lou Gehrig, Jimmie Foxx, Al Simmons, and Joe Cronin in the 1934 All-Star Game probably constituted the best compressed piece of pitching in baseball history. When that string was over, Lefty Gomez came to the plate and told Gabby Hartnett, "You are now looking at a man whose batting average is .104. What the hell am I doing up here?" And as the third inning ended, Frank Frisch of the Cardinals, the National League second baseman, said to Hubbell's teammate Bill Terry, "I could play second base fifteen more years behind that guy. He doesn't need any help. He does it all by himself.'"

What is largely forgotten about Hubbell's strikeout string is what came immediately before: the first American League batter was Charlie Gehringer, who singled, and the second was Heinie Manush, who walked, and the two men executed a double steal when Foxx was at the plate.

Zeke Bonura was a pure hitter whose .307 lifetime average was all the more impressive for his painful slowness—as a runner, and as a thinker. Playing in Chicago for Jimmy Dykes, who called him "my pet ox," Bonura often stood uncomprehending outside the batter's box, unable to fathom the signs flashed from third base. On one occasion, Dykes became so exasperated as Bonura tried to puzzle out the sign that he shouted, "Bunt, you meathead. Bunt. Bunt! B-U-N-T."

After Bonura was traded to the Senators before the 1938 season, the White Sox didn't bother to change their signs for their first series against Washington and Bonura. Dykes told Coach Bing Miller, "Why should we? He couldn't remember them when he was with us." But when Bonura, leading off third, saw Dykes absently swing his scorecard at a dugout mosquito, he unexpectedly rumbled toward home, his 210 pounds separating the ball from the catcher's embrace. Afterward, Bonura explained his dash (one of only 19 stolen bases in his entire career): "I saw Dykes give the sign to steal, and I forgot I wasn't on his team anymore."

Nineteen thirty-nine was in some ways a sad year for the Yankees, what with the passing of Ruppert and the diagnosis of Gehrig's illness. But the team on the field rivaled the '27 Yankees, winning 106 games and losing only 45 to finish 17 games ahead of the Red Sox. One of DiMaggio's chief henchmen was the powerful outfielder, Charlie "King Kong" Keller. Keller's nickname derived from his huge muscles and bushy eyebrows, and when he reported to the Yankees, Lefty Gomez cracked, "Why, he's the first player brought back by Frank Buck." (Buck was a famous big-game hunter of the period.)

The Yankees swept the Reds in the 1939 Series. In the first game, Keller tripled and scored the winning run in the ninth. In the third game, he hit two homers. The fourth game went into extra innings, and in the tenth, Keller reached on an error, then slammed into catcher Ernie Lombardi as he tried to score after DiMaggio singled and Reds outfielder Ival Goodman bobbled the ball. Keller knocked the ball loose and Lombardi silly, and during what came to be known as "Lombardi's Snooze," DiMaggio came all the way around to score.

The Yankees had become the first team to win four straight World Series, and they had taken the last two in four-game sweeps. The cry, "Break up the Yankees," was heard throughout the land, although one Cincinnati fan had something more specific in mind. "The hell with breaking up the Yankees," began his immortal utterance, "I'll be satisfied if they break up Keller."

Another Yankees outfielder in the late '30s was Jake Powell, a man with a variety of demons racing around his skull. Although Powell was a pretty good player, he became more famous for something he said than anything he did. It was during a pre-game radio interview in Chicago that Powell noted that during the offseason he was a policeman in Dayton, Ohio, and kept in shape "cracking niggers' heads." When Powell's remark was circulated, it naturally started a storm of controversy. He was suspended for a while, but there was still talk of a boycott by blacks of all Yankee games.

When Powell returned to New York, he went up to the top of Harlem, alone and after dark. Working southward, he stopped in every saloon he came across, introducing himself as Jake Powell, apologizing for his foolish words, and buying everyone a round of drinks. It was a strange form of penance, but it took guts and helped the storm subside.

The storm inside Powell raged on, however. After his playing career was over, he was arrested in 1948 for passing bad checks in Washington, D.C. In full view of the officers at the police station, Powell shot himself twice—first in the chest, then in the head.

One of the most celebrated of baseball photographs shows the old National League umpire, big George Magerkurth, on his back at Ebbets Field being pummeled by an irate Brooklyn fan. The man had chosen those rather extreme means to protest a call by Magerkurth, who had reversed a pro-Brooklyn decision by fellow umpire Bill Stewart.

It turned out that the mugger was an ex-con, and he was returned to the penitentiary for violating parole. A few years later, Brooklyn Judge Samuel Liebowitz encountered the man, now on trial as a pickpocket, in court. Having established this was the fan who had jumped the umpire, Liebowitz asked him, "How did you come to lose your head that day? Were you really as stirred up as all that? Hot enough to slug the umpire, and especially a big one like Magerkurth?"

"I was pretty stirred up," the pickpocket acknowledged. "But just between you and me, Judge, I had a partner in the stands that day. We were doing a little business."

VANDER MEER'S NO-HITTERS

It was in the first night game in Ebbets Field that Johnny Vander Meer threw his second consecutive no-hitter, on June 15, 1938. He barely made it. To the first batter in the ninth inning, Buddy Hassett, he threw three wild pitches before getting him out on a ground ball.

Then he walked Babe Phelps. He walked Cookie Lavagetto. And, loading the bases, he walked Dolf Camilli on four pitches. He still had a 6-0 lead, and manager Bill McKechnie was probably going to let Vander Meer keep walking batters until the score was 6-5.

He managed to get Ernie Koy on a fielder's choice, and then all that stood in his way was Leo Durocher—"The All-American Out," he'd once been called. With the count at two strikes, Vander Meer threw a pitch that, to his mind, got a chunk of the plate, but umpire Bill Stewart said it was a ball. Durocher finally made the game-ending out, and as the celebrations began the umpire came to the mound. "John," he said, "I blew that pitch. If you hadn't gotten him out I was the guy to blame for it."

Said Vander Meer to Donald Honig nearly forty years later, "If Durocher had got a base hit, would he have come out and said it anyway?"

ERNIE LOMBARDI

His hands were so big he could hold seven balls in one of them. He ran so slowly he was once thrown out at first on a line shot off Crosley Field's left-field wall. His enormous nose brought on the nickname "Schnozz," and it made him such a formidable snorer, said Bill Rigney, that "The entire train would shake."

But what Lombardi mostly was was a hitter, a creator of fearsome line drives with his 46-ounce bat that dented walls and caused pitchers to tremble in every National League city. Had he had any foot-speed at all, he would have won many more than his two batting championships. Opponents played him so deep that Lombardi himself once said, "It took me four years to find out Pee Wee Reese was an infielder." Arthur Daley once wrote, "When you look back on him and his seventeen years in the majors, you almost come to the conclusion that he was the greatest hitter of all time."

But praise such as Daley's (or, implicitly, Reese's) did not make up for the general ridicule Lombardi was subject to. After his career was over, he attempted suicide in 1953. He later worked as a press box attendant in San Francisco, and in 1974, having been rebuffed repeatedly for the Hall of Fame, Lombardi said, "If they elected me, I wouldn't show up for the ceremony. . . . All anybody wants to remember about me was that I couldn't run. They still make jokes. Let them make jokes."

TED WILLIAMS

As a rookie, Ted Williams said, "All I ever want out of life is that when I walk down the street folks will say, 'there goes the greatest hitter who ever lived.'" By the time his career ended twenty-one years later, he may well have been granted his wish.

If the greatest hitter ever wasn't Ruth, then it could only have been Theodore Samuel Williams (actually, his birth certificate read "Teddy"; the "Theodore" came later). His father was a portrait photographer whom he rarely saw, and his mother was a missionary for the Salvation Army, known throughout San Diego as "Salvation Mary." She would often drag Ted along with her on her rounds, but she did allow him to play baseball, and he loved the game. His first offer to play baseball for money, though, came from a semi-pro team sponsored by the Texas Liquor House. As Williams told John Underwood, "I came home and told my mother about the money, and she said that was fine. 'Who will you play for?' 'Uh, the Texas Liquor House.' If I had said Murder, Inc., I wouldn't have gotten a quicker refusal."

Williams's pro career began with the San Diego Padres of the Pacific Coast League in 1936. The team was trailing by 10 runs late in the game when he volunteered to pitch. Manager Frank Shellenback put the 6'3", 148-pound youth into the game as a pinch-hitter, and Williams doubled his first time up. He got through one inning on the mound unscathed, and doubled his second time up as the Padres rallied to within one run. But Williams got shelled in the next inning, and when Shellenback came to get the ball from him, Williams said, "Skip, I think you've got me playing the wrong position." From then on, he was a left-fielder.

Williams didn't make the Red Sox after his first spring with the club, and ended up in Minneapolis, where he hit .366 with 142 RBIs and 43 homers, smashed every available water cooler and generally drove his manager, the former Tigers shortstop Donie Bush, to distraction. At one point, Bush told the Boston front office, "Either Williams goes, or I go." But Bush backed down when the Red Sox informed him that he was the more expendable.

Williams was up for good in 1939, and he hit .327 with a league-leading 145 RBIs. He had one of his more memorable days that year in Detroit's Briggs Stadium. His first time up, the count went to 3 and 0 when Rudy York, who was catching, said, "You're not hitting, are you, kid?" Williams replied, "I sure as hell am," and proceeded to knock the pitch on top of the upper deck in right field. As Williams described it, "I got to first base and Greenberg was still looking where the ball had gone. I reached second and Gehringer, who hadn't said a word to anybody in 20 years, was still saying nothing. Frank Croucher at short just looked, and Billy Rogell, playing third base, didn't say anything either, but I could see him watching me closely. I got home, and York said, 'You weren't kidding, were you?'

"The next time up there were two men on, and this is the one I hit out of Briggs Stadium. I got to first base and Greenberg was still looking, and Gehringer still hadn't said anything in 20 years, and Croucher at short was scraping the ground. Then I got to Rogell at third base and he said, 'What the hell you been eating?' "

In 1941 Williams hit his mythic .406; no batter in the previous 10 years had hit .400, and no batter has done it since. He was able to prime himself for the season especially well because of a fortuitous ankle injury. For the first two weeks of the season, he could only pinch-hit, so he took a lot of extracurricular batting practice against Joe Dobson, a pitcher who felt he needed work. "Dobson had a hell of a curve and a good overhand fastball," said Williams, "and he always bore down. Every day that his arm held out and the blisters on my hand held out, we'd go at it there like it was all-out war, one-on-one. Well, for me, it was great fun, and I was about as sharp as I could ever be."

Thus sharpened, Williams rapped out 185 hits, 37 of them homers, while walking 145 times. He won the All-Star Game that year with a two-out, ninth-inning, three-run homer off Claude Passeau. He slumped a little towards the end of the season, but he came into the last day of the season, a double-header in Philadelphia, with a batting average of .39955, which would have rounded out to .400. In one of the more celebrated instances of managerial courtesy on record, Joe Cronin asked Williams if he wanted to sit out, but Williams said if he couldn't hit .400 all the way, he didn't deserve it.

It was a cold, miserable day, and when Williams came up to bat for the first time, the home plate umpire, Bill Mc-Gowan, stepped in front of him to dust off the plate and said, "To hit .400 a batter has got to be loose. He has got to be loose." Williams couldn't have been looser. He singled off Dick Fowler that first time up, homered the next at-bat, then got two more singles off relief pitchers. In the second game, he hit a ball off the loudspeaker horn in right field for a double. With .400 on the line, Williams went six for eight. And in the off-season, Connie Mack had to replace the horn.

BOB FELLER

The same year Joe DiMaggio came onto the major league scene, another rookie made his debut: Robert William Andrew Feller. Feller was just seventeen when he appeared for the Cleveland Indians in that summer of 1936. He went 5-3 with a 3.34 ERA and 76 strikeouts in 62 innings, and then returned to Van Meter, Iowa, to finish high school.

Feller developed his great fastball doing heavy chores on the family farm and pitching into a backstop of two-by-fours and chicken wire made by his father. Until Dwight Gooden came along in the early 1980s, Feller was the youngest pitcher ever to win 20 games—he was 20 when he went 24-9 in 1939. That same year, Feller threw a pitch that a batter tipped back into the stands, hitting Feller's mother and sending her to the hospital.

He pitched three no-hitters, one on opening day of 1940, and 12 one-hitters, and he ended his career after 1956 with

266 wins, 162 losses, 2,581 strikeouts, and an ERA of 3.25. A statistician once figured that if Feller had not missed four seasons during World War II, he would have had 357 wins and 3,516 strikeouts. In a famous newsreel, Feller "raced" his 95-mile-an-hour fastball against a motorcycle—and won.

Long after his active pitching career ended, Feller continued to travel America, pitching in exhibitions in minor league parks. When he was sixty-six, he was asked how hard he could throw. "I can still throw it in the 70s. And I can throw it in the 80s if I don't want to comb my hair for a week."

Feller's opening day no-hitter came against the White Sox. Mike Kreevich, at bat in the first inning, acknowledged the pitcher's overwhelming speed when he turned to the umpire to contest a called strike. "What was wrong with it?" the umpire asked. "It sounded a little high," Kreevich said.

When Feller was nine years old in 1928, he wanted to see a barnstorming game in Des Moines between teams "managed" by Babe Ruth—the Bustin' Babes—and Lou Gehrig—the Larrupin' Lous. More than that, he wanted one of the baseballs autographed by both men and advertised at $5. He didn't have the money, but as it happened, the county treasurer was offering a ten-cent bounty for every groundhog brought into his office. So Feller and a friend got an old Dodge truck, and put one end of a hose over an exhaust pipe and the other inside a mound full of gophers. When Feller stepped on the gas, his friend bagged the gophers as they bolted out of the ground. "I got 50 of 'em," Feller later told Malcolm Moran of the *New York Times*, "and I went to the county treasurer's office. My dad drove me there in the old Rickenbacker car we had. And I got five bucks. Went down and got Babe Ruth's and Lou Gehrig's autograph on a baseball. And I still have it at home. The first gopher ball I ever had."

What Feller didn't say is that there are actually three signatures on the baseball: those of Ruth and Gehrig and also the scrawl of the then nine-year-old Robert W. A. Feller. He knew, it appeared, what was in store for him.

DiMAGGIO'S STREAK

In mid-May of 1941 the Yankees were foundering in fourth place. People hardly noticed that Joe DiMaggio was on a 10-game hitting streak. On June 2, Gehrig died and DiMaggio extended his hitting streak to 24. Immediately ahead was the Yankees record of 29, shared by Roger Peckinpaugh and Earle Combs, and beyond that the AL record of 41 held by George Sisler, and the major league record of 44 owned by Willie Keeler. "That's when I became conscious of the streak," said DiMaggio, "when the writers started talking about the records I could break."

On June 17 he broke the New York record with a bad-hop single off the shoulder of White Sox shortstop Luke Appling— one of his few lucky hits in the streak. In the thirty-sixth game, he needed an eighth-inning single off rookie Bob Muncrief of the St. Louis Browns, who could have given him a pass to first. "It wouldn't have been fair to walk him—to him or me," said Muncrief. "Hell, he's the greatest player I ever saw."

There were tenser moments yet to come. In the eighth inning of the thirty-eighth game, Tommy Henrich asked McCarthy if he could bunt, so as not to hit into a double play and deny the as-yet-hitless DiMaggio a chance. McCarthy agreed, and DiMaggio thereupon doubled off Eldon Auker. Johnny Babich, a renowned Yankee killer for the Athletics, vowed to stop DiMaggio's streak at 39; he walked him the first time on four pitches, and took him 3-and-0 on his second time up. But McCarthy gave DiMaggio the green light, and Joe lined an outside pitch right through Babich's legs. "His face was white as a sheet," DiMaggio remembered afterward.

The biggest threat, though, came the next day, during a doubleheader in Washington. DiMaggio tied Sisler's AL record in the first game, but between games a fan jumped on the field near the Yankee dugout, stole DiMaggio's favorite bat, and slipped back into the stands. Fortunately, Tommy Henrich was using another DiMaggio bat, and with that one Joe singled in the seventh inning to extend his streak to 41. But he missed his own bat. "I had sandpapered the handle of this one to take off one-half to three-quarters of an ounce," he said at the time. "It was just right. I wish that guy would return it. I need it more than he does."

The bat thief was never identified, but he was from Newark, and he had bragged about having the prized piece of lumber. Some friends of DiMaggio eventually tracked him down, confiscated the bat, and returned it to Joe on July 4. But now it was July 1, a doubleheader with the Red Sox in Yankee Stadium, and DiMaggio was still using Henrich's bat. In the fourth inning of the opener, DiMaggio hit a tricky bouncer to third baseman Jim Tabor, who hurried his throw and fired wildly past first base. It was a borderline call, and Dan Daniel of the *New York World-Telegram,* ordinarily a tough scorer, ruled it a hit. "Damn you, DiMaggio," Daniel hollered in the press box. "I gave you a hit this time, but everything has to be clean from now on." It was the only hit he got in that game.

Keeler's record fell with a fifth-inning homer the next afternoon off the mellifluously named Heber Hampton Newsome of the Red Sox. DiMaggio actually started to relax after that, and in the next 11 games he batted .545. Along the way he even singled in the All-Star Game in Detroit, scoring the third run in the AL's 7-5 victory on a single by his brother Dom. (Red Sox fans had a song that went, "Who can run and bat and throw? Who hits the ball both high and low? Who's better than his brother Joe? Dom-in-ic Di-Magg-io." It wasn't true, but it had a catchy little tune.)

Joe kept the streak going in St. Louis and Chicago and through the first game in Cleveland. As DiMaggio and Gomez got into a cab to go to Municipal Stadium for a night game against the Indians on July 17, the streak stood at 56.

The cab driver looked in his rear-view mirror, recognized DiMaggio, and said, "I got a feeling if you don't get a hit the first time up, they're going to stop you tonight."

Gomez chastised the driver. "What the hell is this? What are you trying to do, jinx him?" DiMaggio just smiled and left the driver a big tip.

In the first inning, DiMaggio hit a smash down the third base line, but Ken Keltner backhanded it and made a fine throw from foul territory. DiMaggio walked in the fourth. He hit another hot shot at Keltner in the seventh, but the third baseman again threw him out. On a 2-and-1 pitch from Jim Bagby, Jr., in the eighth, DiMaggio hit a hard grounder to shortstop Lou Boudreau, who played a bad hop and started a double play.

DiMaggio simply rounded first, picked up his glove and trotted to center. According to one account, "There was no kicking of dirt, no shaking of the head." Said DiMaggio as he arrived at his locker after the game, "Well, that's over."

Astonishingly, DiMaggio went on a 16-game hitting streak after the big one ended. In fact, from May 2 to August 3 of 1941 he was on base in every game. The Yankees ran away with the pennant, beating the second-place Red Sox by 17 games, and then took the Brooklyn Dodgers in five games in the World Series. DiMaggio was named MVP over Ted Williams, who had hit .406. But the biggest award DiMaggio received that season was given to him by surprise on August 29.

The Yankees had just arrived at Washington's Hotel Shoreham, and Gomez was taking an unusually long shower. "C'mon, Lefty," said his roommate, DiMaggio. "All the steaks will be gone." Gomez got out of the shower and told Joe to relax. On their way out, Lefty said, "I just remembered something. I have to stop by Selkirk's room." DiMaggio said he would go ahead to the dining room and order, but Gomez insisted he come with him. "It'll only take a minute," he said.

When DiMaggio walked into George Selkirk's room, there were 40 men—Yankees and sportswriters—with champagne glasses raised for a toast. Gomez presented DiMaggio with a silver cigar humidor which pitcher Johnny Murphy had ordered from Tiffany's. On the cover was a relief likeness of DiMaggio in mid-swing, on one side was the number 56 and on the other side the number 91, signifying each hit he had during the streak. And there was an inscription: "Presented to Joe DiMaggio by his fellow players on the New York Yankees to express their admiration for his consecutive-game hitting record, 1941."

DiMaggio was suitably humble for a star of his magnitude, but he knew his role in baseball. The Yankees once had a doubleheader in sweltering St. Louis against the last-place Browns, a prospect hardly worth relishing. Yet DiMaggio made an off-hand comment that he was looking forward to playing that day.

"In this heat?" said a writer. "How can you enjoy playing a doubleheader in this heat?"

"Well," said DiMaggio with a glance towards the stands, "maybe somebody never saw me before."

MIND GAME

During the 1941 pennant race, the Dodgers met their chief competition, the Cardinals, in St. Louis. In the first game, the score tied in the ninth, Fat Freddy Fitzsimmons faced the St. Louis slugger Johnny Mize. Umpire Al Barlick called a ball that Fitzsimmons didn't like, and the pitcher stormed in to argue, enraged.

In the heat of the argument, Fitzsimmons caught Mize smiling at him. He turned his wrath away from the umpire, shouted a few imprecations at Mize, and then scowled, "Three straight fastballs and you're out of there."

Mize doubted the pitcher, even in his anger. Fitzsimmons was past his prime, out of condition, and relying almost exclusively on the knuckleball that had made him a success in the first place. But the first pitch came in a fastball, which Mize let pass for a strike. Then another, on the outside corner, also a strike. Mize reasoned that now was the time for Fitzsimmons to let loose the knuckler. Came another fastball, and Mize was caught flatfooted and struck out.

The Dodgers went on to win in eleven.

TWO EXITS

With war on the horizon, baseball was about to undergo changes as profound as those that had occurred at the turn of

the century and in the wake of the Black Sox scandal. Appropriately, 1941 was the year in which Bill Klem, that direct
link to the early years, chose to give up the ghost. He had
broken in back when baseball was a rough, small-time en-
deavor, featuring such dimly remembered lights as Joe Mc-
Ginnity and Deacon Philippe; as his career moved toward its
close, such young stars as Stan Musial and Ted Williams had
captured the nation's attention. Klem was a relic, but he didn't
accept this until one otherwise ordinary afternoon in Brooklyn.

St. Louis was playing the Dodgers, and when Billy Herman
made a tag play on a Cardinals runner at second, Klem called
him out. As the runner protested that Herman had never actually tagged him, Klem turned and walked away. "I'm almost certain Herman tagged him," the umpire said to himself. "Then," he recalled later, "I almost wept. For the first
time in all my career I only 'thought' a man was out."

Immediately after the game, Bill Klem retired.

The golden age of baseball that filled the years between the
wars didn't truly end until several years later—until the death
of Ruth. Although he was never told of the diagnosis, Ruth
was discovered to have cancer in 1946. Sunday, April 27, 1947,
was declared Babe Ruth Day all throughout baseball, and
60,000 people appeared in Yankee Stadium to honor the Bam-
bino, who was dressed in his familiar camel's hair coat and
cap but looked and sounded horribly different from the man
the crowd had once known. "Thank you very much, ladies and
gentlemen," he told hushed fans. "You know how bad my voice
sounds. Well, it feels just as bad."

Ruth went through a brief period of remission, but he again
fell ill in the summer of 1948. He came back to the Stadium
one last time, on June 13, for the twenty-fifth anniversary of
the House That Ruth Built. He was helped into his uniform
by his male nurse and posed with the other '23 Yankees. He
stood in the middle of the group, with Joe Dugan placing his
hand on one of Ruth's shoulders, Wally Pipp putting his hand
on the other.

Ruth was the last player introduced to the crowd, and W.C.
Heinz wrote, "He walked out into the cauldron of sound he

must have known better than any other man." After a short speech, Ruth walked back into the clubhouse, and was soon joined by Dugan.

"How are things?" Dugan asked him.

"Joe, I'm gone," said Ruth. "I'm gone, Joe."

Both men started to cry.

At Ruth's funeral, Dugan and Waite Hoyt were two of the pallbearers. It was an extraordinarily hot day, and Hoyt allowed that he could sure use a beer. Replied Dugan, "So could the Babe."

That same day, the old baseball writer Tommy Holmes said to Red Smith, "Some twenty years ago, I stopped talking about the Babe for the simple reason that I realized that those who had never seen him didn't believe me." It could have been an epitaph for the entire era.

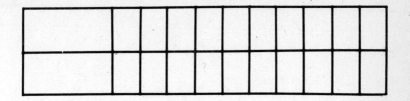

INTERLUDE
Wartime

Even before the Japanese bombed Pearl Harbor, there were signs that things were slightly amiss. At the conclusion of the 1940 season, the Indians lost the pennant to Detroit by one game. Unable to proceed into the 1940 World Series, after his team lost, Cleveland third baseman Ken Keltner made a formal application for unemployment benefits from the state labor department.

But sacrifice was the order of the day. Beginning with men like Hugh "Losing Pitcher" Mulcahy and Hank Greenberg, ballplayers were rapidly enlisting or accepting induction, even before Pearl Harbor. It was somewhat different from the attitude that prevailed, at least in some quarters, during the First World War; back then, Cubs pitcher Harry Weaver made a formal request for a deferment on the grounds that "we have a good chance to win the pennant."

But some things stayed the same, too. When Al Lopez, then with Pittsburgh, stepped out of the batter's box while Brooklyn's Hugh Casey entered his wind-up in a game during the 1941 pennant race, the Dodgers pitcher dropped his hands. Lopez screamed "balk", umpire George Magerkurth fell for the ruse, and the tying run trotted in from third. The Dodgers came apart—not least because Casey walked the next hitter while trying desperately to hit Magerkurth with a pitch—and lost.

After the game, Leo Durocher hurled a chair through the window of the umpires' room. He broke every light bulb he encountered on the way to his own clubhouse. And the next day, he punched an AP reporter whose questions he didn't like.

But then the bombs came, and on January 16, 1942, President Roosevelt issued his famous "green light" letter, giving organized baseball the permission, and the encouragement, to play through the war. "I honestly feel that it would be best for the country to keep baseball going. . . . These players are a definite recreational asset to at least 20,000,000 of their fellow citizens—and that in my judgment is thoroughly worthwhile."

Roosevelt's decision was widely supported; polls showed that substantial majorities believed that the war effort would be helped by the game's continuation. Journalist Quentin Reynolds wrote, "Hitler has killed a great many things in the past few years. Do not let him kill baseball."

And so the game went on, as Richard Goldstein reports his fine history of wartime baseball, *Spartan Seasons*—with bond drives and victory rallies on its fringes, cut-rate subscriptions to *The Sporting News* being sent to servicemen, and the nation's finest, hardiest athletes entering the armed forces. What was left was baseball, yes, but a very different game from what went before or came afterward. For one thing, the St. Louis Browns won a pennant during the war years—but that's getting ahead of things.

Early in the war, baseball broadcasters were forbidden to give information about weather conditions over the air, for fear it might be of aid to enemy bombers. On one St. Louis broadcast, Dizzy Dean and his play-by-play partner Johnny O'Hara filled a rain delay with about an hour of aimless palaver, never mentioning why there was no action on the field. Finally, Dean "ran out of words," as O'Hara explained it, and said, "If you folks don't know what's holdin' up this game just stick your heads out the window."

Throughout the war, blackouts at night games were practiced, sometimes at a pre-determined hour by which time the game was expected to be finished, sometimes for brief periods during the course of the game. In August of 1942, a Dodgers-Giants game at the Polo Grounds came to an abrupt conclusion with the Giants ahead. But as the Dodgers had been leading after the last full inning, the game was awarded to the visitors. Vociferous booing ensued, even drowning out a performance of the national anthem by a 150-member chorus that had been lined up for the occasion. Only when a spotlight was beamed onto the American flag atop the stadium did the hooting stop.

During a mid-game blackout in Philadelphia, Shibe Park announcer Babe O'Rourke noticed the glowing tips of several cigars and cigarettes in the right-field stands. "You gentlemen who are lighting cigarettes and cigars, if you are Americans, you won't do it," O'Rourke intoned over the public address system.

And in a minor league game in Florida, a pre-arranged blackout struck in midpitch. Wrote John Kieran in the *New York Times,* "The catcher later claimed it was a perfect strike whereas the batter said it was a foot outside. The umpire said nothing. He went home to bed."

Travel restrictions had big league teams forgoing warm-weather sites for spring training by 1943. The Red Sox worked out in suburban Medford, the Pirates in Muncie, Indiana, the Dodgers in Bear Mountain, New York. The Giants went to the New Jersey resort town of Lakewood, where in 1944 inclement conditions and inadequate indoor facilities enabled them to manage only eight exhibition games. Manager Mel Ott called his team "the worst-conditioned club in Giant history."

The need for a new baseball that didn't consume war-essential rubber led to the "balata ball," introduced at the beginning of the 1943 season. Remarkably unresilient, it led to sharply deflated batting performances until it was replaced by a quickly redesigned model. Through the first 72 games of the '43 season, only nine home runs had been hit by American

League batters; with the introduction of the revised version, AL hitters managed six home runs on its first day in use.

Across the Pacific, the Japanese made some adjustments in their version of baseball, too. In the half-century or more that baseball had been played in Japan, much of American baseball language had become part of standard Japanese usage, too. But after war broke out, "strike" and "ball" were expunged from the acceptable lexicon, and Japanese words were inserted in their place.

Of course, American baseball changed its perspective on the Japanese version, too. The game's popularity in Japan had long been a point of pride inside the game, but now some disowning had to be done. *The Sporting News*'s J. G. Taylor Spink, proprietor of the game's semi-official house organ, editorialized that the major leagues should "withdraw from Japan the gift of baseball which we made to that misguided and ill-begotten country."

In fact, as William Mead reported in the excellent *The Ten Worst Years of Baseball* (from which many of these anecdotes are drawn), Japan itself did the honors, eventually abolishing baseball during the war years as an insidious American influence.

But the biggest change occurred on the line-ups of the teams themselves. Strapped for real talent, baseball had to look for likely suspects who had something wrong with them—something serious enough to keep them out of the service.

The player shortage became so severe that in 1943 the Cardinals took out a two-column help-wanted ad in *The Sporting News:* "If you are a free agent and have previous professional experience, we may be able to place you . . . on one of our clubs. We have positions open on our AA, B, and D classification clubs."

The Dodgers were so badly depleted by enlistments and the draft that by 1944 Dixie Walker and Mickey Owen were the only regulars left from their 1941 pennant team. Billy Herman, one of the last of the Dodgers starters to go into the service, left such a gaping hole at second base that Leo Durocher, then thirty-eight, announced he would become Herman's replacement. Durocher had played in only 24 games in the three preceding years combined.

Inevitably, on his first fielding chance, Durocher took a bad throw from his 18-year-old shortstop, Gene Mauch, and broke his thumb in two places.

So the game turned to the old, the young, the too-tall, the too-fat, or—in the case of the St. Louis Browns—an all-4F infield. Joe Nuxhall, who pitched two-thirds of a nightmarish inning for the Reds in 1944 when he was still a month-and-a-half shy of his sixteenth birthday, was the youngest player brought up to fill a roster hole. The A's used sixteen-year-old pitcher Carl Scheib, and seventeen-year-old Granny Hamner played 21 games for the Phillies. At their training camp in 1944, the A's had sixteen-year-old Nellie Fox at first base, and Earle Mack, who looked after such details for his father, carried Fox's work permit with him whenever the boy was on the field.

At the other end of the age scale, the Phillies had 12 players aged thirty-five or over, including thirty-seven-year-old Jimmie Foxx, who converted to pitching near the season's end in 1945, compiling a 1.59 ERA in 23 innings. Bill Steinecke, who had played four games for the Pirates in 1931, suddenly found himself a member of the Yankees; and in Detroit, Chuck Hostetler became a major league rookie at 40. Babe Herman came back to the Dodgers, who also signed up both Paul and Lloyd Waner; Joe Cronin activated himself as a player; and forty-year-old Doc Cramer became an outfield regular for the pennant-winning 1945 Tigers.

In that most awful of World Series in 1945, at one point Cramer and Roy Cullenbine stood immobile as Phil Cavarretta of the Cubs hit an easy fly ball between them. Asked afterward to explain how it happened that the ball had dropped unmolested, Cramer said, "I could have caught the ball, but Cullenbine kept shouting, 'all right, all right.' When I heard this I stopped and then to my surprise the ball plopped to the ground. I asked Cullenbine why he didn't make the catch, and he told me, 'When I called all right, all right, I meant all right, you catch it.' "

There were also several big leaguers who got there because they were too tall for the military's six-foot six-inch height limit. The Dodgers had 6′6½″ Howie Schultz; 6′8″ Mike Naymick won five games for the Indians; and 6′9″ Johnny Gee, who had actually appeared in six games before the war, pitched for both the Pirates and the Giants.

After his stint with the Dodgers, in 1944 Paul Waner moved to the Bronx to finish up with the Yankees. He was forty-one years old, and by his own admission barely a shadow of the player he'd once been. In one game, a fan shouted, "Hey, Paul, how come you're in the outfield for the Yankees?"
Waner shouted back, "Because Joe DiMaggio's in the army."

In 1945, Bert Shepard, a war veteran with an artificial leg, pitched a game for the Senators; he gave up three hits in five and one-third innings. The Yankees activated their batting-practice pitcher, Paul Schreiber, who had last appeared in a major league game in 1923. In the minors, York (Pennsylvania) of the Inter-State League pitched fifty-seven-year-old Lefty George, who had played for the Browns in 1911. And the Browns—in 1945, the Browns played the one-armed outfielder Pete Gray in 61 games.
Gray had managed to win the Southern Association MVP Award the previous season, largely on the strength of his speed and his drag-bunting ability. But in the majors, even the wartime majors, he was badly overmatched. To compensate for his disability, he began his one-armed swing early, and major league pitchers soon realized he couldn't handle a change-up. In the outfield, his need to remove the glove from his hand before making a throw enabled batters who had singled to take second base. And the Browns' use of him, however crowd-pleasing, created dissension on the team. Mike Kreevich, who had starred for the 1944 pennant winners, found himself spending more and more time on the bench to make room in

the lineup for Gray, and it led him to retire. "If I'm not playing well enough so that a one-armed man can take my job," Kreevich said, "I quit."

The owners, of course, sought ways to turn the war to their advantage by using it as an excuse to hold the line on salaries. After Joe DiMaggio's 1941 season, in which he assembled his 56-game hitting streak and was named Most Valuable Player, Yankees General Manager Ed Barrow tried to cut his salary. But in St. Louis Sam Breadon, who owned the world champion Cardinals, wouldn't budge past $13,000 for National League MVP Marty Marion in 1944. He told Marion that he had held the line with Mort and Walker Cooper, and had also promised the Cooper brothers they'd be the highest-paid players on the club.

Still, Marion insisted, and got Breadon to agree to $15,000; the Cardinal owner in turn kept his promise to the Coopers and brought them up to the same level. In gratitude for winning him a raise, Mort Cooper bought Marion a hat.

Emblematic of the players who made it to the big leagues during the war was Lou Novikoff. "The Mad Russian" was a minor league hitter of prodigious accomplishment, but a fielder of dreadful incapability. From Ponca City to Moline to Tulsa to Los Angeles, he produced such staggering batting statistics—.367, .368, .363; 112 RBI, 114, 171; 23 triples one season, 41 home runs two years later—that the Cubs finally determined to promote him in 1941, and to ignore his distaste for encountering a live ball in the field.

But, with the Cubs, Novikoff's hitting was nearly as pathetic as his fielding. Philip K. Wrigley, who owned the club, determined that Novikoff had become too cautious: notorious as a free-swinging, bad-ball hitter in the minors, he apparently now felt he had to be more diligent in his appraisal of each pitch. Novikoff consequently stared at too many hittable pitches, and his hitting suffered.

Wrigley decided that he needed to provide suitable reward for Novikoff to revert to his more instinctive hitting style. Thus did the owner give Novikoff a bonus of $5.00 for every time he struck out swinging. This bizarre approach actually seemed to work; playing as a regular in 1942, Novikoff batted .300. But the Wrigley system had its flaws, too. This became clearest in one game when Novikoff was at bat with the bases loaded, two outs, and two strikes on him. The pitch came in over his head, and Novikoff swung—and missed. As he dejectedly walked away, Novikoff was stopped by coach Charlie Grimm, who said, "You must be awful short of dough."

Novikoff hung on with the Cubs through 1944, occasionally hitting, frequently singing and playing his harmonica in the clubhouse, constantly pleasing the Chicago fans. He blamed his poor performance on what he insisted was a crooked left-field foul line, and he had a morbid fear of contracting a terrible disease from the ivy on Wrigley's outfield walls. As Grimm said years later, "Louie was a terrific showman. People wanted to see a ball go through his legs."

The greatest symbol of the period, of course, was the American League championship won by the St. Louis Browns in 1944. The Browns had been baseball's doormat for so long that they were barely considered major league. They had never won a pennant; before the war they hadn't been in the first division since a fourth-place finish in 1929.

And they weren't held in any higher regard by their fans. In all of 1935, the Brownies had appeared before only 81,000 fans at home—an average of fewer than 1,100 spectators per game. And at one home game in 1933, the total turnstile count was 34 people.

Nor did the Browns begin their pennant year with St. Louisans as believers. Thirteen of the team's players were classified 4-F for various physical infirmities, and the rest weren't terribly hale either. So, despite winning their first three games in Detroit, only 3,395 fans showed up for their home opener, and a thousand of those were servicemen and children who were admitted free.

One thing the Browns did have going for them was their manager, Luke Sewell. An old catcher with 20 years of playing experience, he held his team together with baling wire, magic, and generous helpings of intuition. The Washington sportswriter Shirley Povich came especially to marvel at Sewell's roster manipulations near the season's end, as the St. Louis manager did everything he could to keep his team in the race. As Povich told William Mead, "I said, 'What's going on here, Luke?' You change these lineups every day! You must smell these guys on the bench getting hot.'

"And he says, 'No, Shirley, I smell those bums out there on the field getting cold.' "

Other than for his miracle-working with the Browns, Sewell might best be remembered for his retort to those who insisted the curveball didn't curve, but was merely an optical illusion. "Isn't it strange,'" Sewell said, "that the optical illusion only happens when someone tries to throw a curve ball, and never when a fast or straight ball is attempted?"

The night before the pennant-deciding game against the Yankees in 1944, the Browns' scheduled starting pitcher, Sig Jakucki, was spotted by trainer Bob Bauman entering the team hotel carrying a bag of whiskey bottles. Jakucki was a terrible drinker, and Bauman—seeing the Browns' first pennant about to disappear in a Jakucki bender—accosted the pitcher. "You're not going to take that to your room," Bauman shouted. Jakucki resisted, and swore he wouldn't drink that night.

The next morning, at the ball park, Bauman immediately realized that the pitcher had indeed been drinking. Jakucki defended himself: he admitted he had promised not to have a drink the night before, and insisted he hadn't. But, he added, "I didn't promise I wouldn't take one this morning."

He proceeded to outpitch the Yankees' Mel Queen, taking the game 5-2. The Browns had won the pennant with an all-time American League low winning percentage of .578.

And then came the Series itself, against the team with whom they shared Sportsmen's Park, the Cardinals. It was nice for the city of St. Louis, but awkward for the two managers; Sewell and Billy Southworth had shared an apartment all year, as one was on the road whenever the other was at home.

Remarkably, the Browns won the first game, 2-1, even

though they managed only two hits off of Mort Cooper. Then came the second game and a deeply symbolic play that Sewell later described to Donald Honig:

"Emil Verban [of the Cardinals] got a single and [Max] Lanier bunted. He popped the ball up between the pitcher and the foul line. [Nelson] Potter and [Marv] Christman ran over, looked at each other, and let it hit the ground . . . Then Potter grabbed the ball and it rolled up his arm. That's two misplays. When he threw it to first, he threw wild. That's three. [Don] Gutteridge was covering, and he tried to keep his foot on the bag as he reached for the ball instead of getting off and grabbing it. That's four. The ball went down into the corner, where Chet Laabs got after it. It hit the fence and bounced back between his legs. That's five. Then he picked it up and made a bad throw to second. That's six . . .

"If it hadn't been for that, we would have beat them and then the next day had them down three games to none."

And so the Browns lost the Series, four games to two, with a team batting average of .183. Years later, whenever Sewell was asked about the most memorable play he ever saw, he'd say it was a pop fly that George McQuinn caught in foul territory. " 'What was so great about it?' they'll ask. 'It was the last out of the last game of the 1944 season,' I tell them."

Worse still, though, was the 1945 Series between the Tigers and the Cubs. Frank Graham called it "The fat men against the tall men at the office picnic"; Chicago writer Warren Brown said, "I don't think either team is capable of winning." Charles Einstein said that the sixth game, in which the Cubs prevailed in 12 innings, was "The worst game of baseball ever played in this country."

On the apparent principle that "bad pitching will go seven games against bad hitting any time," the Tigers were the last to hit the mat, and prevailed in Chicago on October 10, 9-3. Warren Brown summed it up brilliantly: "It went the full seven games before the Tigers took the odd contest and became the world's champions. Long before that point was reached, even the players themselves had given up trying to figure out what might happen next. Fly balls were dropping beside fielders who made no effort to catch them. Players were tumbling going around the bases. The baseball was as far removed from previous major league standards as was possible without its perpetrators having themselves arrested for obtaining money under false pretenses."

Finally, the real players came home, and the full measure of wartime weakness became clear when the 1946 season began. Of the 128 non-pitchers who had been regulars the previous season, only 32 remained full-time players in the year that the vets came back. The season before, Red Barber would later say, "was just a matter of playing anyone who was breathing."

PART										
4										

THE RETURN TO GLORY

From the Arrival
of Jackie Robinson
to Casey Stengel's
Last Hurrah

As the deal that sent Babe Ruth to New York would shape baseball in the twenties and thirties, the postwar era would take its definition from another front-office action. The office was the Montague Street headquarters of the Brooklyn Dodgers, and the actors Branch Rickey and Jackie Robinson.

Rickey was unquestionably the greatest non-playing figure baseball ever knew. A mediocre catcher and an at best passable field manager, once he moved into general management he exerted a force on the game as strong as the laws of nature. He was a Bible-quoting teetotaler who presided over some of the roughest, hardest-living teams in baseball; he was a sanctimonious defender of justice and fair-play who used cunning and guile to make a fortune in the game. His invention of the farm system in the 1920s made his Cardinals the dominant National League team from the early thirties through the middle forties. And his signing of a former UCLA star named Jack Roosevelt Robinson made his Dodgers the successors to the Cardinals. This last act, of course, also removed from baseball's ledger the official institutional racism that had disgraced the game since the time of Cap Anson.

It is a sign of Rickey's skills of calculation, persuasion, and timing that he was able to become baseball's Great Emancipator. Integration had been discussed for years, and at least two of the game's major figures had made some effort to pull it off. The first was John McGraw, and indirection was his technique.

In 1901, McGraw's Baltimore Orioles conducted their spring training in Hot Springs, Arkansas. A bellboy at their hotel was a young, light-skinned black man named Charles Grant, who had played for a Negro team in Chicago the previous year. Several members of the hotel staff played pick-up baseball during their off-hours, and McGraw noticed that Grant had major league abilities. He decided he would try to squeeze the bellboy into the American League by giving him a new name, Tokohama, and passing him off as a Cherokee.

Charles Comiskey of the White Sox was the first member of the lodge to object. "I'm not going to stand for McGraw bringing in an Indian on the Baltimore team," he said. "Somebody told me that the Cherokee of McGraw's is really Grant, the crack Negro second baseman from Cincinnati, fixed up with war paint and a bunch of feathers."

Still, Grant and McGraw tried to keep up the ruse, the player insisting that his mother was a Cherokee, his father a white man. But as the spring wore on, McGraw backed down.

Thirty-two years later, when Jimmy Powers of the New York *Daily News* conducted a poll of major league figures on the desirability of integrating baseball, McGraw was the only one who went on record *against* the idea. Of course, this was the same year in which National League president John Heydler said with an apparently straight face, "I do not recall one instance where baseball has allowed either race, creed, or color to enter into its selection of players."

And nine years after that, with such managers as Leo Durocher, Gabby Hartnett, and Bill McKechnie beginning to make the case for dropping the color bar, Commissioner Landis had the temerity to say, "Negroes are not barred from organized baseball by the commissioner and never have been during the twenty-one years I have served . . . If Durocher, or any other manager, or all of them, want to sign one, or twenty-five, Negro players, it is all right with me. It is the business of the managers and the club owners."

And so came effort number two, as if a direct challenge to Landis's remark. Problem was, the owner who wanted to integrate was, at the time, only a *potential* owner: Bill Veeck, Jr.

The roots of Veeck's first effort to buy a major league club go back to his own youth as the son of the Cubs' president, and to a less likely torch passing in Philadelphia. There, when Phillies owner William Baker died in 1930, an improbable character named Gerry Nugent took over.

It was Nugent's luck that his wife had been Baker's secretary for years, and when the old man's will was probated it was learned that he had left a majority interest in the club to the faithful May Mallon Nugent. Her husband, a former shoe salesman, took control of the club. In ten years, his teams finished seventh four times, and last six times. The National League took over the club in receivership in 1943, and put it up for sale.

Enter Bill Veeck, by now a minor league operator. His notion was to stock the team with players from the black leagues; with wartime rosters so grievously depleted by the draft, he reasoned that such an aggregation would vault the Phils to the pennant.

As Veeck recalled it, he went to Judge Landis, for whom he had great respect, to inform him of his plan. His candor was an error; almost immediately thereafter, the team was no longer available, sold instead to lumberman William D. Cox.

As it happened, less than ten months later Landis kicked Cox out of baseball for having bet on Phillies games. In the press, the reaction was not that Cox was corrupt, but that he was stupid—he had bet on the Phillies to win.

JACKIE ROBINSON

Then came Rickey, who at least knew enough to wait for Landis's death, and who then saw his chance in the ascendance to the commissionership of Happy Chandler, a U.S. Senator from Kentucky.

When Chandler's appointment was announced, Ric Roberts,

a sportswriter for the black *Pittsburgh Courier,* rushed to Capitol Hill. Roberts was the best-known black journalist in the country, and knew Chandler slightly. When he found him, he asked the new commissioner, "What about black boys?" And Chandler, who had just returned from an inspection tour of Pacific battlefields, replied, "If they can fight and die in Okinawa, Guadalcanal, in the South Pacific, they can play baseball in America. And when I give my word, you can count on it."

The next day, the black newspapers bannered the story across their front pages; and before Chandler even resigned from the Senate and assumed the commissionership at the end of October 1945, Jackie Robinson signed his contract with Rickey's Dodgers.

Clyde Sukeforth is properly remembered as the scout who brought Robinson to Rickey's attention. But before putting Sukeforth on the case, Rickey had already had Tom Greenwade—who, working for the Yankees, would later sign Mickey Mantle—take a look at other potential pioneers. Greenwade, working in the Caribbean, sent telegraphed reports to Brooklyn using a code known only to Rickey: If the first word of the cable began with a letter from N-Z, he was reporting on a white Latin American player; if it began with a letter from A-M, it was a report on a black man.

Robinson wasn't the best young player in the black leagues— that was probably Monte Irvin, who would later join the Giants. But Robinson had all the qualities that Rickey thought his grand experiment would require, most notably patience and a pride that could withstand daily assault.

Both qualities were tested early on. Robinson's first manager in the Dodgers system was Clay Hopper, a Mississippian who headed Brooklyn's Montreal farm team in the International League. Hopper had pleaded with Rickey not to make him the first white man to manage an integrated team and then, according to Rickey, Hopper asked him, "Do you really think a nigger's a human being?"

But at the end of Robinson's season in Montreal, after a

year of insults, cold shoulders, and the banking of the player's urge to retaliate, Hopper approached him and said, "You're a great ballplayer and a fine gentleman. It's been wonderful having you on the team."

And then came the move to Brooklyn. As he expected, Rickey was immediately confronted by a group of players, mostly Southerners, threatening a revolt.

Their manager, Leo Durocher, was more direct. Pitcher Kirby Higbe recalled that he was among five players who had gone to Durocher, as they had to Rickey: the others were Carl Furillo, Dixie Walker, Bobby Bragan, and—surprisingly— Kentucky-born Pee Wee Reese, later Robinson's most supportive teammate.

As Higbe recalled it, Durocher explained that Rickey was willing to trade them, but that so long as Durocher was manager he wouldn't let him: he thought the team might win, and Robinson could only help them. It was Durocher's belief, simply put, that the black man would help put money in their pockets.

According to traveling secretary Harold Parrott, Durocher made a more public appeal to his players one midnight in Panama, where the team was playing some exhibition games against the Montreal club. Said Durocher, "I don't care if the guy is yellow or black or if he has stripes like a fuckin' zebra. I'm the manager of this team, and I say he plays. What's more I say he can make us all rich."

Of the five rebels, Furillo, Reese, and Bragan all relented before the season began (later, Bragan would say that his experience with Robinson made him "a better, more enlightened man"). Higbe was traded to Pittsburgh on May 3. And then there was the Georgia-born Walker, the most popular of the pre-Robinson Dodgers and probably their best player as well. After Durocher took the air out of the wider effort to block Robinson from joining the team, Walker sent this letter to Rickey:

"Recently the thought had occurred to me that a change of Ball clubs would benefit both the Brooklyn Baseball Club and myself. Therefore I would like to be traded as soon as a deal can be arranged. My association with you, the people of Brooklyn, the press and Radio has been very pleasant and one I can truthfully say I am sorry it has to end. For reasons I don't care to go into I feel my decision is the best for all concerned."

Walker's wish was granted, and when writer Maury Allen asked him, 35 years later, about the events of 1947, he replied, "I've said all I'm going to say on that subject." Then Walker broke. "There is one more thing I'll add. Jackie Robinson was a great ballplayer."

Once the battle for his own team's loyalties was won, Robinson still had to face the assault of other National Leaguers, most notably members of the Phillies and the Cardinals.

After Bob Carpenter, the DuPont heir who was by now the Phillies owner, tried in vain to talk Rickey into sitting Robinson down when the Phils and Dodgers met, Carpenter threatened to pull his club off the field. Rickey said he'd be happy to accept a forfeit, and Carpenter never acted on his threat. But his players, encouraged by manager Ben Chapman, subjected Robinson to relentless, vicious vituperation. According to Rickey, Chapman had done the Dodgers a favor—the Philadelphia assault on Robinson had united the Brooklyn players behind him.

Then, in early May, as the Dodgers prepared to visit St. Louis for the first time that season, word leaked from the Cardinal clubhouse that the players were planning a last-minute protest strike. The story was broken in the *New York Herald Tribune,* and National League president Ford Frick reacted immediately. His statement to the St. Louis players read:

"If you do this you will be suspended from the league. You will find that the friends you think you have in the press box will not support you, that you will be outcasts. I do not care if half the league strikes. Those who do it will encounter quick retribution. They will be suspended and I don't care if it wrecks the National League for five years. This is the United States of America, and one citizen has as much right to play as another.

"The National League will go down the line with Robinson whatever the consequence. You will find if you go through with your intention that you have been guilty of complete madness."

One year earlier, while Robinson was playing for Montreal, Frick had been the co-author of the major league report that recommended against the integration of baseball.

The hot-headed, vituperative Chapman was nearly a sociopath; his assaults on Robinson from his manager's perch in the Phillies dugout were utterly in character, the racism only adding a dimension to a nastiness that had long been in his makeup.

This violent, untrammeled combativeness was, apparently, precisely the quality which made Herb Pennock, the old Yankees pitcher who was Philadelphia's general manager, give him the manager's job. Pennock and Chapman had gotten to know each other when the older man was coaching, and Chapman playing the outfield, for the Red Sox in the late 1930s.

The most memorable encounter the two men had in Boston was, however, hardly the sort of meeting of minds that would lead one to think Chapman was managerial material. In the 1938 season, Chapman came to the plate with two men on; Pennock relayed the bunt sign from manager Joe Cronin. On the first pitch, the runners broke and Chapman's mighty swing produced a loud foul. Again, on the second pitch, the same result. Finally, with two strikes on him, Chapman hit into a double play.

Furious, Pennock accosted him as the teams changed sides, wanting to know if Chapman had missed the sign. Chapman acknowledged that he had, indeed, gotten the sign, which only infuriated Pennock more. He demanded to know why Chapman had ignored it.

The player glared at his coach. "Because," he said evenly, "I don't bunt." He was traded to Cleveland at season's end.

Robinson himself was probably Chapman's equal in combativeness, if not in the other aspects of his personality. After his rookie season—he was the overwhelming choice as Rookie of the Year—and with the removal of Rickey-imposed constraints on his behavior, Robinson backed down from no one. He was a hyperkinetic competitor who seemed to try, in every game, to make up for the years he had lost to the color line. At bat, he produced far more RBIs than a player of his relatively limited power should have been able to; on the bases, he was the most adept, and feared, runner since Cobb; and in the field, he made up for a weak arm and somewhat limited range with a deep knowledge of hitters and positioning.

But more than anything, Robinson was characterized by his unquenchable competitiveness. When Bobby Thomson ended the 1951 season with his epochal home run against Brooklyn in the Polo Grounds, the stadium all but exploded and the Brooklyn players ran speedily for the shelter of their clubhouse. But Robinson stood at his position in the field—watching with care as Thomson circled the bases, making certain that he touched every one.

As noble a figure as Robinson was, his career ended in 1956 under something of a self-wrought cloud. With the help of a ghostwriter, he had composed an article announcing his retirement for *Look* magazine. Part of the deal was that he would keep it quiet, so that the magazine would have an exclusive. When the Dodgers announced they'd traded him to the Giants for pitcher Dick Littlefield, Robinson only said he wouldn't report, mentioning nothing about his planned retirement.

The consequences, wrote Red Smith at the time, were that "he has embarrassed the Dodgers, dislocated the plans of the Giants, and deceived the working newspapermen whose friendship he had and who thought they had his confidence."

Robinson said, "I think they [newspapermen] will understand why this was one time I couldn't give them the whole story as soon as I knew it." Answered Smith, "He is probably correct. Those who feel he has flim-flammed them will understand that he did it for the money."

The postscripts to the Robinson saga were manifold: the signing of scores of others who had previously been barred from baseball; the rise to dominance of the National League, where integration began and took its firmest hold; and, inevitably, the death of the old Negro Leagues, whose last major product was a young shortstop-turned-outfielder named Henry Aaron.

The saddest of the Negro League stories might have been Ray Dandridge's. Dandridge was the leading third baseman in the black leagues from 1933, when he broke in, until 1949, when he at last signed a contract with the New York Giants' top farm club in Minneapolis. That season, at forty, he was rookie of the year in the American Association; the next year, at forty-one, he was voted the league's Most Valuable Player.

Dandridge didn't expect to start a major league career at his advanced age, but he had hoped that he would at least appear for a few games in a major league uniform before he retired. It never happened though, and when his career was over he asked Giants owner Horace Stoneham why he was never called up for the chance to play with the big club. Replied Stoneham, "You were the drawing power of Minneapolis."

THE INCREDIBLE SERIES

The 1947 World Series was notable for a number of reasons: it was the first in which a black man—Jackie Robinson, of course—appeared; it was the first of six in seven years, seven in nine years, won by the New York Yankees; and it was the scene of three of the most unlikely events in World Series history.

Going into the fourth game, the Yankees held a 2-1 lead over the Dodgers. Pitching for the Yankees was an undistinguished right-hander named Floyd Bevens, who had managed but a 7-13 record on a Yankees team that had gone 97-57 over the season. Bevens had little control, but a great deal of luck.

Over the first eight innings, he had walked eight men, but allowed only one run—and had yet to give up a single hit. After three batters in the ninth, holding a 2-1 lead, Bevens was one out from the first no-hitter in Series history. It was an astonishing accomplishment.

Inevitably, perhaps, the wild Bevens would not retain center stage on this day, and the second of the '47 Series' memorable events took place. With two out, and Brooklyn's Carl Furillo on first via a walk, Pete Reiser came up to pinch hit for Dodger pitcher Hugh Casey, while reserve outfielder Al Gionfriddo went in to run for Furillo. Like Bevens, whose nascent no-hitter was totally unexpected, Gionfriddo surprised his opponents and everyone else in the park: he stole second base. It was his third stolen base of the entire year. Yankees Manager Bucky Harris, who had last managed in a World Series in 1925, for the Washington Senators, had Reiser—the winning run—walked intentionally; Brooklyn manager Burt Shotton put in Eddie Miksis to run for Reiser, and then had Cookie Lavagetto bat for Eddie Stanky. A fairly decent hitter before World War II, Lavagetto had but 18 hits, only four for extra bases, as a reserve for the Dodgers in 1947. It was perhaps inevitable, on this peculiar day, that the mild Lavagetto would send a drive deep to right field, scoring the unlikely Gionfriddo (and Miksis), and beating the improbable Bevens.

Two days later, back in the Bronx, Gionfriddo returned to register a feat that dwarfed his stolen base and entered Series lore along with Lavagetto's hit and Bevens's thwarted no-hitter. The Yankees led in games, 3-2; the Dodgers led in the sixth inning, 8-5; Joe DiMaggio was at bat, with two men on base. Gionfriddo had come into the game just minutes earlier. Were the game played in virtually any other park but Yankee Stadium, the huge drive DiMaggio hit, 415 feet into the stadium's yawning prairie of a left field, would have been a game-tying home run. As it was, it was intercepted just as it was about to clear the bull-pen fence, caught on the dead run, horribly out of position, his body twisted away from the fence at the last minute, by Al Gionfriddo.

Though the Dodgers prevailed in that sixth game, the Yankees went on to win the Series the next afternoon, and five more over the next six years. The Dodgers remained their favored opponent, facing off against the Yankees five times in nine years. And Bevens, Lavagetto, Gionfriddo, the unquestioned stars of the '47 Series? Not one of them ever appeared in another big league game.

THE TRIUMPH OF CASEY STENGEL

From 1949, when Casey Stengel first took over as manager of the New York Yankees, until 1960, when he was forced into retirement, the Bronx Bombers won seven World Series. He had a constellation of stars playing for him—Joe DiMaggio, Yogi Berra, Phil Rizzuto, Whitey Ford, Mickey Mantle, Elston Howard, Roger Maris—but Stengel himself was the constant. The Yankees knew how to execute, and although they may not have stolen many bases—no one did in those power-mad years—they went from first to third better than any team in baseball. Stengel did for platooning what Bach did for the harpsichord, and he was a skillful handler of pitchers. Old as he was—he was fifty-nine when he became the Yankees manager—he was willing to give young players every chance. He even conceived of the instructional league (the "instructural league," he called it) to smooth the way for rookies.

He could be irascible and downright nasty, but he could also be sensitive and understanding. He was a proud man who mentally kept tabs on the ghost of John McGraw, and like McGraw he ended up with ten pennants to his credit. He did wonderful things with English and with mime, and he was always good for a laugh. But as Red Smith once wrote, "It is erroneous and unjust to conceive of Casey Stengel merely as a clown. He is something else entirely—a competitor who always had fun competing, a fighter with a gift of laughter."

On October 12, 1948, twenty-five years to the day after Casey had hit the second of his two game-winning homers in the 1923 World Series, he was named the Yankees manager. The baseball world was a little skeptical given Stengel's earlier failures as a manager with the Braves and the Dodgers, and Stengel was uncharacteristically nervous and edgy at the press conference that day. Later he said, "I could hear the hum and I knew what they was talking about. They was saying, 'This bum managed nine years and never got into the first division.'" But he loosened up after awhile, and after photographers persuaded him to don a Yankees cap and jersey, he posed for a comic picture in which he is peering over a backlit baseball as if it were a crystal ball. The photograph received wide attention, and when one member of the team's business staff saw it he said, "We have hired a clown."

Stengel had made a few enemies along the way, and one of them was Dave Egan, a Boston columnist. Egan wrote of the signing, "Well, sirs and ladies, the Yankees have now been mathematically eliminated from the 1949 pennant race. They eliminated themselves when they engaged Perfesser Casey Stengel to mismanage them for the next two years, and you may be sure that the perfesser will oblige to the best of his unique ability."

Another doubter was Bill Veeck: earlier in the decade, Veeck had called Stengel "a second-division manager, entirely satisfied with a losing ball club as long as Stengel and his wit are appreciated."

For the most part, Stengel walked as if on eggshells that first year. He was wary of the old guard Yankees, particularly DiMaggio, who didn't play that season until June 28 because of a heel injury. Stengel had left it up to DiMaggio to decide when he would return, and before the game, reporters were pestering the manager for the starting lineup. "I can't give you the lineup yet," Stengel said as he glanced over at DiMaggio, who was bent over, tying his shoes, on the bench. Joe said nothing, and Casey continued chatting with the reporters, his eyes still stuck on DiMaggio. Finally the Yankees' best player straightened up and nodded his head. "Now I can give you the lineup," Stengel said.

The Yankees were hanging onto first place when DiMaggio returned, and they proceeded to put some distance between themselves and the rest of the field. But then the Red Sox, managed by old friend Joe McCarthy, got hot, and the Yankees started getting hurt and sick. DiMaggio came down with viral pneumonia and lost 10 pounds. The Yankees trailed Boston by one game with two games left to play, in Yankee Stadium against the Sox. Boston led 4-0 in the first of the games, but the Yankees came back to win. The second game was also a cliff-hanger, with the Yankees fighting off a late Boston rally to win 5-3. When the last out was made, coach Bill Dickey leaped up and split his head open on the concrete roof of the dugout. Red Patterson, the Yankees' PR man, dutifully informed the press that the injury was the seventy-fourth disability suffered by the team that season.

After the Yankees swept the Dodgers in the 1949 World Series, Casey could finally be himself. He was still deferential to DiMaggio, but he started changing the rest of the cast, discarding or ignoring Snuffy Stirnweiss, Joe Page, Charlie Keller, and Tommy Henrich, and promoting Jerry Coleman, Billy Martin, and a young left-hander then known as Ed Ford. Stengel also hurt DiMaggio's pride when he 1) tried to get him to play first base, 2) moved him down to fifth in the lineup, and 3) sat him down for a few games during a slump. DiMaggio responded with a sensational six weeks that carried the Yankees to another pennant, although he refused to talk to Stengel. "So what if he doesn't talk to me?" said Stengel. "I'll get by and so will he. DiMaggio doesn't get paid to talk to me, and I don't either."

Although Stengel and his wife Edna were childless, he had at least three Yankees sons: Berra, Mantle, and Billy Martin. He was the first to really see Berra's true potential, and he treated him with great kindness. Frank Graham wrote: "Aware, as no one before him had been, that here was a truly sensitive young man who was hurt by many of the quips made about him, yet had the guts to smile through them, Casey acted as a buffer between Berra and those on his own club who poked fun at him. It wasn't long before the slower thinkers among the Yankees gained a realization of what Yogi meant to them."
Stengel had Martin back when he managed Oakland in the

Pacific Coast League in 1948, and he loved him. "He's a fresh kid, ain't he?" Casey would say with admiration. He hit Martin countless grounders, schooled him on the double play, wheedled and cajoled him. In turn, Martin loved Casey, and repaid him with inspired play for several seasons. It did not escape Stengel's attention that in 1954, when the Indians interrupted the Yankees's string of pennants, Martin was in the Army.

But the two men had a falling out when general manager George Weiss sent Martin packing to Kansas City in 1957. Stengel called Billy into his office and said, "Well, you're gone. You're the best little player I ever had. You did everything I ever asked." For years, Martin thought Stengel had betrayed him by not sticking up for him. Finally, Mantle talked Billy into going over to Casey before a game, saying, "Look, you're a lot younger than he is and one of these days he'll be gone and you'll regret it."

Mantle led Martin over to the dugout, and as Mantle later recalled, "Billy had tears in his eyes and he was crying, and the old man had tears in his eyes and he was starting to cry. And I had tears in my eyes, too, and I was crying."

Mantle was the son who was always a disappointment to Casey. He wanted Mickey to be the best player ever, partly because he wanted a personal monument to himself, but also because he didn't want to see an ounce of Mantle's great talent wasted. Casey tried to get him to cut down on his swing, figuring a 450-foot homer was just as good as a 565-foot homer, but Mantle wouldn't listen. "I never learned anything," Mantle admitted. Martin once said, "Once I saw the old man grab Mickey by the back of the neck and shake him hard when he did something the old man didn't like. He said, "Don't let me see you do that again, you little bastard!"

When Stengel at last accepted the fact that Mantle was too stubborn to change, the two got along well enough. But when Stengel retired from the Yankees and was asked to name his all-time, all-star team, Mantle was not on it, even though Berra, Rizzuto, and DiMaggio were.

The Yankees won 103 games in 1954, but unbelievably—at least to Stengel—the Indians won 111. "Those plumbers," he called them, and he refused to believe they were better than his team. That year a comic fantasy by Douglas Wallop entitled *The Year the Yankees Lost the Pennant* was published (it was the basis for the musical *Damn Yankees*) and when someone saw the book on Stengel's desk, he asked the manager what he thought of it. "I ain't read it," he said. "Some guy sent it to me the other day and it's just been laying there ever since. It ain't a true story. It's fiction."

But losing the pennant finally dawned on Stengel after a doubleheader loss to Cleveland before 86,563 in Municipal Stadium on September 12 dropped the Yankees 8½ games back. On the Monday morning following the double wipeout, the departing Yankees were gathered in the lobby of their hotel. The traveling secretary saw some of the regular beat writers standing around and shouted, "Come on, you guys, you'll miss the train." But the writers had been instructed by their offices to stay in Cleveland to do Indian stories, and one of them said, "Don't worry about us. We're staying. We're picking up the Indians."

Stengel, watching this byplay, responded with genuine shock. "You mean they ain't coming?" he said. "Jesus, I'm losing my writers."

They were his writers, all right. He knew what they wanted, and he always had time for them. One reporter remembered asking him a question once, and Stengel talking for 40 minutes in response. Finally the reporter said, "Casey, you haven't answered my question." Stengel said, "Don't rush me."

Another time a writer left the press room to talk to Casey in the late afternoon before a night game. When the writer returned after an hour, a colleague asked, "Did Casey tell you who's going to pitch tomorrow?" The writer said, "He started to, but he got talking about McGraw and the time he managed in Toledo and the Pacific Coast League and God knows what else. I think tomorrow's starting pitcher is Christy Mathewson."

A verbatim transcript of Stengel's response to the spring training question, Who will your third baseman be this year?: "Well, the fella I got on there is hitting pretty good and I know he can make that throw, and if he don't make it that other fella I got coming has shown me a lot, and if he can't I have my guy and I know what he can do. On the other hand, the guy's not around now. And, well, this guy may be able to do it against left-handers if my guy ain't strong enough. I know one of my guys is gonna do it." Reporters with the team knew that Casey was talking about Gil McDougald, Andy Carey, Billy Martin, and Bobby Brown.

The convolutions were almost always for effect. When Red Barber became the Yankees broadcaster before the 1953 season, he asked Casey to go over the players with him when he had a few spare moments. Stengel immediately sat down and went over the roster. "He went down the list, man by man, in detail," said Barber. "There was no double-talk, none at all. In 30 minutes he gave me a detailed, analytical report on every last man on his roster. It was remarkable. And all season long, everything he told me about every man held up."

Stengel's wit could sting. "I'm not tired," a pitcher told him when Casey came out to the mound, and Stengel said, "Well, I'm tired of you." Watching second baseman Jerry Lumpe hit rope after rope in batting practice, Stengel said, "He looks like the greatest hitter in the world until you play him." Of slumping pitcher Bob Turley, Casey once said, "Look at him. He don't smoke, he don't drink, he don't chase women, and he don't win." He came and sat down on the bench next to big outfielder Bob Cerv before one game and said, "Nobody knows this, but one of us has just been traded to Kansas City."

He could even turn on members of the media. After the Yankees had lost the first two games of the 1958 Series, a television interviewer thrust his microphone toward Casey and asked, "Do you think your team is choking?" Stengel barked, "Do you choke on that fucking microphone?," turned his back to the camera and pointedly scratched the seat of his pants. Later, Stengel said, "When I cursed, I knocked out their audio, and when I scratched my ass I ruined their picture."

But Stengel's most famous speaking performance came off the field, in a hearing before the Senate Subcommittee on Antitrust and Monopoly on July 9, 1958. Several baseball people were called to testify the day after the All-Star Game in Baltimore to speak about a bill to exempt baseball from antitrust restrictions. As often as it has been quoted, it merits repeating here:

SENATOR ESTES KEFAUVER: Mr. Stengel, you are the manager of the New York Yankees. Will you give us very briefly your background and your views about this legislation?

STENGEL: Well, I started in professional ball in 1910. I have been in professional ball, I would say, for 48 years. I have been employed by numerous ball clubs in the majors and in the minor leagues.

I entered in the minors with Kansas City. I played as low as Class D ball, which was at Shelbyville, Kentucky, and also Class C ball and Class A ball, and I have advanced in baseball as a ballplayer.

I had many years that I was not so successful as a ballplayer, as it is a game of skill. And then I was no doubt discharged by baseball in which I had to go back to the minor leagues as a manager, and after being in the minor leagues as a manager, I became a major league manager in several cities and was discharged, we call it discharged because there is no question I had to leave.

And I returned to the minor leagues at Milwaukee, Kansas City, and Oakland, California, and then returned to the major leagues. In the last 10 years, naturally, with the New York Yankees, the New York Yankees have been a tremendous success and while I am not a ballplayer who does the work I have no doubt worked for a ball club that is very capable in the office.

I have been up and down the ladder. I know there are some things in baseball 35 to 50 years ago that are better now than they were in those days. In those days, my goodness, you could not transfer a ball club in the minor leagues, Class D, Class C, Class A ball.

How could you transfer a ball club when you did not have a highway? How could you transfer a ball club when the railroads then would take you to a town you got off and then you had to wait and sit up five hours to go to another ball club?

How could you run baseball then without night ball? You had to have night ball to improve the proceeds, to pay larger salaries, and I went to work, the first year I received $135 a month. I thought that was amazing. I had to put away enough money to go to dental college. I found out it was not better in dentistry. I stayed in baseball.

Any other questions you would like to ask me?

KEFAUVER: Mr. Stengel, are you prepared to answer particularly why baseball wants this bill passed?

STENGEL: Well, I would have to say at the present time, I think that baseball has advanced in this respect for the player help. That is an amazing statement for me to make, because you can retire with an annuity at 50 and what organization in America allows you to retire at 50 and receive money?

Now the second thing about baseball that I think is very interesting to the public or to all of us is that it is the owner's fault if he does not improve his club, along with the officials in the ball club and the players.

Now what causes that? If I am going to go on the road and we are a traveling ball club and you know the cost of transportation now—we travel sometimes with three Pullman coaches, the New York Yankees on the road and all, that it is the best, and we have broken records in Washington this year, we have broken them in every city but New York and we have lost two clubs that have gone out of the city of New York.

Of course, we have had some bad weather. I would say that they are mad at us in Chicago, we fill the parks. They have come out to see good material. I will say they are mad at us in Kansas City, but we broke their attendance records.

Now on the road we only get possibly 27 cents. I am

not positive of these figures, as I am not an official. If you go back 15 years or if I owned stock in the club, I would give them to you.

KEFAUVER: Mr. Stengel, I am not sure that I made my question clear.

STENGEL: Yes, sir. Well, that is all right. I am not sure I'm going to answer yours perfectly, either.

Stengel delivered seven thousand words of testimony over 45 minutes, pausing occasionally to let the laughter die down. But the best line of the hearing was delivered by the next witness, Mantle. Asked by Kefauver if he had any observations on the antitrust measure, Mickey said, "My views are just about the same as Casey's."

In his book, *Stengel,* Robert Creamer described Casey in the locker room at 70:

"He was a bizarre spectacle, this naked old man parading through a room full of hard-muscled young athletes, but Stengel never gave a sign that he recognized the incongruity. On the contrary, he was vain about his body, even as an old man, as he was vain about many things. He loved to pose for photographers, mugging extravagantly, twisting his leathery face into grotesque winks, wearing odd bits of clothing for props, doing almost anything the photographers wanted when he was in the mood to do it. And he was something special for them to photograph, with his craggy seamed face, jutting jaw, wide mobile mouth, huge hooked nose, amazingly blue eyes, great pendulous ears, long arms, crabbed stooped body."

Casey was aging faster in his body than in his mind, but when the Yankees finished third in 1959, people began to think he might be losing it. There were reports of Stengel falling asleep on the bench. Bill Veeck, who owned the pennant-winning White Sox, didn't think Stengel was at fault. "I know Casey well," said Veeck, "and he's no different now from the way he was when he was winning pennants. He just hasn't got the horses."

After the season, Stengel got a new horse from Kansas City,

right-fielder Roger Maris. Maris won the MVP award in 1960, the year before he hit 61 home runs, and he and Mantle became the Yankees' most potent one-two punch since Ruth and Gehrig. Casey was hospitalized for chest pains in May, leaving Ralph Houk to run the club, but he returned after two weeks as spry as ever. "They examined all my organs," said Casey. "Some of them are quite remarkable and others are not so good. A lot of museums are bidding for them."

The Yankees won 15 in a row at the end of the '60 season to outdistance the Baltimore Orioles, and they were heavily favored against the Pirates in the World Series. Asked if he would quit if he lost the Series, Stengel said, "Well, I made up my mind, but I made it up both ways."

It was a bizarre Series, one in which the Yankees outscored the Pirates 55-27 and blew a 7-4 lead in the eighth inning of the seventh game when Bill Virdon's double-play grounder hit a pebble and bounced up into shortstop Tony Kubek's throat, setting the stage for a five-run rally. The Yankees tied the score in the top of the ninth, but Bill Mazeroski hit a home run off Ralph Terry in the bottom of the ninth to give the Pirates the championship.

It was a bitter defeat for Stengel, and five days later the Yankees called a press conference at the Savoy Hilton in New York to announce that Stengel would not be back. "Casey, were you fired?" one reporter shouted, and Casey replied, "No, I wasn't fired. I was paid up in full. Write anything you want, quit, fired, whatever you please. I don't care." Later Stengel would say, "I'll never make the mistake of being 70 again."

RALPH KINER

He still holds the record for the most consecutive seasons leading a league in home runs, and Ralph Kiner's most famous utterance underscored his special talent: "Home run hitters drive Cadillacs, and single hitters drive Fords."

Actually, it was Fritz Ostermueller who made the automotive comparisons, in a comment to Kiner. The Cadillac driver's best *bon mot* came at his own expense, during his Hall of Fame induction speech. Recalling his days with the Cubs, when he played a lead-footed left field and Hank Sauer played an immobile right while Frank Baumholtz was compelled to cover center, Kiner said, "Between us, we shortened Baumholtz's career by three years."

STAN MUSIAL

If ever a ballplayer played out a long career wanting in classic anecdotes, it was Stan Musial: a gentleman, respected by all, modest in habit and in language, he simply went about his business—and his business was hitting.

What the record reveals is three stories, all of them strikingly similar in message, and all of them likely to be true:

Before Willie Mays's first appearance against the Cardinals, Leo Durocher ran down the St. Louis batting order for him, telling the rookie how the various hitters should be played. He described the lead-off batter, and the number two man, and then moved to the clean-up hitter.

Mays interrupted to ask about number three.

"The third hitter," Durocher said, "is Stan Musial. There is no advice I can give you about him."

Before the 1951 All-Star Game, Ed Lopat of the Yankees told Brooklyn's Preacher Roe that he'd figured out a way to pitch to Musial. In the fourth, Musial stood against Lopat and lined his first pitch into the right-field seats. Thereupon Roe shouted to Lopat, "I see what you mean, but I found that way to pitch to him a long time ago, all by myself."

Finally, Roe again, in 1957 explaining how he pitched to him, as Musial's illustrious career—more than 3600 hits, 475 home runs, a lifetime average of .331—was winding down: "I throw four wide ones, and then I try to pick him off first."

ENOS SLAUGHTER

The 1946 Series is remembered for two events: Ted Williams bunting against the Cardinals' over-shifted defense, and Enos Slaughter scoring the Series' winning run from first base on Harry Walker's single.

Slaughter's "Mad Dash Home" was re-enacted twenty-five years later, in St. Louis. Several of the original participants took part in the staged event, including pitcher Joe Dobson and Boston shortstop Johnny Pesky, who had often been held responsible for holding the ball as Slaughter scored from first on Walker's single. In fact, Pesky's back was to the plate as he took the relay from the outfield, and the roaring crowd at Fenway Park made it impossible for him to hear the alarms shouted by his Boston teammates.

After the 1971 re-enactment, Slaughter suggested that the same participants all gather again 25 years after that, and do it again. Pesky scoffed at the notion, but as Slaughter told Donald Honig, "You can't tell. I'll be only eighty years old then, and you know I keep my legs in shape."

TOMMY HOLMES

For a few seasons one of the finest hitters in the game, Holmes was desperately loved by the bleacherites at Braves Field in Boston, who rarely had anything else to love. After a few seasons together, Holmes and the right field fans developed a standing routine enacted at the beginning of each game. As Holmes would come out to right field, a designated ringleader would croak, "Wait until he picks up his glove." Then, as one, the bleachers would erupt with "How many hits today, Tommy?" and Holmes would answer back with a finger signal.

But a personnel change upset the routine. When Johnny Barrett arrived in Boston from Pittsburgh in the 1946 season, Braves Manager Billy Southworth planned to use him in left. But Barrett had never played left, and with Holmes's agreement Southworth put the newcomer in right, with Holmes on the other side of the outfield.

The day the reassignments were put into effect, the right-field fans were outraged. They chanted for Holmes all day, and when Barrett came out to the field each inning, they insulted him mercilessly. He received nothing but boos from Holmes's faithful from first inning to last. After the game, Barrett said he'd had enough, and the next day he became a left-fielder.

The following season, when Holmes was hit in the wrist on a pitch from Alpha Brazle of St. Louis, Southworth put Nanny Fernandez in for him. Fernandez had been with the Braves for three seasons and knew what to expect. When he reached his position, he cupped his hands and shouted at the fans, "Holmes hurt his wrist. He can't play!"

Came back the reply, "Send him out anyhow. He'll do better hurt than you'll do healthy."

FRONT OFFICE FOLLIES: MacPHAIL, RICKEY, O'MALLEY

Brooklyn was a singular place, and not just because of Rickey. In fact, he was only the middle man in a string of three Dodgers chief executives as distinctive as one could wish.

The first was Larry MacPhail—Leland Stanford MacPhail, actually—at various times a practicing lawyer, a banker, a car dealer, a department store executive, an army officer in both World Wars—and John Foster Dulles's bridge partner at George Washington University.

He was a protégé of Rickey's (of whom he once said, paraphrasing Churchill, "There but for the grace of God, goes God") who ended up a bitter rival; a high-living carouser who played a major role in getting Leo Durocher suspended from baseball for a year for similar behavior; a Barnum-like promoter who nonetheless built league champions in Cincinnati, Brooklyn, and the Bronx; a driven baseball executive who led the Yankees to a world championship shortly after becoming the team's general manager—and then announced his retirement at the team victory party.

When Durocher was manager of the Dodgers, MacPhail would go into periodic rages, often fueled by drink, and fire him. But clerks in the team's front office learned to type the press releases announcing such dismissals very slowly, for they knew MacPhail would change his mind before they got to the bottom of the page. As Durocher himself said, "They say there is a thin line between genius and insanity, and MacPhail was constantly wandering over the line."

One of MacPhail's more uncontrolled moments came when Joe Medwick, playing for the Dodgers, was beaned by Bob Bowman, a former St. Louis teammate with whom he hadn't gotten along. While Medwick was being carried off the field on a stretcher, MacPhail abandoned his private box in the upper deck, raced to the Dodgers clubhouse, through the dugout, and onto the field. He strode out to the mound to challenge Bowman, then went directly to the St. Louis dugout and challenged the whole Cardinal team. MacPhail was still screaming when coach Charlie Dressen and pitcher Hugh Casey wrestled him away.

Years later, writer Gerald Holland was dispatched by *Sports Illustrated* to do a profile of MacPhail, and he brought up the famous day on which the now-retired executive had charged on to the playing field. MacPhail denied it ever happened. Holland read to him the *New York Times* of the day following, but MacPhail was steadfast. "I went right from my box to the dressing room to see how Medwick was," he said. Then Holland read another eye-witness version from another of the New York papers. Again MacPhail denied it, as he did with each subsequent clipping Holland pulled out.

Finally, MacPhail challenged the writer directly: "Are you going to pay attention to all that garbage, or are you going to believe *me?*"

MacPhail's disavowal of the Medwick incident wasn't really in character, or perhaps it reflected the mellowing that comes with age. Back in 1936, while running the Reds, a story broke that he had punched a Cincinnati detective (this was before he actually punched the Reds' chief owner, Powel Crosley). A member of the Reds' board of directors rushed to MacPhail's office to offer his sympathies for the plainly unfair treatment MacPhail had gotten in the press.

But MacPhail surprised him. He was sitting at his desk going through the clips, a grin on his face. "How do you like *that* for publicity?" he asked happily.

Branch Rickey arrived in Brooklyn when MacPhail left to join the army, and the families that owned the team granted him a 25 percent share of the club. Building on what MacPhail had already accomplished, he quickly made the Dodgers the National League's pre-eminent team.

Success of this nature did not, however, make Rickey any less parsimonious. Emerging from contract talks with Rickey after a particularly good year, Brooklyn outfielder Gene Hermanski seemed pleased when a reporter, who was waiting in Rickey's outer office, saw him. (Brooklyn reporters, incidentally, liked to call the orotund Rickey's office "The Cave of the Winds.") "It looks like you got a raise," the reporter said. "No," Hermanski replied, "I didn't—but I didn't take a cut either."

Bobby Bragan was managing the Dodgers farm team in Fort Worth, under Rickey's instructions to economize. At one point he got a telegram from Rickey asking, "Do you need a shortstop or can you go with your present infield?" Mindful of—and no doubt a little peeved by—the economy dictum, Bragan wired back a one-word reply: "Yes." Came Rickey's next wire, which said "Yes, what?" And Bragan responded, "Yes sir!"

Rickey's business sense served him well in 1950, when Walter O'Malley and John L. Smith, his partners in the Dodgers, let him know that they were about to boot him as the club's president. The Dodgers paid no dividends, and Rickey's 25 percent share of the club could be rendered all but worthless. From this disadvantage, Rickey persuaded William Zeckendorf, the New York real-estate mogul, to make an offer of $1,050,000 for his share of the club; under the terms of the partnership, O'Malley had to meet that price to keep control. "Zeckendorf," wrote Red Smith, "got $50,000 for his trouble, while Rickey got his million and O'Malley's enduring hostility."

O'Malley was a politically savvy Brooklyn lawyer who would, in time, grab total control of the Dodgers, move them to Los Angeles, and turn them into the most profitable sports franchise in the world.

But that didn't make him careless with his cash. Harold Parrott, who worked for O'Malley for close to two decades, related how the boss insisted that front office employees who were granted World Series rings were required to turn them in when the Dodgers next won a pennant.

But O'Malley—who late in life estimated his personal net worth at more than $20,000,000, irrespective of the 300 acres of downtown Los Angeles real estate the Dodgers owned—reached the pinnacle of meanness in 1956. The Dodgers were planning their first post-season trip to Japan, and Mrs. Harry Hickey, whose husband was a member of the Dodgers board, called to say that she and her husband wished to join the party. Hickey had been very ill but was now feeling well enough to travel.

O'Malley ordered the Hickeys off the travel list. "Have you stopped to think," he said to Parrott, who was making the arrangements, "what it would cost to send a body home from Japan? We can't take that chance."

In 1966, Sandy Koufax stunned O'Malley by engaging in a joint hold-out with Don Drysdale. Correctly perceiving that their concerted action would enhance their individual bargaining positions, Koufax and Drysdale declared that until they both were signed, neither would report to camp in Vero Beach.

O'Malley eventually had to give in—the two men had won 49 games, more than half the Dodgers' total victories, the season before. But while O'Malley waited out Koufax and Drysdale, he turned his attentions to the other pitchers on his staff, notably Claude Osteen, the number three starter. When Osteen, who had won 15 games in 1965, reported to Dodgertown,

O'Malley asked a nearby Dodgers factotum, "Does this man have a nice room? Give him a suite."

THE MOVE WEST

The new era of franchise-shifting—the first such upheaval in half a century—began in 1953, when the Boston Braves moved to Milwaukee. The Philadelphia A's soon jumped to Kansas City, while the St. Louis Browns transmogrified into the Baltimore Orioles. But baseball's empire did not take on its modern shape until after the 1957 season, when the Los Angeles Dodgers and the San Francisco Giants were born.

At the time of the move, both clubs were still profitable in New York. But Walter O'Malley, who never smelled a dollar he didn't like, sniffed countless millions of them awaiting baseball in southern California. O'Malley also knew that it would be hard to justify the sudden implantation of just one franchise on the West Coast, so he turned his attention to Horace Stoneham.

Stoneham, who owned the Giants, listened to O'Malley the way some other gullible sorts had once listened to Tom Sawyer describe the joys of whitewashing a fence. San Francisco, he was persuaded, was the pearl of the West—not least because a city-financed stadium would be built for him there. He quickly picked up on O'Malley's suggestion, and on Opening Day in 1958 metropolitan New York was without National League baseball for the first time since 1882.

For most of the next three decades, the Giants suffered amid small crowds in cold, drafty, ill-planned Candlestick Park. And Walter O'Malley, who'd made the suggestion to move in the first place? He got the Los Angeles sunshine, sole ownership of a ballpark (and its adjacent parking lots) on 307 acres of prime L.A. real estate, more than seven million dollars in various grants from local governments, and a lock on what would quickly become—and remain—the most profitable franchise in baseball history.

O'Malley would have to wait a few years for his new stadium in Chavez Ravine to open. In the interim, the Dodgers played in the old Los Angeles Memorial Coliseum—a stadium that was great for a track meet, all right for a football game, and absolutely ill-suited to baseball.

The Coliseum's football-style rows of seats were so gently elevated that fans in the tenth row felt they were miles from the action. The elongated shape of the playing field created enough foul territory along the third base line to accommodate virtually another entire infield. Although close down the foul-line, the right-field fence curved so outrageously distant that it became almost unreachable: Duke Snider, whose left-handed bat had accounted for 40 home runs the team's last year in Brooklyn, managed only fifteen his first year in California.

But the Coliseum's most distinguishing characteristic was the so-called "Bamboo Curtain," a 42-feet-high wire-mesh screen that stretched from the left-field line 140 feet toward center. The Curtain was necessitated by the odd dimensions of the Coliseum, which placed the left-field foul pole only 251 feet from home plate. Despite the screen, right-handed singles hitters became sluggers, and of the 193 home runs hit in the Coliseum in 1958, fully 182 of them reached the seats in left.

Pitcher Don Drysdale, who himself once hit two home runs over the Curtain in one game, expressed the problem aptly after watching a skinny radio announcer hit a pop fly over the screen in a sportswriter-broadcaster exhibition game. "See how easy it is?," Drysdale asked. "And in an hour or so I have to pitch to Ernie Banks!"

When the Dodgers became the first team to bring a World Series championship to Los Angeles in 1959, they did it on the unlikely shoulders of Wally Moon. Moon was a good enough ballplayer, but it didn't figure that, as a lefty, he could do much damage to the distant fences in right.

But Moon knew how to adapt and, using a peculiar inside-out swing, learned to slice the ball to left. His 19 home runs in '59 included fourteen over the Curtain—more than any right-handed hitter on the team.

YOGI

Stengel once said of Yogi Berra, "They say he's funny. Well, he has a lovely wife and family, a beautiful home, money in the bank, and he plays golf with millionaires. What's funny about that? Money is the last thing Yogi thinks about at night before he goes to sleep."

Before he was Yogi Berra, he was Larry or Lawdie Berra, the son of Italian immigrants who lived in the Dago Hill section of St. Louis. Joe Garagiola was a childhood friend, and the broadcaster has since made an industry out of telling Yogi stories. According to Garagiola, Berra got his nickname simply because "he walked like a yogi."

When Berra first came up to the Yankees, then-president Larry MacPhail said he looked like "the bottom man on an unemployed acrobatic team." But with Stengel's careful nurturing, he soon became the best catcher in baseball. As funny-looking as he was, he played like a cat behind the plate. At bat he swung at everything with unusual success. And he handled pitchers and defensive alignments so well that Stengel would introduce him as "Mr. Berra, which is my assistant manager."

But always, there were what came to be known as Berra-isms. Take his very first season, in 1947. When the Yankees came to St. Louis to play the Browns, they had a Yogi Berra Night at Sportsman's Park, and the honoree said, "I want to thank all those who made this night necessary."

"I didn't say everything I said," Yogi once insisted. But the following selections are varifiably on the record:

On his beautiful new house: "It's nothing but rooms."

Giving directions to the house: "It's pretty far, but it doesn't seem like it."

On being told by the wife of New York Mayor John Lindsay that he looked very cool in his summer suit: "Thanks. You don't look so hot yourself."

On being given a check, made out to Bearer, by St. Louis announcer Jack Buck for appearing on a pre-game show: "How long have you known me, Jack? And you still don't know how to spell my name."

After seeing the movie *Dr. Zhivago:* "It sure was cold in Russia in those days."

A radio interviewer once told Berra before a broadcast, "We're going to do free association. I'm going to throw out a few names, and you just say the first thing that pops into your mind."

"Okay," said Berra.

On the air, the announcer said, "I'm here tonight with Yogi Berra, and we're going to play free association. I'm going to mention a name, and Yogi's just going to say the first thing that comes to mind. Okay, Yogi?"

"Okay."

"All right, here we go then. Mickey Mantle."

"What about him?" said Berra.

Berra was a sensitive man, as this passage in *Yogi,* his 1961 autobiography (written with Ed Fitzgerald) shows: "I worry about getting old. I worry about not getting around on the fastball. I worry about keeping Carm [his wife Carmen] happy so she won't be sorry she married me, about the kids growing up good, and about keeping out of trouble with God. I worry a lot."

Always Berra had a wonderful innocence about him, and the tastes of a child. Many Yogi stories surround his attachment to comic books, which he read faithfully. But when his teammates kidded him about his comics, he knew enough to say, "If that's so silly, how come every time I put one down, somebody else picks it up?"

BILL VEECK

Bill Veeck first got the idea of playing a midget from John McGraw, a friend of Veeck's father. When the Veecks invited McGraw over for dinner, he would regale them with tales of his old Giants, and one time, he talked about a hunchback batboy he employed named Eddie Morrow, adding that he was often tempted to send the little fellow to the plate just to get a walk.

The younger Veeck never forgot that. He bought the moribund St. Louis Browns in 1951, the year the American League was celebrating its fiftieth anniversary, and Veeck decided to have a big birthday party during an August 19 doubleheader against the Tigers. At the time, the Browns were some 36 games out of first. All the fans received free ice cream, cake, and beer—the Falstaff Brewery was also celebrating its fiftieth anniversary—and in between games, the crowd was entertained by jugglers, acrobats, fireworks, a band led by Satchel Paige, and baseball clown Max Patkin. A huge cake was rolled out to the pitcher's mound. PA announcer Bernie Ebert told the crowd that the club was giving manager Zack Taylor a present of a little Brownie, and the people assumed he meant the camera of the same name. Out of the cake popped a midget in a Browns uniform, No. ⅛, Eddie Gaedel. People laughed, but they assumed the joke was over.

Of course, Veeck had something more in mind. A theatrical agent had sent him in the 3′7″, 65-pound Gaedel, the most athletic midget he could find. Veeck interviewed him, offered him $100, told him what he wanted him to do, measured his strike zone in a crouch as 1½ inches high, and threatened to shoot him if he tried to take a swing. But Gaedel had thoughts of glory and kept trying to show off his swing. Gaedel asked Veeck, "How tall was Wee Willie Keeler?" Veeck said, "Wee Willie Keeler was six-foot-five."

The first batter for the Browns in the second game was outfielder Frank Saucier, but then Ebert announced, "For the Browns, number one-eighth, Eddie Gaedel, batting for Saucier." Gaedel came out of the dugout carrying three little bats. Home plate umpire Eddie Hurley summoned manager Taylor, who came out to show him a sheaf of papers validating Gaedel's status as a bona fide member of the team. Hurley could do nothing but wave Gaedel into the batter's box. Tigers catcher Bob Swift went out to the mound to discuss how to pitch to the midget with pitcher Bob Cain. When Swift returned to the plate, he knelt down on both knees to make a target. To Veeck's horror, Gaedel ignored his instructions to crouch, assuming "a fair approximation of Joe DiMaggio's classic style," as Veeck recalled it. But Cain was laughing too hard to get the ball over the plate, and Eddie walked on four pitches. Jim Delsing came in to pinch-run for Gaedel, who patted Delsing on the butt in true professional style. Eddie then shook hands with the first-base coach, waved to the crowd, and took a long, triumphant walk across the field.

Naturally, baseball took every step to assure that a midget never batted again. As for Gaedel, Veeck later employed him for various other stunts. The last one was at Comiskey Park, when Veeck was owner of the White Sox. Gaedel and three other midgets, all dressed as Martians, dropped from the sky in a helicopter, landing right behind second base. The Martians quickly captured the White Sox tiny double-play combination of Nellie Fox and Luis Aparicio, made them honorary Martians, and informed the crowd that they had come down to aid Nellie and Luis in their battle against the giant Earthlings.

Gaedel died about a year later of complications from a mugging. Among those at his funeral was Bob Cain, the pitcher who walked him.

Veeck wasn't just a showman. He was also a shrewd trader who built the Cleveland clubs that won the AL in '48 and '54, as well as the '59 AL champion White Sox. He was also a pioneer who had tried to integrate baseball in 1944, when he'd made his effort to buy the Phillies.

This is not to say Veeck wasn't a promoter; he was the greatest in baseball's long history. He used to encourage players to hold out in spring training, hoping thereby to garner a little extra publicity. He once insured the face of his good-looking infielder Johnny Berardino—he later became an actor—for $1,000,000 against line drives and other mayhem. When a night watchman named Joe Early wrote a letter to the *Cleveland Press* asking why ballclubs always had special days for baseball players who didn't need the loot instead of for fans, Veeck put on "Good Old Joe Early Night." Among the gifts Early received were an outhouse, one of those circus cars that backfired and reared up on its back tires, and a swaybacked horse. But he also received a new Ford convertible, appliances, clothes, and a nice watch.

A year after the Indians' 1948 championship, on the day the team was eliminated from the race, Veeck held a funeral for the pennant. To the accompaniment of a dirge, the flag was lowered and folded into a pine coffin. The pallbearers, who included manager Lou Boudreau and his coaches, slid the coffin into a horse-drawn hearse. Veeck, dressed as a mortician and dabbing his eyes with a handerchief, drove the hearse slowly towards an open grave in center field, the Cleveland players joining the procession.

After he sold the Indians, Veeck bought the Browns in mid-season 1951. Wrote John Lardner, "Many critics were surprised to know that the Browns could be bought because they didn't know the Browns were owned." In the preceding five years, they had finished sixth once, eighth once, and three times in seventh place. They were utterly overshadowed by the Cardinals and didn't draw at the gate.

Veeck couldn't build a winner, but he could use his other tricks. As he later wrote, "Satchel Paige was the first player I brought in. Max Patkin and Jackie Price came back to entertain. Within the first month we had a miniature circus, featuring 'Millie the Queen of the Air' sliding down a tight-wire that extended from right field to third base."

One of his first successful promotions was Grandstand Managers' Day, for a game against the A's. The fans sitting behind the St. Louis dugout—among them, a smiling Connie Mack—were given large cards with YES printed in green on one side, and NO on the other. Manager Zack Taylor was outfitted for the game in civilian clothes and bedroom slippers, and sat in a rocking chair on top of the dugout. Fans had been asked to pick the starting line-up from a ballot in one of the St. Louis papers. At each strategic juncture in the game itself, Veeck's publicity man, Bob Fishel, would hold up a sign reading "SHALL WE WARM UP PITCHER?," or "INFIELD

BACK?," or whatever the particular situation would call for. A circuit judge would quickly tally the votes and relay the result to Johnny Berardino, in the third-base coaching box.

The Browns won 5-3, ending a four-game losing streak.

One of the players Veeck brought to the Browns was a pitcher named Bobo Holloman. Like Newsom, this Bobo was a character. "He could outtalk me, outpester me and outcon me," wrote Veeck. "Unfortunately, he could not outpitch me."

Holloman kept bugging Veeck and manager Marty Marion for a starting assignment, and they finally gave him one against the Athletics. Everything the A's hit was a rocket—right at somebody. The Browns never fielded better. Just when he appeared to be tiring, a rain delay would refresh him. With two outs in the eighth, second baseman Billy Hunter made an impossible play behind the bag. With two outs in the ninth, Vic Wertz caught a screamer down the first base line. Holloman had a no-hitter—the first twentieth-century no-hitter achieved by a pitcher in his first major league start.

That was the only complete game Holloman would ever have in the majors. By the end of the year, he was back in the minors, never to be seen again in the big leagues.

As much as he loved to put on a show, Veeck did know how to watch his dollars. In 1951, Ned Garver won 20 games for the last place Browns. He'd earned $18,000 that year, and he wanted a substantial raise for the '52 season. Veeck declined with a piece of unerring logic: "We finished last with you," he told the pitcher. "It's a cinch we can finish last without you."

Veeck claimed that his best gimmick was the exploding scoreboard he installed at Comiskey Park in Chicago. He got the idea from a William Saroyan play, *The Time of Your Life,* in which a pinball machine erupts in flashing lights just before the final curtain. Veeck had ten mortars put on top of the scoreboard, and every time the White Sox homered, Roman candles would fly out of the mortars while members of a fireworks crew behind the board shot off bombs and rockets. For special occasions, the scoreboard's loudspeakers would reverberate to the strains of the Hallelujah chorus from Handel's *Messiah*.

Veeck's influence on the game is still felt—in the ivy he planted on the Wrigley Field wall as a young man, in the face of the laughing Indian Cleveland still employs as a symbol, in the scoreboard that still explodes after every White Sox homer. He was a maverick and a character—he would throw his cigarette butts into the hollow of his wooden leg—and baseball needed him more than it ever realized. After Veeck sold the White Sox in the '60s because of illness, pitcher Early Wynn asked the *Chicago Sun-Times* to print this letter:

"Dear Bill, I'm a better pitcher than I am a letter writer—at least I hope I am—but I'm writing now, not just for myself but for all the other fellows who have played and worked for you on the White Sox . . . I know I speak for all of us when I say that you've been a helluva lot more than just a boss. You've been a wonderful friend. All of us will always cherish your friendship. . . . The most important thing, though, is that you enjoyed it. . . . You enjoyed seeing someone stand at home plate and discover that he had just won two dozen live lobsters or a barrel of chocolate-covered butterflies. You weren't the only one who laughed. We all did."

But not all of his employees liked Veeck's shenanigans. In spring training of 1952, shortly after Veeck signed Rogers Hornsby to a three-year contract as manager, the Browns were working out when a carload of performing midgets came into the field. The ferocious Hornsby told them to leave and not come back—in the process, picking up one midget and throwing him over the railing.

In his autobiography, Hornsby recalled, "We didn't have any more midgets around after that. But of course I didn't stay for all three years."

PETE REISER

Charles Einstein wrote that "Pete Reiser busted more fences than busted him—though the margin wasn't very big." He was an exceptional talent from the moment he broke in, but a series of injuries—mostly from collisions with outfield walls—soon blunted Reiser's potential.

The horrifying crash into the center-field wall that most severely hampered his career came on a drive by Enos Slaughter in July 1942. The Dodgers had a 13½-game lead at the time, but this game, against St. Louis, was in the thirteenth inning. After making the catch and slamming head first into the concrete wall, Reiser dropped the ball, then somehow managed to pick it up and relay it to Pee Wee Reese before collapsing, unconscious.

After Reiser was hospitalized, his doctor told the newspapers he was out for the season, and in the hospital for a while. But Reiser got up out of his bed—"the room started to spin," he acknowledged—sneaked out of the hospital, took a train to Pittsburgh to catch up with the Dodgers, and went to the park.

He put on his uniform, but told Durocher he couldn't play. The manager wanted him on the bench, though, where Pirates manager Frank Frisch would see him, and maybe manipulate his pitching changes accordingly.

The game went into the fourteenth inning. Ken Heintzelman, a lefty, was pitching for the Pirates, with men on first and second. Durocher was out of pinch-hitters, and Reiser offered himself. He hit what looked like a possible triple to right center, scoring both runners, but collapsed rounding first. The Dodgers won the game, and the next day Reiser was back in the hospital.

Eventually, he returned to the lineup. But he wasn't the player he had been, having trouble both at the plate and in the outfield. In time, the Cardinals came from eight games back to take the pennant from the Dodgers. And several years later, Reiser told W. C. Heinz, "I'd say I lost the pennant for us that year."

Still, Reiser later insisted that, despite the 13½-game lead, he was right to take on the wall. No matter the circumstances, he told Donald Honig, "You slow up half a step, it's the beginning of your last game."

Reiser's .343 had won the National League batting title the year before and, at the time of his injury, 23 years old, he was hitting .380. He only once batted over .300 again.

The last great accomplishment of Reiser's career came in 1946, when he set a record by stealing home seven times. He always maintained, though, that he actually stole eight—once, against the Cubs, he slid in safely under a pitch from Chicago's Johnny Schmitz.

As Reiser recalled the incident to Donald Honig, umpire George Magerkurth threw up his thumb, yelled "You're out!", and in the next breath said, "Goddam, did I blow that one. Called you out, kid. Sorry."

LEO DUROCHER

For most of his career, Reiser's manager was Leo Durocher, the man who was also responsible for starting the careers of Jackie Robinson and Willie Mays. He was combative, independent, extremely bright, and extremely dislikable. Happy Chandler said, "He would hold the lamp while his mother was cutting wood."

Umpire Harry Wendelstedt was far blunter: "Call me anything," he said, "call me motherfucker, but don't call me Durocher. A Durocher is the lowest form of living matter."

And that was just after Durocher's twenty-fourth year as a big league manager, when he was sixty-nine years old.

Durocher's career in Brooklyn ended under two clouds: his one-year suspension for consorting with gamblers (a charge made by Larry MacPhail, as a way of striking at Rickey) in 1947, and his departure during the 1948 season to the hated Giants.

But while he was in Brooklyn, the fans loved him. Foremost among these was Hilda Chester, a leather-lunged denizen of

Ebbets Field who incessantly rang a cowbell she carried with her, knew all the players, never missed a game, and generally comported herself in the Ebbets fashion—which is to say, un-predictably.

In the early '40s, in the middle of a game, she shrieked "Hey, Reiser," and got the attention of the Dodgers center-fielder. Dropping a piece of paper onto the field from her perch in the bleachers, she asked Reiser to "give it to Leo."

As the inning ended and he came in from the field, Reiser chatted briefly with Brooklyn General manager Larry Mac-Phail, who sat in the box next to the home dugout. Finally, arriving on the bench, he gave Hilda's note to Durocher.

In the next inning, Whitlow Wyatt, who was pitching for Brooklyn, gave up a hard out and then a hit. Durocher pulled Wyatt, brought in Hugh Casey from the bullpen, and saw Casey get hit hard and virtually blow a big Dodgers lead.

After the game, after steaming behind the closed door in his office for several minutes, Durocher came out and screamed at Reiser: "Don't you *ever* give me another note from Mac-Phail as long as you play for me."

Reiser corrected his manager. "That note was from Hilda."

Durocher exploded. "From *Hilda!* You mean to say that wasn't from MacPhail?" The note, which Reiser hadn't looked at, read, "Get Casey hot, Wyatt's losing it."

MORE DODGERS

Durocher was succeeded in Brooklyn by Burt Shotton, an old Rickey retainer who ran his team while dressed in street clothes (he and Connie Mack were the last managers to eschew uni-forms). Shotton's successor was Charlie Dressen. Dressen was an excellent sign stealer, and like most such types he knew when his own team's signs were being stolen. Once when the Dodgers were playing Cincinnati, he came to the mound and told Kirby Higbe that the Reds were on to the Brooklyn sig-nal.

Higbe doubted Dressen, and before the next inning told his

catcher to signal for a curve on the first pitch, but to expect a fastball. Frank McCormick was leading off for the Reds, and Higbe threw a fastball right at his head. McCormick strode right into it, as if the pitch were going to break, and it hit him in the ear.

Higbe apologized to Dressen for doubting him, and that night, at the hospital, to McCormick for throwing at him.

After the Dodgers lost two straight pennants on the final day of the season in 1950 and 1951, Dressen allowed a magazine article entitled "It Won't Happen Again" to be published under his name.

Cautioned about the reckless assertion, Dressen said there was no risk at all: "The three grand [he received for the article] is found money. If the Dodgers lose this year, I'll be fired anyway."

Dressen once found himself without a warmed-up reliever when his starter lost control of the game. He brought Clyde King in from the bullpen, but King immediately showed he wasn't ready, loading the bases.

Trying to buy time for King to throw some warm-up pitches, Dressen had Pee Wee Reese feign a problem with his eye. But while Reese acted out his little show, with Jackie Robinson and Billy Cox assisting as he tried to get the imaginary something that was in his eye, the agreeable King left the mound to help out as well.

The most peculiar of Dressen's Dodgers was Billy Loes, an occasionally effective pitcher whose successes could not be attributed to his brain power. His most famous utterance, made during the 1952 Series, was his assertion that he had misplayed Vic Raschi's grounder because "I lost it in the sun." But perhaps more noteworthy was his public explanation of why the ball popped out of his glove during the same game, causing an automatic balk. "Too much spit," Loes said.

Just before that same Series began, a reporter asked a number of players for their predictions. Dressen read the next day that Loes thought the Yankees would win in seven. Nearly strangling on his disbelief, the manager confronted his pitcher, who acknowledged that he was, indeed, misquoted. "I picked 'em in six," he said.

COMMISSIONERS

Kenesaw Mountain Landis may have been a racist, was certainly a mountebank, and no one would challenge the assertion that he was as arrogant as a man could be. But no one was ever able to challenge Landis's independence and his absolute control of the baseball world.

Such was not the case with his successors; after Landis was gone, the owners would for the next forty years make it very clear who was in charge: They were. No one was more aware of this than the great Red Smith, who summarized the careers of the Judge's two immediate successors with stunning succinctness:

Smith on Happy Chandler: "Happy left office for reasons of health; that is, the owners got sick of him."

And Smith on Ford Frick: "As National League president, he'd often say, 'That's not in my jurisdiction.' As Commissioner, he'd say just as frequently, 'It's a league matter.' "

UNLIKELIES

Eddie Stanky was famous as the man "who couldn't run, hit or throw—all he could do was beat you." His techniques were best described by Branch Rickey, who liked to gather the Dodgers farmhands during spring training and ask, "If you had the bases loaded in the ninth with two out, and the pennant depended on it, who would you want to bat for you?"

The crowd would shout the expected names—DiMaggio, Williams, Musial—and Rickey would say, "You're wrong! You'd call in Ed Stanky! Eddie would get up to bat and throw dirt on the plate, the ump would go and clean it off. He'd throw dirt on the plate again, and the ump would clean it off again.

He'd take a swing back with his bat and hit the catcher in the mask, who by this time was so riled up he'd give the sign for a knockdown pitch that would make your hat stand up. Stanky'd take the pitch for ball one and proceed to laugh at the pitcher and scream how he couldn't throw a fastball. Then he'd get knocked down with Ball Two. He'd get on base using all these tricks."

Jackie Price was a facsimile of a shortstop who played in seven games for the Indians in 1946. But his real skills were of the performing variety: he could play catch while standing on his head, he could put two balls in his throwing hand and release them simultaneously, one a fastball and the other a curve; he could place three men several feet apart and in one motion throw a ball to each of them.

The man who brought him up to the big leagues, of course, was Bill Veeck, who used him as a pre- and post-game entertainer in Cleveland. Among Price's non-athletic idiosyncrasies was a fondness for snakes, an attachment so binding that he would actually wear live snakes around his waist as belts. "Jackie was one of the most identifiable men I have ever known," Veeck once wrote. "I mean, he was the one with the snake around his waist."

When Veeck actually put Price on the Cleveland active roster, manager Lou Boudreau was less than happy about it; though Boudreau would learn to play along with Veeck's gags and promotions, he was at the time still a serious young man who mostly wanted to win baseball games. Thus it was utterly in keeping with the Veeckian atmosphere that when the Indians were on a train during spring training in 1947, Price released the snake from his belt loops in a crowded dining car. As the resultant turmoil peaked, the conductor accosted Price and demanded to know his name.

Naturally enough, the player answered, "Lou Boudreau," and at the next stop two detectives tried to throw the Cleveland manager off the train.

One of baseball's very best autobiographies is Kirby Higbe's *The High Hard One,* a bruisingly honest account of the fastball pitcher's checkered career, his alcoholism, and his brushes with the law. In it he recounts his precipitous descent from the majors. Released by the Giants, he went to Minneapolis; from there, down to Double A Montgomery; then to Rock Hill, in the Carolina League. About Rock Hill, Higbe wrote, "That was a poor excuse for a ball club at Rock Hill. They were buying players for as little as $100 when you couldn't get a good batboy for that. . . . We had a third baseman whose arm was so bad he would field a ground ball and toss it to the pitcher for a relay to first. He was hitting .250 and was, outside of me, our top hitter."

Finally, the former major leaguer, who had once enjoyed seven straight years winning in double figures, found himself in 1953 at Forest City, in the Western Carolina League, his last stop in professional baseball. In 1955, a friend asked him to pitch for his semi-pro team. "I told him I hadn't thrown a ball for nearly two years," Higbe wrote. But, he added, "I needed the $25." He was forty years old.

Van Lingle Mungo threw as hard as he drank, which means that he threw very hard indeed. But his fondness for anything alcoholic didn't help his stamina any, and he rarely could throw very hard for very long. Consequently, when they were teammates with the Giants, Mungo and relief pitcher Ace Adams were as if an entry in a thoroughbred race: Mungo would start, falter, and be replaced by Adams. It became so commonplace that one spring Adams wired New York management in advance of his arrival at their training base, "Will report Tuesday in good shape and ready to relieve Mungo in the fifth inning."

Blix Donnelly was a right-handed pitcher with a formidable curveball and not much else who began his career with the Cardinals in 1944. In an early 1946 game in which Donnelly was pitching, St. Louis manager Eddie Dyer came out of the dugout to make a change. But as Dyer advanced toward the mound, the pitcher told his manager that if he took another step he'd hit him between the eyes with the ball.

Donnelly stayed in the game; he was shipped to the Phillies not long after.

He was chiefly celebrated for his immensely slow, arching, too-tantalizing blooper pitch, the "Eephus," but Rip Sewell was also a tough, competitive player. When Joe Garagiola was a rookie with the Cardinals, he was knocked down by a Sewell fastball; angered, he determined to bunt on the first-base side so that he might throw a body block at Sewell as the pitcher covered first.

But Sewell didn't present the target. Anticipating Garagiola's intent, he headed toward first but veered sharply right before he got there, clobbering Garagiola as the young catcher raced down the line.

SATCHEL PAIGE

Late in Jackie Robinson's rookie season, Bill Veeck integrated the American League when he signed outfielder Larry Doby. And the next year he brought to the majors black baseball's greatest star, Satchel Paige.

According to both Dizzy Dean and Charlie Gehringer, Paige was the greatest pitcher who ever lived. He was as confident of this fact as anyone, as evidenced by an incident that took place in Pittsburgh on July 21, 1942. Pitching against the Homestead Grays, Paige found himself leading 4-0, with two out in the seventh inning. Then the Grays' next batter, Jerry Benjamin, tripled.

Paige called his first baseman, Buck O'Neil, over to the mound and informed him he was going to walk the next two hitters, load the bases, and pitch to Josh Gibson—the Babe Ruth of the black leagues. As he threw four straight balls to Buck Leonard, who batted just before Gibson, he called out to the Homestead star in the on-deck circle, "I'm gonna put Buck on and pitch to you."

Before his first pitch, Paige told Gibson he was going to throw a fastball. Gibson watched it pass, for strike one. He told Gibson another fastball was coming, and again Gibson let it by, for strike two. And on the third pitch, Paige whipped another fastball, right past Gibson's knees. The inning was over.

In Oakland, the season before Joe DiMaggio came up, the Yankees sent a scout to see him play against a Paige-led barnstorming team. Richard Donovan said the Yankee scout wired the home office, "DIMAGGIO ALL WE HOPED HE'D BE. HIT SATCH ONE FOR FOUR."

When Veeck signed him in '48, Paige was already past forty. In *The Sporting News,* editor Taylor Spink wrote, "To bring in a pitching 'rookie' of Paige's age casts a reflection on the entire scheme of operation in the major leagues. To sign a hurler at Paige's age is to demean the standards of baseball in the big circuits. Further complicating the situation is the suspicion that if Satchel were white, he would not have drawn a second thought from Veeck."

As Veeck would later write, "If Satch were white, of course, he would have been in the majors twenty-five years earlier, and the question would not have been before the House." And as it turned out, Paige won six games and lost only one for the pennant-bound Indians that season—and after each victory, Veeck would send a telegram to Spink, adjusted to the circumstances: "NINE INNINGS. FOUR HITS, FIVE STRIKEOUTS. WINNING PITCHER: PAIGE. DEFINITELY IN LINE FOR THE SPORTING NEWS AWARD AS ROOKIE OF THE YEAR."

There is no end to Satchel Paige stories, just as there was in his lifetime no end to writers who tried to pry them out of him. Though generally obliging, Paige could at times get resistant. According to Richard Donovan, when Paige was finishing up his second career, the one in the major leagues, he said about all the questioning, "Who's gonna straighten out 2,500 ball games in my head? How many cow pastures you played on, Satchel? they wanta know. How many bus rides you took? Who put the spike scars on your shinbone? Why is your feet flat? Who was it offered you $50 to pitch a triple-header that time?

"Man," he concluded, "the past is a long and twisty road."

"THE SHOT HEARD 'ROUND THE WORLD"

Of all baseball events, the one that requires the least retelling is Bobby Thomson's home run that won the pennant playoff for the Giants over the Dodgers in 1951. There is little to add to the well-known tale of how the Giants had come from 13½ games back on August 12 to tie Brooklyn for the pennant; that the combatants split the first two games of the best-of-three playoff; that rookie Willie Mays was shaking nervously in the on-deck circle, fearful that he'd have to come to bat after Thomson; that pitcher Ralph Branca, untimely brought in from the bullpen, had given up a home run to Thomson two days earlier; that Clem Labine, who had the day before struck out Thomson with the bases loaded, was available in the bullpen when Charlie Dressen made his decision to go with Branca.

The words of Red Smith in the *New York Herald Tribune* the next day best summarize the afternoon of October 3: "Now it is done," Smith wrote, "now the story ends. And there is no way to tell it. The art of fiction is dead. Reality has strangled invention. Only the utterly impossible, the inexpressibly fantastic, can ever be plausible again."

WILLIE MAYS

When the nineteen-year-old Willie Mays was in Minneapolis in his second season of organized baseball, the Giants sent the old Brooklyn catcher Hank DeBerry to report on his progress. This is what DeBerry, who had been in professional baseball for three decades, wrote:

"Sensational. Is the outstanding player on the Minneapolis club and probably in all the minor leagues for that matter. He is now on one of the best hitting streaks imaginable. Hits all pitches and hits to all fields. Hits the ball where it is pitched as good as any player seen in many days. Everything he does is sensational. He has made the most spectacular catches. Runs and throws with the best of them. Naturally, he has some faults, some of which are: charges low-hit balls too much, runs a bit with head down. There have been a few times when his manager needed a rope. When he starts somewhere, he means to get there, hell bent for election. Slides hard, plays hard. He is a sensation and just about as popular with local fans as he can be—a real celebrity. The Louisville pitchers knocked him down plenty, but it seemed to have no effect on him at all. This player is the best prospect in America. It was a banner day for the Giants when this boy was signed!"

Mays was hitting .477 for Minneapolis in 1951 when Leo Durocher brought him up to New York. In his first 26 at bats, he managed only one hit, but by June had his average up to .314.

Still, it was a defensive play that established Mays as the extraordinary talent that he was. In August the Giants were playing Brooklyn, the score tied in the eighth inning with one out and Dodgers on first and third. Carl Furillo hit a drive to deep right center; the man on third, Billy Cox, playing cautiously, tagged.

When Mays made the catch after a long sprint, he was heading toward right and had to pivot against his momentum to make his throw. Cox, a fast runner, dashed for the plate but Mays's throw, which carried to the plate on the fly, beat him there: double play.

Furillo, celebrated for his own arm, said, "He'll never make a throw like that again."

Well, not exactly. First game, 1954 World Series, the Polo Grounds. Vic Wertz at bat, Don Liddle pitching. Score tied 2-2, two men on. Wertz sends a monstrous drive to straight-away center field, and Willie Mays makes a catch known forever after as The Catch.

Mays insists he never said, "I don't rate 'em—I just catch 'em." But he did talk about The Catch:

"As for there being anything difficult about the catch, though, the answer is there wasn't. Any ball you go a long way for is exciting to the fans in the stands, because they're not looking at you when you get your jump on it—they're looking at the hitter. But I'd gotten the good jump, and I had running room, and the ball stayed up for me. I didn't have to pick it off the grass, I didn't have to avoid another fielder, I didn't have to crash the wall, I didn't have to jump in the air, I didn't have to gauge the wind (there was none) or some eccentric thing the ball itself did (it didn't rise, fall, curve, swerve, or bend too much).

"I doubt there's a day goes by in the big leagues but some outfielder doesn't make a more difficult play than I did on that Wertz ball." But the throw—the brilliant, dead-on-the-money throw into the infield, a throw that carried more than 300 feet in the air—may have been the greatest play Mays ever made.

In fact, Mays threw as well as he did everything else—which is to say, as well as it could be done. In Arizona in 1958, Giants Manager Bill Rigney gathered his rookie infielders and told them, "If they hit a ball to the center fielder, please go to a base. Don't confuse the issue by asking me why. Just go there." Rigney's timing was apt: in that day's exhibition game, with one out and a man on first, Orlando Cepeda saw Mays execute a somersault as he dove for a sinking liner. "The next thing I knew," Cepeda said later, "there was a baseball in my face. I threw up my glove to protect myself. Nobody could make a catch like that and come up throwing."

"The ball ricocheted off Cepeda's glove," wrote Charles Einstein. "The runner advanced. The official scorer, an understanding man, gave the error to Mays."

Hitting? Twice he hit more than 50 home runs. He scored more than 100 runs in a season 13 times, knocked in more than 100 ten times. For one 12-year stretch, he hit under .300 twice, but never under .290. That he was an all-purpose talent was demonstrated by a writer's comment after the 1959 All-Star game, in Pittsburgh. Mays knocked in the winning run in the bottom of the eighth with a long triple into the distant reaches of immense Forbes Field—a ball hit so hard, in such a large park, that Bob Stevens wrote, "The only man who could have caught it, hit it."

Mays is one of several ballplayers who have "written" more than one autobiography; for some, like Mickey Mantle, it simply seems a way to make a few dollars every several years. The definitive Mays book was an as-told-to set to paper by the gifted Charles Einstein, who wrote for the San Francisco *Examiner*. In the season they worked together on *Willie Mays: My Life In and Out of Baseball*, Einstein would interview Mays periodically about his career.

When Einstein repaired to his typewriter in the off-season to put the book together, he called Mays to clairify a few matters. "Hello, Willie? This is Charley."

There was silence at the other end of the line. Then, "Charley who?"

"Charley Einstein." Another pause. "You know, Charley Einstein, who is doing the book with you."

And Mays responded, "What book?"

BONUS BABIES

The bonus babies were the creatures of bidding wars between clubs—usually, high school boys with great promise. The owners, unable to control their crazed desire to get their hands on raw talent, would spend whatever it took. Except in a few cases—Al Kaline, Sandy Koufax—they usually spent poorly, too.

One of the most well rewarded of the bonus babies was Dave Nicholson, whose major league career was primarily distinguished by his tying or setting major league records in five categories, all of them pertaining to strikeouts. The home runs that were supposed to punctuate his prodigious strikeout streaks proved all too rare, and neither did Nicholson make up on defense for what he cost on offense. The Cleveland sportswriter Gordon Cobbledick, reporting on a particularly exasperating spring training session in which Nicholson worked, however vainly, on his fielding, wrote, "He is improving in the outfield. To be sure, he hasn't caught a ball yet, but he's getting closer to them."

Twice the owners tried to control their appetites for the bonus babies. First they instituted a rule that required the signing club to keep the bonus baby on the major league roster for two full seasons; rare was the Kaline who could enter a major league lineup without minor league seasoning. Soon many major league teams used up valuable roster spots and retarded the progress of the bonus babies by having them spend two years on the bench before going down to the minors.

The bonus baby system wasn't truly dead until 1965. That year, making effective use of the game's exemption from antitrust laws, baseball instituted the first draft of amateur talent—the clubs protecting themselves from themselves.

THE RICKEY PIRATES

After Walter O'Malley squeezed him out of Brooklyn, Branch Rickey found his way to Pittsburgh. In time, the team he built there would win the 1960 World Series. But in the early days, it seemed unlikely that the Pirates could win a sandlot championship.

The team Rickey inherited was a remnant of the 1948 Pittsburgh team that had been called "the casino on wheels." Pitcher Tiny Bonham said that "when we pull into Las Vegas nobody gets off because there's more action on the train." Such behavior was inevitable; in 1947, manager Billy Herman had said, "Rules are made to be broken, so there won't be any rules."

Herman's replacement, Billy Meyer, won 83 games with "the casino on wheels" gang, then 71 in 1949, 57 in 1950, a surprising 64 in '51—and then 42 in 1952.

That '52 team had the worst marks in the league in batting average, slugging average, errors, fielding average, complete games, saves, and earned run average—the first team ever to compile a clean sweep (the '42 Phillies had been the first to take last in six of the seven categories). Their infield, whose tallest member was 5'11", was called "The Singing Midgets." The team as a whole was called "The Rickeydinks." Joe Garagiola, traded from the Cardinals, said it was like "getting out of a Cadillac and into a wheelbarrow." When they finished 22½ games out of seventh—54½ out of first—Rickey announced that his goal was a pennant in 1955.

In 1955 the Pirates finished last for the fourth consecutive year. Rickey acknowledged that "I force-fed the youngsters and it failed." By then manager Fred Haney had taken to wearing a batting helmet on the bench—he had bumped his head too often on the dugout roof.

But '56 dawned bright, and Rickey now fielded a team that included, wrote Marshall Smith, "a mink trapper, a Mormon minister, a man who studied two years for the Catholic Priesthood, a former maitre d'hotel of a swank Palm Springs nightclub, an x-ray technician, two players who are refugees from pro football, half an All-American basketball team, and a man who describes himself as the nation's only professional foot-racer beside Wes Santee."

It all worked. The '56 Pirates finished seventh.

ROBERTO CLEMENTE

But those Pirates did have a young Puerto Rican outfielder named Roberto Clemente. He hit only seven home runs in '56— he had only 26 through his first five full seasons—but he soon became Pittsburgh's greatest postwar player. Clemente only became a Pirate because of Dodger arrogance: confident that they could hide Clemente from the eyes of other scouts, Brooklyn officials left him unprotected from the major league draft (the outfielders they held onto were Snider, Furillo, Sandy Amoros, and Gino Cimoli).

But Branch Rickey, who still had good sources in the Dodger organization, dispatched his son to Havana to report on Clemente. Branch, Jr., wired his father: "Clemente is undoubtedly good draft at 4000 or even at 10,0000." The Pirates got him for $4,000, and he remained with the team until his death while on a charity mission to Nicaragua in 1972.

Dodgers official Al Campanis later said, "He was the most complete ballplayer I ever saw." His .317 lifetime average remains the highest compiled by any right-handed hitter in the post-World War II era.

LOPEZ'S INDIANS

The only two times the Yankees didn't win the pennant between 1949 and 1964, Al Lopez did. The manager of the Indians in '54 and the White Sox in '59, Lopez was, inevitably, a protégé of Casey Stengel, for whom he'd caught in Brooklyn and Boston. Lopez, in fact, caught more major league games than anybody ever had, until Bob Boone broke his record in the 1980s. And in all the games he caught, he dropped exactly two foul popups.

In a profile of Lopez for *Sports Illustrated,* Gilbert Rogin wrote, "In the course of time, Al Lopez, the manager of the Chicago White Sox, has been called, by various enlightened members of the working press, the Señor, the Stylish Señor, the Good Señor, the Happy Hidalgo, the Spanish Don, the Clever Caballero, the Cagey Castilian, the Calm Castilian, the Happy Castilian, the Cast-Iron Castilian, the Capable and Courtly Castilian, the Personable Skipper and Frolicsome Al. . . . For the most part, these sobriquets fairly delineate Lopez, and furthermore, inform those who might assume his name to be of Eskimo origin of his true lineage."

The Indians won in '54 because they had one of the finest pitching staffs ever assembled: Bob Lemon (23-7), Early Wynn (23-11), Mike Garcia (19-8), Bob Feller, Hal Newhouser, and two superlative young relievers, Don Mossi and Ray Narleski.

Lemon was a converted third baseman-outfielder. Bill Dickey had seen him pitch in Hawaii during World War II and told Cleveland player-manager Lou Boudreau that Lemon should be pitching on a permanent basis. On opening day in 1946, Lemon was the center-fielder for the Indians, and he made a game-saving catch to give Feller the victory. But his hitting, alas, made the decision to switch him a little easier.

Courtly off the field, Early Wynn was ferocious out on the mound. Bill Veeck once said to him, "You'd hit your poor old mother."

"Only if she were digging in," said Wynn.

Although Wynn never actually pitched to his mother, he did pitch to his son. "I was pitching batting practice to the kid," said Wynn, with a certain amount of paternal pride, "and he hit my outside curve against the left-field wall." Wynn knocked him down with the next pitch.

Wynn could do more than pitch; he could write. While many ballplayers had newspaper columns, most of them were ghost-written and innocuous. Wynn wrote his own column for the *Cleveland News,* in which he took shots at visiting managers like Casey Stengel and even at his own front office. After he blasted the Indians for trying to trade him, they did trade him, along with Al Smith, to the White Sox for Minnie Minoso and Fred Hatfield. Chicago papers were soon bidding for Wynn's sportswriting services. Naturally, the *Cleveland News* sports department was upset at having lost a valued member of its staff, so Frank Lane, the general manager of the Indians, sent them a telegram in Spanish. Translated, it read: "Understand you have lost Early Wynn of your writing staff. This is to advise you that I am available and will be pleased to do a column for you at the same salary you paid Wynn. All you will need is a translator. When do I start? Saturnino Orestes (Minnie) Minoso."

Both Wynn and Minoso went on to long careers. Wynn won his 300th game when he was forty-three, and Minoso played in five different decades, although his last appearance in 1980, when he was fifty-eight, was a publicity stunt—engineered of course by Veeck, who owned the White Sox at the time.

The flamboyant Minoso, who liked to get hit by pitches, was a very popular player wherever he went, and many stories are told about him, most of them having to do with his command of English. In 1958 he was late for spring training with the Indians in Arizona, as was his annual custom. One night Nate Wallack, the club's PR man, got a phone call from Cuba, some 1,800 miles to the southeast. "I no mean to be late," Minoso told Wallack. "I be there. Only I can get no plane reservation. No room on the planes." Wallack offered to work something out. "I no place to stay," said Minoso. Wallack said there was plenty of room at the hotel.

After a small silence, Minoso asked, "Rain there?" Wallack wondered why Minnie would be asking about the weather, but he told him that the sun was shining every day. "No, not rain," said Minoso. "Rain. Ballplayer Larry Rain. He there?" Taking the non sequitur in stride, Wallack said, "Oh, Larry Raines. Yes, he's here." "Okay," said Minoso, buoyed by the social note. "I be there right away."

Minoso's popularity on the Indians was exceeded only by that of Rocky Colavito, a Bronx-born slugger with matinee idol looks. Cleveland bobby-soxers swooned at the sight of the Rock, and it didn't hurt that he hit 83 homers in '58 and '59. The motto in Cleveland became "Don't Knock the Rock." But the day before the start of the 1960 season, Frank Lane traded Colavito, the AL home run champion in '59, to Detroit for outfielder Harvey Kuenn, the league's batting champ in '59. It was one of the most talked-about trades ever, and to make matters worse for Lane in Cleveland, he was quoted as saying, "It was like trading hamburger for steak."

Lane recalled the reaction some years later. "When I traded him, they wanted to lynch me. I went back to my hotel that day and there was this dummy hanging in effigy from a lamp post. 'Frank Lane,' it said on the dummy. I guess they wanted it to be reality instead of effigy. They must have thought, here's our handsome Rocky gone and all we've got is an ugly slob of a general manager."

It turned out to be a bad trade for Lane. Kuenn lasted only one year with the Indians before they dealt him to the San Francisco Giants, while Colavito averaged 39 homers a year the next few years for Detroit. Said Detroit General Manager Bill DeWitt, "I like hamburger."

WHITEY AND MICKEY

Whitey Ford grew up right in New York City, in the Astoria section of Queens. Signed by scout Paul Krichell, Ford received $7,000 in two installments. When he got the first installment, he cashed the check and then went to Times Square to flash the roll. The police tried to arrest him on suspicion of something or other, and Ford had to call his mother so she could explain to them how he came by the money.

The Yankees called him Slick, for the expected reason: Ford cheated, or (to put it more politely) he practiced gamesmanship. He often loaded up the baseball, and later in his career, he wore a ring with a rasp on it to cut the ball.

But Ford won 236 regular season games for the Yankees, and another ten in the World Series, because he knew how to pitch: his winning percentage of .690 is third on the all-time list, and his ERA over 16 years was 2.75. He had fun doing it, too. The week after Billy Martin was traded to Kansas City, the Athletics came to New York, and Ford found himself with a big lead and a shutout going in the ninth. Martin came up, and Ford threw a big, slow curve for a called strike. As he wound up for the next pitch, Ford yelled to Martin, "Same pitch." Martin hit the second big, slow curve into the seats.

Ford's confidence was such that on the days he was the starter he would set up a table for the men in the bullpen, place on it a red checkered tablecloth and a candle in a Chianti bottle, and make sure the relievers all had hero sandwiches. He figured since they weren't going to work that day, they might as well be comfortable.

Mickey Mantle came from the mining town of Commerce, Oklahoma, near the Ozark Mountains in the northeast corner of the state. His father Elven, better known as Mutt, was a zinc and lead miner and a good ballplayer in his day, and he named his son after Mickey Cochrane. Tom Greenwade, the Yankees scout who discovered Mantle, once told a writer, "I don't quite know how to put it, but what I'm trying to tell you is that the first time I saw Mantle I knew how Paul Krichell felt when he first saw Lou Gehrig. He knew that as a scout he'd never have another moment like it."

Mantle was a shortstop back then, with great speed, great power, and the ability to hit from both sides of the plate. Stengel fell in love with him, as did everyone else who ever saw him play. Casey moved him to the outfield because he already had Rizzuto at short, and he didn't want to wait for Mantle to mature in the minors. So he rushed him, and Mantle went north with the club in '51. Mantle was overmatched the first few months, and hot-headed to boot, so Stengel had to send him down to Kansas City.

The slump continued in Kansas City, and after going 0-for-22, Mickey made the famous phone call to his father: "I don't think I can play baseball any more." The senior Mantle showed up in Kansas City the next day, barging into his son's room and throwing Mickey's clothes into a suitcase. Asked a bewildered Mantle, "What're you doing?"

"Packing. You're going home. You're going to work in the mines, that's what we'll do. You can work back down there."

Mantle ended up hitting .360 for Kansas City, and went back to New York to stay. He later said of the confrontation with his father, "That was the turning point of my life."

In the beginning, Mantle was pure country boy. He roomed with Hank Bauer and Johnny Hopp in an apartment over the Stage Delicatessen on Seventh Avenue in Manhattan, and Bauer, the ex-Marine with the face that someone once said looked like a clenched fist, introduced Mickey to the good life, which included countless meals at the Stage. Mantle gained 25 pounds that first year on the sandwiches, matzoh ball soup, and cheesecake from downstairs.

In 1956 Mantle hit .353 with 52 homers and 130 RBIs to lead both leagues in all three categories. Only three men—Hornsby, Gehrig, and Williams—had done it before. He had finally lived up to his promise, and he did it wearing a brace on his right knee much of the time. Early Wynn described an encounter with Mantle at the All-Star Game: "I watched him dress. I watched him bandage that knee—that whole leg—and I saw what he had to go through every day to play. And now I'll never be able to say enough in praise. Seeing those legs, his power becomes unbelievable."

The commercial offers came pouring in after the Triple Crown, and Mantle could have become a rich man. But while Berra had a Midas touch, the naive Mantle invested in losing venture after losing venture. Right after the '56 season, a man named C. Roy Williams approached Mickey and his wife Merlyn about an insurance company he was starting, the Will Rogers Insurance Company. It sounded natural enough—"I never met a man I couldn't insure"—and Williams offered Mantle half of the company for $5,000. He had just gotten his World Series check and had $10,000 in the bank, so he agreed to Williams's proposal and gave him a check.

A few weeks later, the FBI showed up to inform Mantle that C. Roy Williams was an escaped fugitive, who had dreamed up the insurance scam in prison while reading about Mantle's banner year.

Mantle always kept a sense of humor about such things, though. In his Hall of Fame induction speech in 1974, he recalled a fried-chicken chain that carried his name but wouldn't use the slogan he had thought up: "To get a better piece of chicken, you'd have to be a rooster."

UTILITY MEN

Every team has players like him: a useful defensive talent with limited offensive skills. Sometimes the utility infielder has a little power, often a modicum of speed. But the apotheosis of the utility man, Dick Schofield, had neither. All he had was longevity.

His career began with the Cardinals in 1953, when he signed a $40,000 bonus contract. In the ensuing 19 years, he played for eight different teams. Only three times did he play in more than 95 games. His lifetime batting average was .227; he stole only 12 bases and hit only 21 home runs.

The road ended for Schofield with the Angels, who released him after a seven-inning tryout in 1972. His uniform number with California was 58—which led pitcher Eddie Fisher to ask, "Is that your age, or the number of teams you've been with?"

Schofield was determined; his contemporary, Rocky Bridges, was nuts. He played eleven years for seven different clubs, and described the utility man's plight in one perfect aphorism: "My wife had to write to me care of Ford Frick."

Rocky's most striking season was probably 1956, with the Reds, when he was deployed almost exclusively for defense and pinch running duties: he had but 19 at bats in 71 games. Thus it was somewhat understandable when he hit a home run in 1961—his first in two years—and said, "I'm still behind Babe Ruth's record, but I've been sick. It really wasn't very dramatic. No little boy in the hospital asked me to hit one. I didn't promise it to my kid for his birthday, and my wife will be too shocked to appreciate it. I hit it for me."

Phil Linz was a Yankees utility infielder of no special accomplishment, remembered more for playing a harmonica than for playing baseball. In 1964 in the middle of the pennant race, on a bus ride from Comiskey Park to O'Hare International, quiet reigned; New York had just dropped a double-header to the White Sox. Linz, who was in the back of the bus, pulled out a harmonica he was learning to play and quietly tooted "Mary Had a Little Lamb," the only song he knew. Berra, the Yankees manager at the time, shouted toward the back, "Knock it off." Linz didn't hear him, so he asked Mickey Mantle what the manager had said. "He said to play it louder," said Mantle.

Which Linz did. Berra went to the back of the bus and told Linz, "Shove that thing up your ass," then knocked the harmonica out of his hand. The instrument hit Joe Pepitone on the knee, and Pepi yelled in mock pain. Soon everybody but Berra was laughing.

After Berra returned to his seat, Mantle retrieved the harmonica and said to Whitey Ford, who was sitting across the aisle, "It looks like I'm going to be managing this club pretty soon. You can be my third-base coach. And here's what we'll do. One toot, that's a bunt. Two toots, that's a hit and run."

Linz was fined $200. But he also got a $20,000 endorsement contract from a harmonica company.

AARON, BANKS, KLU, AND STRETCH

No player has ever enjoyed a career of such sustained excellence as Henry Aaron. He obliterated Babe Ruth's career home-run record without ever hitting more than 44 homers in a season. His lifetime hit total is the third highest in history, even though he managed 200 hits only three times in his career (by contrast, the two men ahead of him—Pete Rose and Ty Cobb—had ten and nine such seasons respectively). When he was 39, Aaron batted .301—*and* hit 40 home runs.

Aaron was never especially colorful, and his unrelenting consistency had the peculiar effect of diminishing his light—an Aaron season of 35 homers, 120 RBIs, and a .310 average was merely typical. But to Aaron himself, there was no question what he was accomplishing: "I came to the Braves on business," he said, "and I intended to see that business was good as long as I could."

The Cubs of the '50s were nearly as woeful as the Pirates. Chicago newspaperman Warren Brown, sympathizing with Cubs manager Phil Cavarretta, wrote, "Cavarretta should get a bonus for watching the Cubs every day." At least one player was sad to leave the Cubs, though: traded to Philadelphia before the 1955 season, pitcher Dave Cole complained, "They're the only team I can beat."

If nothing else, at least from late 1953 on the Cubs had Ernie Banks. He was a shy, awkward kid from Texas.

"During my half month stay with the Cubs in September,

1953," he said years later, "I met more white people than I had known in all my 22 years." But in time he would become the only shortstop to lead his league in both fielding percentage and home runs; one of the few men to play 1,000 games at two different positions; and a two-time MVP with a mediocre club.

By the time Banks retired, he had amassed 512 home runs for a team that never finished first. But as Jimmie Dykes had said years before, "Without Banks, the Cubs would finish in Albuquerque."

Once, when Leo Durocher was asked who he thought the strongest man in the National League was, he suggested Gil Hodges. "What about Kluszewski?," someone asked. "Kluszewski!," Durocher shouted. "'Hell, I thought we were talking about human beings!"

Umpire Larry Goetz, describing Ted Kluszewski as a hitter: "The first man in the history of the game to be killed by a batted ball will be an innocent stranger. He will be walking down the street in back of Crosley Field in Cincinnati and he will be hit on the head by a ball driven out of the park by Ted Kluszewski."

As strong as he was, as hard as he swung, Kluszewski very rarely struck out; in 1954, he hit 49 home runs, batted .326, and struck out only 35 times. A sudden loss of power after the 1956 season kept him out of the Hall of Fame; still he had four straight seasons with more than 35 home runs, and retired with a lifetime average of .298.

Fortunately for those who would cross him, Klu was as mild temperamentally as he was physically imposing. The only time they ever saw him angry, teammates said, was when Milwaukee's Ernie Johnson threw behind his head. Kluszewski dragged a bunt on the next pitch and came down hard with his spikes on Johnson, who was covering first. Johnson lost his temper, but then reconsidered: "I looked at him standing there, just waiting for me, and said to myself, 'You're smarter than this.' "

When he arrived in San Francisco in 1959 to begin a career that would yield 521 home runs and 1555 RBIs, Willie McCovey's impact was immediate: in his first game, he hit two singles and two triples. In his first seven games, he had three home runs, nine runs batted in, and a .467 average. After McCovey's first few months in the league, Robin Roberts said, "He hit everything I threw." And Lew Burdette summarized "the book" on McCovey: "He hits curves, sliders, and fastballs."

And so he did for the rest of his long career. But to McCovey himself, his most memorable moment came in failure: in the ninth inning of the seventh game of the 1962 World Series, with two outs, the tying and winning runs in scoring position, he nailed a line shot toward right field. But Yankees second baseman Bobby Richardson stood right in its path and the game and the Series were over.

When McCovey was inducted into the Hall of Fame he said, "People ask me how I'd like to be remembered. I tell them I'd like to be remembered as the guy who hit the line drive over Bobby Richardson's head."

OTHER YANKEES

Stengel liked Phil Rizzuto a lot more than Rizzuto liked Stengel. The little shortstop had given him the best year of his life, 1950, when he was the American League MVP. But by 1956 Rizzuto was only a spare part, and an expendable one at that. In those days, the Yankees could afford to look weeks ahead to the World Series, and Stengel decided he needed a left-handed hitting outfielder to do battle against the National League-leading Dodgers. The one they wanted was Enos Slaughter, and they had to activate him before September 1 to make him eligible for the Series roster. Which meant that somebody else had to go.

Rizzuto was called into Stengel's office, and, he said, "I couldn't imagine what he wanted." General Manager George

Weiss was there, too, and the two men told Rizzuto about the chance to get Slaughter and the problem they faced. They asked Rizzuto to look over the roster and suggest who might be dropped. Rizzuto naively offered up the names of a spare catcher and a spare pitcher, and Stengel patiently explained why he needed those men. Then it dawned on Rizzuto, and before Weiss could explain that they would keep him on salary and restore him to the roster after September 1, Phil was out the door. He took off his uniform, got dressed, and left the stadium. His playing career was over.

After Slaughter joined the club, he hit .289 in 24 games, then hit .350 against the Dodgers in the Series.

The only man to pitch a perfect game—or a no-hitter, for that matter—in World Series history was an unlikely candidate for immortality. Don Larsen was a 3-21 pitcher for the Orioles in 1954, and although he was 11-5 for the Yankees in 1956, his real claim to fame that season came in spring training when he fell asleep at the wheel and wrapped his car around a tree. The Brooklyn Dodgers had knocked Larsen out of the box in the second inning of the second game of the Series, and many people questioned Stengel's decision to come back with him in Game 5.

It took awhile for the 64,519 fans in Yankee Stadium to sense what was happening. In the second inning, Jackie Robinson hit a sharp grounder to the left side that eluded third baseman Andy Carey but ended up in the glove of shortstop Gil McDougald, who nabbed Robinson at first. It was the first of several close calls Larsen would have that afternoon. Using a no-windup delivery, he had the Dodgers baffled. Mantle's solo homer off Sal Maglie had put the Yankees ahead 1-0 in the fourth. In the fifth, Gil Hodges hit a shot to deep left-center, but Mantle caught it at the last instant.

When the Yankees returned to their dugout after the seventh, with the score now 2-0, nothing was said but everything was understood. Infielder Billy Hunter politely asked Mantle to move down the bench since Hunter had been sitting in that particular spot all afternoon, and Mantle complied. Larsen ducked into the runway for a smoke, and when Mantle passed, Larsen asked, "Do you think I'll make it?" Mantle didn't answer.

In the eighth, Larsen got Robinson, Hodges, and Sandy Amoros on easy outs. In the ninth, Carl Furillo fouled off four pitches, then flied out to right. Roy Campanella hit a loud foul, then an easy bouncer to Martin at second. Dale Mitchell, a lifetime .314 hitter recently acquired from Cleveland, came up to hit for Maglie, the last chance. With the count 2-and-2, Larsen threw a fastball on the outside part of the plate. Home plate umpire Babe Pinelli could have gone either way, and indeed he seemed to take an extra split-second. But he raised his arm. Strike three.

Berra rushed out to the mound to give Larsen an airborne bear hug. The Yankees still had to win one more game in the Series, which they did, but the celebration for Larsen rivaled any seventh game victory party. Forgotten in the madness was Pinelli, who wept unashamedly. He had been planning all along to retire after this Series, and Larsen had given him an extraordinary good-bye gift.

BILLY MARTIN

A few words from Billy Martin: "Do you think I can manage? I have all the credentials, you know. I can really run a game, run a team. I'll do it some day. You'll see." That quote appeared in the *New York Post* on May 1, 1950, when Martin was twenty-one years old and had just arrived in New York.

Alfred Manuel Martin grew up in Berkeley, California. His father was Portuguese, his mother Italian. His father left home, though, when Billy was eight months old, so he was raised by his mother and grandmother, who lived next door. He always had his sensitivities: along about 1951, Martin did something few if any ballplayers had ever done. He got a nose job.

After a loss to the Dodgers in the sixth game of the 1956 World Series that some Yankees blamed on Enos Slaughter's fielding, Martin went up to Stengel on the team bus and said, "If you're going to keep playing that fucking National League bobo out there, we're going to blow this Series."

Stengel, who was used to Martin, asked him who Billy would play. Said Martin, "You better put Elston [Howard] out there, and you better get [Moose] Skowron's ass back on first."

Stengel did just that for the seventh game. Howard hit a solo homer in the fourth and Skowron hit a grand slam in the seventh as the Yankees beat Brooklyn 9-0.

The Copacabana incident that finished Martin in New York was much ado about very little, and it certainly was no match for his later escapades as a manager. Some players and their wives decided to go to the night club to celebrate Martin's birthday and watch Sammy Davis, Jr., perform. Across the room was another big party, a bowling team from the Bronx, and the people at that table were giving Davis a hard time, calling him "little black Sambo" and other lovely things. Outfielder Hank Bauer asked them to knock it off. Naturally, one of the bowlers said, "Well, why don't you make me."

The bowler, who owned a deli, invited Bauer out back, and both Bauer and Martin started to follow him, the other Yankees in pursuit. According to Ford, who had no reason to lie years later when he retold the story, "We got there maybe 10 or 15 seconds [after Bauer and Martin], and by then the guy that told Bauer to come into the back was stretched out on the floor. . . . But I know Bauer didn't hit him, or Billy, either, because they never left our sight, they were just 40 or 50 feet in front of us all the time. And the guy . . . looked like he'd been hit 15 times." Ford surmised that it was a Copa employee who had pummeled the deli owner.

But the incident was all over the newspapers the next day, and Ford, Mantle, Martin, Bauer, Berra, and Gil McDougald were fined $1,000 apiece by Weiss. Pitcher Johnny Kucks, who was also present, only had to pay $500 out of sympathy for his rookie status. The deli owner also brought suit against the Yankees, and the ensuing legal fees cost each Yankee an additional $1,000.

When Berra was asked about the night, he said, "Nobody did nothin' to nobody."

MORE YANKEES

The Yankees were one of the last major league teams to integrate, Elston Howard joining them in 1955, eight years after Jackie Robinson reached the Dodgers. Stengel said of the musclebound Howard, "Well, when they finally get me a nigger, I get the only one who can't run." Howard couldn't run, but he could hit—.348 in '61—and he was a fine enough catcher to eventually move Yogi into the outfield.

Howard was also a quiet man, and didn't like to make waves. Ford remembered a time when Stengel hired out a room in a Baltimore hotel so that Yankee advance scout Rudy York could give the squad a briefing.

"So Rudy York gets up in front of the team in this room, and he was from Alabama and didn't realize Elston was with us now, and he starts to give us his report on the Orioles, who had a black guy pitching for them that night. 'Hi, fellows,' he says, 'tonight Connie Johnson is pitching for Baltimore. And when he holds his full right hand right up in his glove, you know he's going to be throwing a fast ball. When he drops his hand down, and you can see the heel of it below his glove, it'll be a curve ball. You know, niggers have white palms—lighter than the backs of their hands . . .'

"By then it was so quiet in the room, you could hear a pin drop. We were so embarrassed."

The Yankees finished an uncharacteristic third in 1959, but that wasn't bad considering they were in last place in May. Adding to the embarrassment, though, was an appearance by several of them on the Arthur Murray Dance Party television show. Norm Siebern was first up, doing the rhumba. He was followed by Andy Carey, who performed a waltz. Then Bob Cerv performed a polka. Dancing cleanup was Ford, who did the jitterbug. According to the audience, Carey was the best of a bad lot, and he received $500, a color TV, and an invitation to come back for the grand prize dance-off. In conversation with Kathryn Murray, Carey said that his wife was expecting soon.

"How nice," said Mrs. Murray. "Do you hope for triplets?"

Said Carey, "I'm not hitting that well this year."

One of the few Yankees to have a good year that season was Ryne Duren, the fast-balling, bespectacled reliever who saved 14 games in '59. Duren was notoriously wild on and off the field. He got in many scrapes with teammates because of his drinking, and things became so bad for him that one night, when Duren was finishing out his career with the Washington Senators, his manager, Gil Hodges, had to talk him down off a bridge. In his book *The Comeback,* Duren, who became a counselor for substance abusers, said that he could look at a team picture of his old Yankees and spot at least 13 alcoholics.

Jim Coates, another Yankees pitcher of this period, was a mean-spirited guy who slept with his eyes open, earning him the nickname "Mummy." On a bus trip in '59, Coates fell asleep, his eyes open, his head tilted at a funny angle. Edna Stengel, Casey's wife, who was sitting a few rows ahead of Coates, looked back and then said to her husband, "Dear, I think one of your players is dead."

KALINE, CASH, AND KILLER

Al Kaline was the stalwart of the Tigers for 22 years, retiring at the age of 39 after the '74 season with 3,007 hits and a .297 lifetime average. Yet he never quite matched his 1955 season, when, at the age of twenty, he led the American League in batting at .340, drove in 102 runs, and hit 27 homers. He was compared to Ty Cobb and to his contemporaries Mickey Mantle and Willie Mays, but he was never able to fulfill those great expectations.

Kaline was so good so young because he lived and breathed baseball while growing up in Baltimore. Baseball was in his blood—his father Nick, his grandfather Philip, and his uncles Bibb and Fred were all pretty good catchers in their days— and as an adolescent Kaline would play as many as three games in a day. At the mid-season point for one of his many semi-pro teams, the teenage Kaline was batting .924; at season's end he had tailed off to a mere .609.

The Tigers gave him $30,000 when he was eighteen, and brought him immediately to Detroit. Even then he was an extraordinarily gifted outfielder, and in one game against the White Sox when he was nineteen, Kaline threw out Fred Marsh trying to score from second on a single, Minnie Minoso trying to stretch a single into a double, and Chico Carrasquel trying to go from first to third on a single. Once, in the bottom of the ninth at Yankee Stadium with the Tigers leading by a run and two outs and two men on, Mantle hit a ball so hard and so far that broadcaster Mel Allen whooped, "The Yankees win 5-4." The Tigers' clubhouse man angrily shut off his radio, but when the Tigers came in they were laughing and shouting— Kaline had made a leaping, backhanded catch against the scoreboard.

Kaline played with such grace that most Tigers fans never realized he also played in pain because of a bone condition that left him with what he called "a constant toothache in my left foot." Periodically, there was talk of trading Kaline, but as General Manager Jim Campbell noted in 1964, during one period of trade rumors, "I would consider it. Yes, sir, I would. If the Giants would offer Mays and Marichal and Cepeda for Kaline, I would have to give it some consideration."

In 1961 Kaline's teammate Norm Cash won the AL batting title with a .361 average. Cash, who also hit 41 homers and drove in 132 runs, would have been the MVP had he not made the mistake of having his best year in the same season that Roger Maris broke Ruth's home-run record.

But Cash, it turned out, broke the rules of baseball to assemble his impressive statistics. He would bore a hole about half an inch wide and eight inches deep in the top of the bat, plug the top two inches of the hole with cork, sawdust, and glue, then sand the top so no one would notice. Corking a bat makes it lighter, so that a hitter will get the mass of a 36-ounce bat with the whip of a 34-ouncer, resulting in an extra 20 to 50 feet on some line drives.

Cash was proud of his handiwork. Near the end of his career he said, "I owe my success to expansion pitching, a short rightfield fence, and my hollow bats."

Inevitably, they called him "Killer" when he first came up, yet Harmon Killebrew was anything but. He was quiet and unassuming, and his most distinguishing personal character-istic was the best handwriting of anyone who ever played the game. He was signed by the Washington Senators after being discovered by a real life Senator, Herman Welker of Idaho. Those who remember Killebrew trying to play first, third, and left field will find it hard to believe he came up as a shortstop, but he did. He languished on the bench and in the minors for a few years, but then, out of nowhere, hit 42 homers in 1959. By the time he finished his career in 1975, he had 573 home runs, fifth on the all-time list.

Writers were forever trying to colorize Killebrew's life, but Harmon always thwarted them. He didn't even want them to print the fact that he neither smoked nor drank for fear of offending his friends who did smoke and drink. Once asked what his hobbies were, Killebrew replied, "Well, I like to wash dishes, I guess."

THE SADDEST OF THE RED SOX

From 1954 to 1958, the Red Sox outfield was manned by Jimmy Piersall, Jackie Jensen, and Ted Williams, each one extraor-dinarily gifted, each one the product of a broken home, each one tormented in some way. Piersall had a rough time grow-ing up in Waterbury, Connecticut. His father, a house painter, was a very demanding man, and his mother was in and out of mental institutions while Jimmy was growing up. He began to have agonizing headaches when he was fifteen. Still, that did not prevent him from achieving glorious athletic feats in high school, and the Red Sox signed him in 1950.

Boston had great plans for him. Dom DiMaggio himself told Piersall he was already the best center-fielder in the American League, and the kid had played but a handful of games. But Piersall became increasingly paranoid about the way the Red Sox treated him, and he began to behave irrationally. He sat in movie theaters all day, and while packing for spring training in 1951, he purposefully left his glove behind, thinking that would somehow keep him from having to play. Finally, he broke down at the Red Sox hotel in Sarasota. He was committed to Westborough State Hospital in Massachusetts, where he underwent shock treatments and counseling. In his autobiography, *Fear Strikes Out* (made into a movie starring the preposterously unathletic Anthony Perkins), Piersall described looking out his window in the violent room of the hospital at a water tower. "There it stood, high and solid, almost majestic, and more than anything else, normal. . . . That's what I want to be—normal and commonplace—an average guy. I don't ever again want to be different."

Piersall recovered and went on to a 17-year career. But he could never be anything but different. He'd take bug spray out to the outfield, he threw an orange and a baseball at Bill Veeck's exploding scoreboard in Chicago, he trotted backwards around the bases and slid home after a home run.

In 1960 Piersall, then with Cleveland, got into an argument with Detroit manager Jimmy Dykes after Dykes told the umpires to make Piersall wear a batting helmet in the on-deck circle. Piersall pointed to the left-field seats with his bat and proceeded to hit a home run off Pete Burnside. Piersall hotdogged it around the bases, tipping his hat to Dykes as he rounded third and yelling, "Get on that, old man."

His next time up, Piersall went to the plate wearing a large, football-like helmet. Burnside's first pitch wasn't all that close, though, and the catcher, Red Wilson, started yelling at Burnside, telling him he was gutless if he didn't knock Piersall down. The next pitch sailed over Piersall's head, and Wilson got even madder at his pitcher. Burnside missed a third time, and Wilson got so angry that Piersall had to calm him down. The way Piersall described it, "I told him I'd seen a lot of crazy people in the sanitarium, but nothing as bad as that."

Jackie Jensen was known as "The Golden Boy of the Golden Bears." He was an All-American in both football (as a running back) and baseball at the University of California, and his wedding in 1949 to Zoe Ann Olsen, an Olympic silver medalist in diving, was a huge and gala affair. Attendees included Nobel Prize-winning physicist Ernest O. Lawrence, Cal football coach Pappy Waldorf, songwriter Jimmy McHugh, and Jensen's teammate on the Oakland Oaks, Billy Martin.

Bought from the Oaks by the Yankees, Jensen played parts of three seasons in New York before he was traded to the Washington Senators, who in turn traded him to the Red Sox before the '54 season for Mickey McDermott and Tom Umphlett. For Boston, it turned out to be the steal of the decade, as Jensen drove in 97 or more runs in each of the next six seasons. In 1958 he was the American League MVP, batting .286 with 35 homers and 122 RBIs.

But Jensen's career began to crumble as air travel began to replace the railroad. Gripped by an irrational fear of flying, he would drive from Boston to Detroit just to avoid a flight. He sought the help of show biz hypnotist Arthur Ellen, who had once hypnotized the Senators' weak-hitting catcher Bob Oldis, telling him he would perform to the best of his ability the next day, and Oldis went 3-for-3. But Ellen couldn't help Jensen; he surmised that Jensen's fear of flying was a mask for his desire to stay at home and mend his failing marriage.

Sometimes the Red Sox would give him sleeping pills for a flight, and teammates would haul the semi-conscious Jensen aboard. "I would be out when they got me to my seat," said Jensen. "Then when the engines started, I'd be wide awake and everybody else on the plane would be fast asleep."

In 1960 at the age of thirty-two, coming off a 28-homer, 112-RBI season, Jensen finally gave up and quit baseball. He tried coming back the next season, but it was simply too late.

THE LAST OF WILLIAMS

In his classic account of Ted Williams's last game, "Hub Fans Bid Kid Adieu," John Updike wrote: "The affair between Boston and Ted Williams has been no mere summer romance; it has been a marriage, composed of spats, mutual disappointments, and, towards the end, a mellowing hoard of shared memories. It falls into three stages, which may be termed Youth, Maturity, and Age; or Thesis, Antithesis, and Synthesis; or Jason, Achilles, and Nestor."

The spats were fueled by certain members of the Boston press. While Williams, who read every word ever written about him, carried sufficient enmity for the "knights of the keyboard," as he sarcastically called them, the writers were not without blame. In 1947 Williams, who hit .343 with 32 homers and 114 RBIs, lost out to Joe DiMaggio by one point in the MVP voting because a Boston writer named Mel Webb had a grudge against Williams and didn't give him so much as a 10th-place vote.

In time Williams's reputation for nastiness grew as large as his renown for his skills. Sometimes when he traveled, he'd use an alias, and once when he checked into a motel in Fort Myers, Fla., on his way to a fishing spot, he signed the register as "G.C. Luther." The clerk looked at the name and said, "Gee, for a minute I thought you were Ted Williams." Said Williams, "Yeah, a lot of people say that. I think Williams is actually a much older man." The two men got to talking about this and that—fishing, where to eat—and finally the clerk said to Williams, "I have to admit I had my doubts when you signed in, Mr. Luther. I thought you really were Ted Williams. But I can see you're not. You've got a much nicer disposition."

When Joe McCarthy was named manager of the Red Sox for the '48 season, there was much speculation as to how Williams would respond to such a ferocious disciplinarian. Said McCarthy, "If I don't get along with a .400 hitter, it'll be my fault." Their first confrontation was expected to arise over McCarthy's dress code—the manager had always required his

Yankees to wear ties, and Williams to this day refuses to wear one. So at the first formal sitdown meal for the club that spring, the manager himself showed up wearing a brightly colored sport shirt.

Williams lost 4½ seasons of his career to World War II and the Korean War. In his last game before reporting to the Marine Air Corps in 1952, the Boston fans all joined hands to sing him a farewell. He flew 39 missions in Korea and survived a fiery crash of his F-9. He also flew with a young lieutenant named John Glenn.

Pneumonia ended his fighter pilot career in '53, and upon his return late that summer, Williams hit 13 homers in 37 games, while batting .407. General Manager Joe Cronin told him, "Ted, you've set spring training back 20 years."

One might have thought the Boston press would let up on a returning war hero, but they didn't, and Williams returned the enmity. When he hit his 400th homer in '56, he spat towards the press box as he crossed home plate, as if to say, "Here's to you, boys." That started what the writers referred to as "great expectorations," a period of spraying incidents that culminated in a real spitfest in a tight game against the visiting Yankees. Owner Tom Yawkey fined Williams $5,000 for his spitting, although he never actually collected the money.

In 1957 the thirty-nine-year-old Williams hit .388. In 1959 he was suffering from a pinched nerve in his neck, and he hit .254—the only year of his career in which he batted below .316. Yawkey summoned up the courage to ask Boston's greatest star to retire after that season, but Williams, a man of immense pride, refused. "I may not have been the greatest hitter who ever lived," he said, "but I knew I was the greatest old hitter." In 310 at bats the next season, Williams hit .316 and 29 homers.

Towards the end of the 1960 season, before the last game in Boston, Williams told manager Pinky Higgins that he didn't want to accompany the team on its final road trip; he wanted to bow out at home. So on Wednesday, September 26, before

10,454 paying customers on a cold and dreary day at Fenway Park, Williams played his last game. He hit two shots that died in the wind, and in the eighth inning, with the lights on, he faced Baltimore's Jack Fisher. "Twenty-two years coming down to one time at bat," Williams would later recall. "I remember how the fans started applauding when I went to the on-deck circle, and feeling the chills up my spine, and thinking how much I wanted to put one out of there but knowing what the odds were."

With the count at 1-and-1, Fisher tried to throw a fastball past the old man. But Williams turned on the ball and, into the wind, sent it over the fence in right center. "They cheered like hell," said Williams, "and as I came around the cheering grew louder and louder. I thought about tipping my hat, you're damn right I did, and for a moment I was torn, but by the time I got to second base, I knew I couldn't do it."

As Updike wrote, "Gods do not answer letters."

Sometimes they don't even speak to one another. Not too long before he retired, Williams dropped in on Ty Cobb at the old man's home in Arizona. They talked, of course, about hitting and hitters, amiably covering the ground they both knew so well.

When the two men decided to name their all-time all-star team, the amiability suddenly vanished when Williams suggested putting Rogers Hornsby at second base. When Cobb demurred, Williams pointed out that "Hornsby outhit *you* a couple of years."

Cobb's fires had not been banked by old age. He hated Hornsby, and so screamed at Williams, "Get away from me! And don't come back."

Cobb and Williams never spoke again.

FOUR PITCHERS

He pitched his first game in 1942, his 750th in 1965. He started with a terrible team in Boston, finished with a worse one in

New York, and in between starred for some great ones in Milwaukee. He threw a no-hitter in 1961, when he was forty, and in 1963, at forty-two, he was 23-7 with a 2.60 ERA.

It was Stan Musial who uttered the phrase that so perfectly described this indefatigable figure: "I don't think Warren Spahn will ever get into the Hall of Fame," Musial said. "He'll never stop pitching." When he finally did, with the Mets in 1965 ("I'm probably the only guy who worked for Casey Stengel before and after he became a genius," he said), Spahn had won 363 games, more than any other left-hander ever.

Hoyt Wilhelm, baseball's first truly great relief pitcher, the record-holder for most games pitched in a career, hardly began the way he ended up. It took him seven years to emerge from the minors, and when he finally came up—he turned twenty-nine during his rookie year—it was as a starter. In fact, he pitched a no-hitter in his ninth major league appearance. Even more unlikely, he hit a home run in his very first at bat—as it turned out, his only home run *ever*.

By the time Wilhelm's career concluded in 1972, the remarkable knuckleballer was forty-nine years old. But the greatest testimony to his perseverance and his sense of his own skills is revealed in one uncommon statistic: in the course of his 21-year career, he was given his unconditional release *nine* separate times.

Along with Spahn, Lew Burdette pitched the Braves to two pennants and a World Series championship in 1957 and 1958. He was a junk-ball pitcher, guileful and clever; one of his favorite tricks was to shout "Look out!" at the batter as he released the ball. Then he'd simply grin as a dinky off-speed pitch caught the outside corner while the batter ducked away.

He also used one of the best spitters in the game. Wrote Red Smith, "When Lew was a 20-game winner for the Milwaukee Braves, papers needed three columns for his pitching record: won, lost, and relative humidity." But Burdette was coy; he told Jim Murray that batters couldn't hit his spitball because he didn't throw it.

One of baseball's most poignant stories of promise unfulfilled belongs to Herb Score, the Cleveland Indians left-hander who won 36 games and struck out 508 batters in his first two seasons, 1955 and 1956. During Score's fifth start of the '57 season, Gil McDougald of the Yankees hit a line drive directly into the pitcher's right eye.

It took Score a year to recover from the eye injury. The folklore of baseball has it that he came back gun-shy from the line drive, but in truth, Score didn't let balls back to the box bother him. He even pitched a three-hit shutout in April of '58. But then he pulled a tendon in his left elbow and had to go on the disabled list. When he came back, he changed his motion, lost his control and, worst of all, began to think about every pitch. He was traded to the White Sox before the 1960 season, but he was no longer the same Herb Score who had terrified hitters four years earlier.

MANAGERS

A Phi Beta Kappa economics major at Swarthmore, Dick Hall spent 19 years pitching in the major leagues. He also made himself useful one season in Pittsburgh, when he had a sore arm and undertook a research project for his manager, Bobby Bragan, who was searching for a new way to approach making a batting order.

What Hall concluded was that "a man has 17 more times at bat over the course of a season for every notch he advances in the lineup"—a leadoff batter, for instance, comes to the plate 51 more times than the cleanup hitter. Bragan saw that those 51 at bats might mean four or five home runs for a powerful hitter—which led him to create a batting order that started with slugger Dale Long batting first, Bill Virdon second, and so on down the line.

The Pirates stayed with the novel order for 41 games, winning only 16 of them. Even so, it was an improvement—in the preceding 41, they had won just 14.

In Chicago, Houston, and other stops in his itinerant career, Paul Richards developed a reputation as one of the brainiest of managers—or, at least, one of the most original. He certainly employed the most extreme defense against the running game when he was managing Buffalo in the International League. Sam Jethroe, the leadoff hitter for Montreal, set a league record by stealing 89 bases one season; to stop him, Richards actually walked the pitcher, clogging the bases and keeping the double play in effect if Jethroe reached base.

One of Richards's strategies that backfired occurred in Baltimore, where he decided that catchers were disadvantaged in plays at the plate, because it was easier for a sliding runner to kick the ball out of a catcher's mitt than a fielder's glove. So Richards devised a play whereby the pitcher would throw his glove to the catcher on a ball hit to the outfield with a runner in scoring position.

Joe Ginsberg was catching the first time the glove-switching maneuver was in effect. "Here comes this guy galloping like a horse from third," Ginsberg remembered, and as he reached for pitcher Bill Wight's thrown glove, he—and Richards—suddenly realized the play didn't make much sense when a left-hander was pitching.

In 1961, Cub owner Philip K. Wrigley declared, "We certainly cannot do much worse trying a new system than we have done for many years under the old." Thereupon was born the rotating group of coaches who collectively managed the Cubs for the next four years, rotating in and out of the manager's chair every two weeks. Third baseman Ron Santo said, "It was terrible. One day you're stealing bases, the next day you're hitting home runs." Finally, Wrigley gave up on the system. "We have tried both ex-Cub players and ex-Cub managers," he said. "It just doesn't seem to work. The best protection we can give our managers is to advise them to get out of baseball."

ROGER MARIS

On December 11, 1959, the Yankees traded Don Larsen, Hank Bauer, Norm Siebern, and Marv Throneberry to the Kansas City Athletics for Kent Hadley, Joe DeMaestri, and Roger Maris. Even though they were in the majors, people thought of the A's as a Yankees farm team because they sent so many good players to New York. But this trade seemed about even at first.

Maris, though, didn't like it. "I don't want to go to New York," he told his wife. When he arrived in the city for the first time, a man named Big Julie Isaacson met him at the airport. Isaacson was one of those "friends" that every successful team has, and he took a look at Maris's white bucks and said, "Listen, kid, Yankee ballplayers don't dress like you. You got these Pat Boone shoes, they gotta go." The first thing Maris did was have Isaacson take him to a Thom McAn's store. He bought two more pairs of white bucks.

Maris was the MVP in 1960, with 39 homers and 112 RBIs. He had gotten off to such a good start that there was talk of his challenging Ruth's home run record, but he missed a few weeks of the season after a collision with Washington shortstop Billy Gardner. After the season, Stengel was quoted as saying, "Why shouldn't he break Ruth's record? He's got more power than Stalin."

But he started slowly in 1961. Houk, the new manager, had him batting as low as seventh in the order in April. Mantle, on the other hand, was carrying the club. Maris had a little something to do with that. Concerned that Mantle was spending too much money living at the St. Moritz Hotel in Manhattan and drinking too much, Maris had invited him to live in the apartment in Queens he shared with Bob Cerv. Frequently that season the two of them would be shopping in a supermarket in Queens, just rolling their carts along the aisle, when someone would shout, "It's Mantle and Maris." And someone else would say, "Yeah, sure. What would Mantle and Maris be doing in this store?"

They were good friends, but not at all alike. Mantle was

gregarious with the press. Maris was reticent. Mantle seldom complained, even about the pains in his legs. Maris groused a lot—when Ford was elected player representative, he named a mock cabinet in which Maris was Secretary of Grievances.

On May 17, Maris hit his fourth homer of the year; Mantle already had ten. But then Roger found a groove. He hit 24 homers in 38 games, 24 homers in five weeks, something that not even Ruth had ever done. By June 22, Maris had 27 homers and Mantle 22. (In the meantime, the Yankees, who had trailed the Tigers by as many as 6½ games in May, caught Detroit.) The first inevitable question was asked by Joe Trimble of the *Daily News* in the middle of June. "Roger, do you think you can break Babe Ruth's record?" "How the fuck should I know?" Maris replied.

Mantle got hot, and he and Maris were neck-and-neck in the home-run race right up through the All-Star break. After the first game of a doubleheader against the Orioles on July 19, Maris was 19 games ahead of Ruth with 35 homers and Mantle was 8 games ahead with 33. Both of them hit homers in the second game of the doubleheader, but the game was called on account of rain, so both lost a homer. That was a bad day all around for Maris and Mantle. Earlier, Commissioner Ford Frick had announced that no batter pursuing Ruth would be credited with breaking the record unless he accomplished the feat within 154 games—the number of games in the 1927 regular season. Frick, a virtual absentee commissioner who rarely attended ballgames, was one of Ruth's closest friends. He also added that if the record was broken after 154 games, "a distinguishing mark" would be added to differentiate it from Ruth's. The mark turned out to be an asterisk—but it became more of a brand on Frick than on Maris.

All summer baseball fans debated the merits of Maris versus those of Ruth. Not only was Maris playing in more games, he was also facing the watered-down pitching of expansion. On the other hand, Ruth never had to bat under the lights or against the modern-day relief pitcher.

Hardly a day went by when one or the other, Mantle or Maris, didn't hit a homer. "M & M Fail To Connect" was big news. They were so popular a stripper in Texas billed herself as "Mickey Maris." On August 22, Maris hit his fiftieth homer of the year; the previous record date for No. 50 was September 4, set by Ruth in 1927 and matched by Jimmie Foxx in 1932. When Stengel was asked which one of the M's had the better chance, he said, "How the hell do I know when I don't even know where the finish is? I know the young fella with the fine swing has a fine chance since he already got 50, but don't overlook the other fella. He hits a ball a mile from either side of the plate and when he gets hot there ain't nobody stopping him." Maris also benefited from having Mantle hitting behind him; he didn't get an intentional walk all year.

The Yankees knocked the Tigers out of the race on Labor Day, and all the attention fell to Roger and Mickey, something Roger didn't much like. Besides, the fans were rooting for Mantle. At one point, Mantle moved to within 53-51 in the race, but he was nursing a sore forearm, and that was as close as he would come.

Fifty reporters crowded around Maris's locker every night, asking the same questions over and over. The Japanese press sent an 18-question questionnaire for him to answer. With 20 games left in the season, 12 before the artificial limit imposed by Frick, Maris needed four to tie, five to break. Maris started losing his hair. "I can't take this anymore," he told Mantle. "You got to," his teammate answered.

Tony Kubek, the Yankees shortstop that year, wrote in his book *Sixty-One* that the Maris home run he most remembered was his fifty-eighth. "We were playing in Detroit, and I was on second base. Roger was at the plate and stepped out of the batter's box. He seemed to be staring at the upper deck in right field. I looked out there, but I didn't see anything. Suddenly, a flock of about 250 Canadian geese appeared on the horizon, flying right over the right-field roof in Tiger Stadium. Roger took off his cap, wiped his brow, and just watched the geese. I know it couldn't have been more than a minute, but it seemed like about 10 before he put his cap back on and got into the batter's box. Nestor Chylak was the umpire, and I could see he was getting a little nervous because Roger was

holding up the game, but Chylak let Roger stand there looking at the geese. Terry Fox was the Detroit pitcher, and he
wasn't thrilled with the delay. But like Chylak, Terry never
said a word. The game just stopped because Roger Maris wanted
to watch some geese."

Years later Kubek mentioned the scene to Maris, and Maris
said, "Tony, I can still see those geese. Watching them was so
peaceful." Thus soothed, Maris reached out and hit Fox's first
pitch into the upper deck in right, just below where the geese
had flown.

Maris still had 58 homers the day of the 154th game in
Baltimore. While he publicly said he was only concerned about
breaking the record in 162 games, he was very nearly a bas-
ket case. According to Houk, "He came to me and said, 'Ralph,
I don't feel good. I'm not playing.' He looked awful. . . . He
said, 'I'm not playing,' and he was kind of crying. It was sad.
It was just we two in the office alone. He said, 'Ralph, why
don't you just get me out of there?' "

Houk talked to him, told him about all the people who had
come to see him, calmed him down. Maris lined out hard to
right in the first inning off Milt Pappas, but in the third, he
hit No. 59, another liner over the fence in right.

A 32-year-old Baltimore native named Bob Reitz caught the
ball, and he was ushered under the stands to meet Maris, who
came off the field between innings to get the ball. Reitz didn't
give it to him, though. He wanted money. "How much?" said
Maris. "Twenty-five hundred dollars," said Reitz. Maris just
shook his head. "Are you really going to keep the ball?" asked
Maris, and Reitz nodded. "Good luck to you then," said
Maris.

Maris hit a couple of loud fouls in the later innings, but he
finished the game with 59. No one seemed to care that the
Yankees clinched the AL pennant that night.

On the Tuesday before the end of the regular season, Maris
hit No. 60 off Baltimore's Jack Fisher. A small crowd of 19,000
in Yankee Stadium called him out of the dugout to thank him—
a rare thing in those days—and Maris reluctantly complied.

Mrs. Babe Ruth was there to congratulate him. Maris asked Houk for the next day off because his wife was in town, and Thursday was also an off-day, and the manager agreed although he wondered why Maris would forgo a chance for No. 61 with only four games left to play.

Maris showed up on Friday looking like a new man. He went hitless that night, though, and homerless on Saturday, so he still needed one homer to break the record with one day left to play. The crowd numbered only 23,154, small considering the occasion and an offer of $5,000 from a Sacramento, California, restaurateur to anyone who caught the home-run ball. Maris flied out the first time up against Boston's Tracy Stallard, but in the fourth inning he connected with Stallard's 2-and-0 pitch, lifting a high fly that landed in the lower portion of the right-field stands.

IMPROBABLE EVENTS

He was a fine pitcher over the course of his career, but Harvey "The Kitten" Haddix is remembered for a game he lost: a perfect game he took into the thirteenth inning on May 26, 1959, against Milwaukee, when Henry Aaron and Joe Adcock did him in.

After the game, Haddix's opposing starting pitcher, Lew Burdette, said that an experienced competitor like Haddix should have known better than to bunch his hits.

At the end of the 1954 season, when the Indians had already clinched the American League pennant, the Yankees found themselves closing the season at home, against the Athletics. To draw a crowd for the final game, Stengel announced he'd start the most powerful lineup in Yankees history. To get as many big bats as possible into the batting order, he put Mantle at short, Berra at third, and Bill Skowron on second.

The A's won, 8-6.

An especially bizarre play occurred in a 1959 game between the Cubs and the Cardinals. Al Barlick, one of the umpires, described it later:

"Stan Musial was the batter for the Cardinals. The count was three and two and Bob Anderson's next pitch was high and inside. Sammy Taylor, the Cubs' catcher, sees the ball roll to the backstop. He makes no attempt to retrieve it, apparently thinking it was a foul tip.

"Vic Delmore, the umpire behind the plate, signals ball four and Anderson and Taylor begin to argue the call. Two things happen then: Musial jogs off to first and Taylor asks umpire Delmore for a new ball. Vic gives it to him and Taylor promptly flips it to Anderson.

"I'm working at first base and I see Alvin Dark, the Cubs' third baseman, running hard toward the plate. I figure he's going to charge Delmore and I run in to help Vic. Instead Dark rounds right past the plate and goes to the backstop. He returns quickly with the original ball. Meanwhile, the Cards on the bench behind first are telling Musial to take second.

"Now comes something I never want to see happen again. Dark and Anderson both throw out to second base. Dark's throw is low and is fielded by Ernie Banks, then playing shortstop for the Cubs. Anderson's throw is high and sails over the head of Tony Taylor, the Cubs' second baseman. Musial slides into second. When he gets up and starts for third, Banks tags him out with the ball Dark had thrown to him."

Barlick and his colleagues called Musial out, on the grounds that he was tagged with the original ball in play. As it happens, they learned later that the Cubs' public address announcer, who was on the field in foul territory when the comic action began, had picked up the original ball and obliged Dark when the third baseman said, "Give me the ball." At that point, of course, the ball was dead and action should have stopped.

In the argument, the Cards had thought Musial was entitled to third; the Cubs had felt that he was out at second; and in conformity to the rules, he really should have been sent back, safe, to first.

SANDY KOUFAX

"Either he throws the fastest ball I've ever seen, or I'm going blind." Richie Ashburn's comment on Sandy Koufax was certainly underscored by statistics: three seasons with more than 300 strikeouts, another three with more than 200. But Koufax's curve was as good as his fastball, and his control nearly as great as his speed: in 1963, when he struck out 306, he walked only 58. By way of contrast, in Nolan Ryan's first 300 K season, 1972, he walked 157.

Of course, he hadn't always had such command. When Koufax was spotted by part-time scout Jimmy Murphy while pitching for an amateur team sponsored by Nathan's Famous, the Coney Island hot doggery, Murphy said, "He throws harder than any kid I've ever seen." But he was a kid who threw utterly without control at first, and at spring training at Vero Beach he worked out of sight behind the minor league barracks. Duke Snider said standing in against him in batting practice was like playing Russian roulette. In 1958, *Sports Illustrated* called him a "young lefty with a wicked fastball and a minimum of control."

Finally, after overcoming his terrifying wildness, Koufax in six seasons—1961–1966—incontrovertibly established himself as the pre-eminent pitcher of his era. Philadelphia manager Gene Mauch, asked if Koufax was the best left-hander he ever saw, replied, "He was the best right-hander, too."

It was one of the ugliest moments in modern baseball history. The Dodgers and the Giants had been engaged in a beanball war, and when San Francisco pitcher Juan Marichal was at the plate, L.A. catcher John Roseboro buzzed his throw back to the mound a bare inch or so from Marichal's head. The photograph of Marichal hitting Roseboro with his bat was on front pages across the country the next day.

According to Roseboro, the incident wouldn't have occurred if, say, Don Drysdale had been pitching for the Dodgers. In proper retaliation for the Giants pitcher's head-hunting from the mound, Drysdale would have thrown at Marichal when he came to bat.

But Sandy Koufax was the Los Angeles pitcher that day and, said Roseboro, "Sandy was constitutionally incapable of throwing at anyone's head. So I decided to take matters into my own hands."

Throughout those extraordinary six years, Koufax defined the Dodgers, overshadowing even so accomplished a teammate as Don Drysdale.

But even though he would start three games in the 1965 World Series, Koufax did not get the opening game assignment: an observant Jew, he would not pitch on Yom Kippur. Manager Walter Alston consequently gave the ball to Drysdale, who lasted less than three innings in a 8-2 Dodgers loss.

After the game, Lefty Gomez wandered into the Dodgers clubhouse and shouted, "Hey, Alston, I bet you wish Drysdale was Jewish, too."

FUTILE PHILLIES REDUX

They never sank as low as the Pirates of the early '50s, but the Phils of the latter part of the decade were a truly terrible team. Eddie Sawyer, who had managed the 1950 Philadelphia whiz kids to the NL pennant, had been out of baseball for six years when Philadelphia owner Bob Carpenter asked him to come back to manage, midway through the 1958 season. The Phillies finished last that year, and last in 1959. Then, after putting the club through spring training in 1960, coming north, and playing the first game of the season, Sawyer looked at his team and decided to resign.

"I'm forty-nine years old," he said, "and I'd love to live to be fifty."

THREE BROTHERS

It wasn't the sort of opportunity that presented itself every day, so San Francisco manager Alvin Dark grabbed it: on

September 15, 1963, the Giants' starting outfield consisted of the brothers Felipe, Matty, and Jesus Alou.

Between them, the brothers would play more than 5,000 major league games, and assemble a total of 14 seasons of .300-plus hitting.

THE AMAZING METS

"I don't know what's going on," Richie Ashburn said, "but I know I've never seen it before." "It" was the expansion Mets of 1962, who managed to lose 120 games under the bemused leadership of an aged Casey Stengel. Ashburn, as it happened, hit .306 that year, but no other regular topped .275. The team's best pitcher, Roger Craig, lost 24 games. The only category in which any Met led the league was errors. The Mets gave up a staggering 948 runs, some 322 more than the Pirates, who finished fourth. The team ERA was 5.04. And they concluded the season 60½ games out of first place—that is, *two months* out of first.

The paradigm of those Mets was Marvin Eugene Throneberry—appropriately, his initials spelled "MET."

On June 17, 1962, Throneberry had his most memorable day in baseball. In the bottom half of the first inning in a game against the Cubs, he charged into third base with a triple, only to be called out on an appeal by the Cubs' Ernie Banks for not having touched first. That was when Casey Stengel, steaming out of the dugout to protest, was told by first-base coach Cookie Lavagetto that Throneberry had missed second, too.

It was in the top of the inning, though, that Marvelous Marv had established his pattern for the day. The Cubs' Don Landrum had led off the game with a walk, and then Al Jackson picked him off first. Landrum was caught in the ensuing rundown, but the call was negated when Throneberry was called for obstruction.

Finally, in the bottom of the ninth, with the Mets down

8-7, two men on and two men out, Throneberry came to the plate with the opportunity to redeem himself. Needless to say, he struck out.

At season's end, the Mets were 40-120. They had had losing streaks of 9, 11, 13, and 17 games. As he prepared to depart for his off-season recuperation, Throneberry asked, "You think the fish will come out of the water to boo me this winter?"

Leonard Shecter reported this exchange between Throneberry and Johnny Murphy, the old Yankee pitcher who negotiated salaries for the early Mets:

Throneberry: "People came to the park to holler at me, just like Mantle and Maris. I drew people to games."

Murphy: "You drove some away, too."

T: "I took a lot of abuse."

M: "You brought most of it on yourself."

T: "I played in the most games of my career, 116."

M: "But you didn't play well in any of them."

In a game against the Giants during the '62 Mets' 17-game losing streak, Roger Craig threw perilously close to Orlando Cepeda, and shortstop Elio Chacon took umbrage at a Willie Mays baserunning move. In short order, Mays took care of the tiny Chacon, and the 210-pound Cepeda disposed of Craig. The next morning, *Newsday*'s coverage of the game began, "The Mets can't fight, either."

Choo Choo Coleman was supposed to be a catcher, but he moved around so much behind the plate that when pitcher Chuck Churn, who had been his occasional battery-mate with the Phillies, was asked who was the toughest man in the league to pitch to, he said, "Coleman."

With the Mets, it was more of the same. Choo Choo was something of a laughing stock even on this woeful club, a situation he generally shrugged off with his notably taciturn nature. A sample of his conversational style became clear in a dialogue with Mets broadcaster Ralph Kiner.

"Choo Choo," Kiner began his interview, "how did you get your nickname?"

Coleman: "Dunno."

Kiner was forced to grope. "Well, what's your wife's name, and what's she like?"

Coleman: "Her name is Mrs. Coleman, and she likes me."

After that first horrible season, the Mets announced they were calling up their three best minor league pitchers: Larry Bearnarth, who'd been 2-13 at Syracuse; Tom Belcher, 1-12 at Syracuse; and Grover Powell, 4-12 at Auburn and Syracuse.

Still the spring of 1963 dawned hopeful for the Mets, who were confident they were an improved team. Then the Cardinals beat them 8-0 on opening day at the Polo Grounds. Said Stengel, "We're still a fraud."

PART									
5									

MODERN TIMES

From Gibby and Yaz
to the Grounder
That Ate Bill Buckner

BOB GIBSON

The sixties had begun as a time for hitters, but toward the end of the decade, pitchers were dominant. The Dodgers, of course, were the standard-bearers, relying on Sandy Koufax and Don Drysdale, but the Cardinals, Tigers, and Mets also won world championships largely on the strength of their pitching staffs. In 1968 Denny McLain won 31 games, while in that same season, the American League batting champion was Carl Yastrzemski, who hit only .301. Over in the National League that year, Bob Gibson of the Cardinals had an astounding ERA of 1.12 in 305 innings. He pitched 13 shutouts, five in succession, and allowed just one run in 11 other appearances. He completed 28 of his 34 starts and allowed just 198 hits and 62 walks. Even more astonishingly, he still lost nine games. The Cards, who won the NL pennant in that last year before the leagues were each split into two divisions, averaged fewer than three runs per nine innings for Gibson; had they averaged four runs a game, Gibson would have been 30-2. As Amos Rusie had done nearly eighty years earlier, Gibson single-handedly brought about a rule change: In 1969 the mound was lowered five inches.

Gibson was a fierce competitor who wouldn't hesitate to brush back close friends. The first time Bill White, his former roommate, batted against him as a Phillie, Gibson hit him in the arm. Perhaps the quintessential Gibson moment came in the opening game of the 1968 Series against the Tigers at Busch Stadium. As Roger Angell described it in *The New Yorker,* Gibson was leading 4-0 in the ninth with a man on and nobody out. "The next batter, the dangerous Al Kaline, worked the count to two and two and then fanned, swinging away at a fastball, to an accompanying roar from the crowd. A moment later, there was a second enormous cheer, louder and more sustained than the first. The Cardinal catcher, Tim McCarver, who had straightened up to throw the ball back to the pitcher, now hesitated. . . . Gibson, a notoriously swift worker on the mound, motioned to his battery mate to return the ball. Instead, McCarver pointed with his gloved hand at something behind Gibson's head. Gibson, staring uncomprehendingly at his catcher, yelled, 'Throw the goddam ball back, will you! C'mon, c'mon, c'mon, let's go!' Still holding the ball, McCarver pointed again, and Gibson, turning around, read the illuminated message on the centerfield scoreboard, which perhaps only he in the ballpark had not seen until that moment: 'Gibson's fifteenth strikeout in one game ties the World Series record held by Sandy Koufax.' Gibson, at the center of a great tureen of noise, dug at the dirt on the mound with his spikes and then uneasily doffed his cap."

Still anxious to get back to work, Gibson then struck out Norm Cash and Willie Horton to finish off the Tigers. His record of 17 strikeouts in a Series game still stands.

Gibson could be standoffish off the field, too. He broke his leg during the pennant race in 1967 and grew so tired of reporters' questions that he taped a sheet of paper to his shirtfront with this message: "1. Yes, it's off. 2. No, it doesn't hurt. 3. I don't know how much longer." The writers never did much like him, and although he was clearly a Hall of Fame pitcher, they made him wait a year after he was eligible before sending him to Cooperstown.

YAZ

Carl Yastrzemski, Jr., grew up in Bridgehampton, Long Island. Carl, Sr., was a potato farmer and a pretty fair ball-

player. The two Carls played together often for the Lake Ron-
konkoma Cardinals, with junior, the shortstop, batting third,
and senior, the third baseman, batting cleanup. In their last
year together, 1958, Carl, Jr., hit .375, and Carl, Sr., hit .410.

Fourteen of the 16 major league teams actively pursued Carl,
Jr., but Carl, Sr., kept holding them off, and holding them up
for money. The kid, meanwhile, enrolled at Notre Dame. His
father eventually got the stakes up to $125,000, which is what
the Cincinnati Reds offered, but then he decided to take a
more modest offer from the Red Sox because they were closer
to home and he liked their scout, Bots Nekola. Carl, who signed
during his sophomore year, never played varsity baseball in
South Bend. As Notre Dame baseball coach Jake Kline explained it, "I never had the chance to ruin him."

The first time Ted Williams saw Yastrzemski, he must have
recalled what Lefty O'Doul had said to him long before: "Don't
you ever let them change your batting stance." Yaz was a
shortstop at the time, but the Red Sox sent him down to Minneapolis to learn to play left field—Williams was in his last
season. There was a great deal of pressure on "the next Williams" when he first broke in, but in his second season he
drove in 94 runs, and in his third season he won the first of
his three batting titles.

Yastrzemski inherited more than left field from Williams.
He, too, became the focal point for the troubles on the team,
and he took the blame for the constant turnover of managers
in Boston—all of whom, supposedly, couldn't get along with
the star. But in 1967, there was only love, because in the Impossible Dream year he won the batting (.326) and RBI (121)
titles outright, while tying Harmon Killebrew for the home
run title (44), an only slightly tarnished Triple Crown. In the
last two weeks of the season, Yaz hit .523, and in the final
two games, which Boston needed to win, he went 7-for-8. In
the World Series against St. Louis, he batted .400 and made
several outstanding defensive plays.

He was clearly the best player in the land, and a vote by
his fellow major leaguers conducted by the Newspaper Enter-
prise Association confirmed that. In voting for Yastrzemski,
however, the players revealed their own illiteracy. Written in

were such entries as Yaztremski, Yastremski, Yastrezemski, Yastreszski, Yastremzminski, Yastrenski, and Yazstremenski. One player, obviously consulting a boxscore, voted for Y'str'mski, while several others opted for the safe designation "Yaz—Boston."

LOU BROCK

In the most one-sided trade in history, the Chicago Cubs sent outfielder Lou Brock to the St. Louis Cardinals for pitcher Ernie Broglio in 1964. Brock would go on to break Maury Wills's record for stolen bases in a season, and set the lifetime record as well. An amiable man who was extremely popular in St. Louis, Brock was also something of an entrepreneur, with interests in such unlikely businesses as a flower shop, and in an invention he called the BroccaBrella, a small umbrella won like a hat.

His start in baseball was unlikely, too. Brock had entered Southern University in Baton Rouge, La., on an academic scholarship, but he lost the scholarship after his first semester, and with that some of the part-time jobs he held on campus. So he wasn't eating very well when he tried out for the baseball team. The coach didn't notice him until one day, while shagging flies in a broiling sun, Brock collapsed from exhaustion. After he was revived, he was given the chance to hit—a good-will gesture from the apparently guilty coach. Brock took five swings and hit four balls out of the park.

BO BELINSKY

Bo Belinsky was the flip side of Sandy Koufax. Like Koufax, Belinsky was a Jewish lefthander who pitched a no-hitter for a team in Los Angeles. But unlike Sandy, Bo spent his free time carousing with the likes of Ann-Margret and Mamie Van Doren, or palling around with Hugh Hefner, Walter Winchell,

Frank Sinatra, and J. Edgar Hoover. J. Edgar Hoover? "He let me shoot tommy guns at FBI headquarters," said Belinsky. "I told him if I ever quit this game I might need a job. He said, 'Bo, there'll always be a place for you on the force.' "

Belinsky pitched his no-hitter on the night of May 5, 1962. Facing an Orioles lineup that included Brooks Robinson, Dick Williams, Jim Gentile, and Gus Triandos, Bo pitched in and out of trouble all night, and with each inning, the Baltimore bench kept reminding him, "Hey, Bo, you got a no-hitter." With two outs in the ninth, Belinsky threw a 1-and-1 fastball to Dave Nicholson, and Nicholson popped it up into foul territory near third, where Felix Torres caught it. As his teammates rushed out of the dugout, and the home crowd went wild, Belinsky pointed to the stands and said to his catcher, Buck Rodgers, "Hey, look at the blonde with the big tits."

Belinsky finished his career with a record of 28-51 and no regrets. "I don't feel sorry for myself. I knew sooner or later I'd have to pay the piper. You can't beat the piper, Babe; I never thought I could. But I'll tell who I do feel sorry for—all those guys who never heard the music."

MORE PITCHERS

In 1968, Denny McLain became the first pitcher since Dizzy Dean to win 30 games in a season. If anything, McLain was even dizzier than Dean. He played the organ in Las Vegas, flew light planes—calling himself "Sky Young"—dumped water on writers, and carried a handgun.

During a 1969 nationally televised game against the Twins, McLain and Detroit first baseman Norm Cash started thinking more about the post-game show than about the game itself—the star of the game received $100 to appear on the program. Cash had hit a homer and a single, McLain was pitching a shutout, and both men were arguing over who was going to be picked. Wrote Bill Freehan in *Behind the Mask,* "We still had three outs to go. Mayo [Manager Smith] sat there, gritting his teeth and wondering. I was, too. I could see that if McLain started screwing around, I'd have to get on his tail real quick, I knew that his arm had been bothering him the whole game, that he wasn't pitching well. . . . But he went out there, this man who makes at least $150,000 a year from baseball and other interests, and, sniffing that $100, reached back and threw the blazes out of the ball. He struck out Harmon Killebrew on four pitches. Cash was down at first base rooting for Harmon, yelling, 'Hit a home run.'

"But McLain got the Twins out, one-two-three, went on the show, and came back into the locker room with the $100 bill pasted to his forehead. It was the best inning he'd pitched all year."

McLain's career ended in a flurry of bad judgments and unfortunate injuries; he was out of baseball at twenty-eight. Years later, he was imprisoned on extortion charges, then released because of irregularities in the trial record.

Sam McDowell was another pitcher whose character kept him from greatness. When Sudden Sam pitched for the Indians, his fastball and curveball were the best in the American League, but the whole was never the sum of his parts. Alcohol had something to do with it—a reformed McDowell later became a drug counselor—but mostly he seemed a pitcher afraid to succeed. After he won 20 games for the first time, he self-destructed.

In his prime, though, he was the most feared pitcher in the American League. Before a game between the Indians and the A's, Cleveland manager Alvin Dark spotted Oakland pitcher Blue Moon Odom. "Hey, Moon," said Dark, "weren't you supposed to pitch today?"

"Supposed to, Alvin. But I wasn't feeling too good today."

"Jeez, that's too bad, Moon. Sudden will be very disappointed. You know, I was saving Sudden just for you today."

"I appreciate that, but I guess I'd rather pitch tomorrow."

"But we ain't playin' tomorrow."

"I'd still rather pitch tomorrow."

No pitcher—not McDowell, not Koufax, not Bob Feller—ever threw harder than a career minor leaguer named Steve Dalkowski. In 1956 Dalkowski was pitching batting practice for the Orioles before a game with the Red Sox when Ted Williams decided to get a first-hand look. Williams stepped into the cage and motioned for Dalkowski to throw the ball. Williams did not swing. He said he didn't even see the pitch. He also said that it was the fastest pitch he had ever encountered and that he would be damned if he'd ever face Dalkowski again.

But Dalkowski was as wild as he was fast. In 995 minor league innings, he struck out 1,396 batters and walked 1,354. The Orioles tried everything. Thinking he was just too strong, they made him throw on the side before a game until he was exhausted. They bought him thick glasses. They made him pitch batting practice daily for two weeks to get him used to a live batter. They had him throw standing only 15 feet from the catcher, gradually moving him back to the standard 60 feet, 6 inches.

Finally Earl Weaver, in Elmira, decided simply to leave him alone. The year was 1962, and Dalkowski responded with six shutouts and a 3.04 ERA. The Orioles were actually counting on him as a reliever in 1963, but in spring training he hurt his elbow making on off-balance throw to first and he was never the same.

Dalkowski stayed in organized ball until 1968, but his failures led him to wine, and the wine led him to a life as a migrant farm worker in California.

Myron Walter Drabowsky was another free spirit reliever who also may have been the best pitcher ever born in Poland. He was certainly the only one to strike out 11 Dodgers in six innings of relief, as he did for Baltimore in the opening game of the 1966 World Series. Asked if that was the best he ever pitched, Drabowsky said, "Not since 1956 when I was pitching for Trinity against Rensselaer Polytechnic Institute." Something else Drabowsky did during the '66 season lives in baseball legend. During a series in Kansas City in May, Drabowsky, sitting in the Baltimore bullpen, telephoned the

Athletics bullpen. Coach Bobby Hofman picked up the phone. "Get Krausse hot!" Drabowsky barked in imitation of A's manager Alvin Dark.

It was the sixth inning, and starting pitcher Jim Nash was cruising along nicely, but Hofman followed orders and told Lew Krausse to warm up. The next phone call, of course, was from the real Dark, who asked, "Why is Krausse throwing?" Hofman smelled the rat when he saw the occupants of the opposing bullpen doubled over in laughter.

THE SOX OF '67

In 1967 the Red Sox got serious. In the year called The Impossible Dream, they rose from ninth place to first under new manager Dick Williams. They won the pennant thanks to a Triple Crown year from Carl Yastrzemski, 22 wins from Jim Lonborg, and 20 saves from John Wyatt—and despite the tragic beaning on August 18 of Tony Conigliaro, who had 20 homers and 67 RBIs at the time. The pitcher who hit Tony C. was Jack Hamilton of the Angels, and here's how Conigliaro later described the pitch: "The ball came sailing right toward my chin; normally a hitter can jerk his head back a fraction and the ball will buzz by. But this pitch seemed to follow me in. I know I didn't freeze. I definitely made a move to get out of the way of the ball. In fact, I jerked my head back so hard that my helmet flipped off just before impact. . . . When the ball was about four feet from my head I knew it would get me. And I knew it would hurt because Hamilton was such a hard thrower. I was frightened. I threw my hands up in front of my face and saw the ball follow me back and hit me square on the left side of the head. As soon as it crunched into me, it felt as if the ball would go in one side of my head and come out the other; my legs gave way and I went down like a sack of potatoes. Just before everything went dark I saw the ball bounce straight down on home plate. It was the last thing I saw for several days."

A doctor later told Conigliaro that had the pitch been two

inches higher, he would have been dead. As it was, Conigliaro's left cheekbone was fractured, and when he took his first look at his own face, after regaining his sight, he could make out the imprint of the stitches where the ball had hit him. Hamilton came to see him in the hospital, as did most of Tony's teammates. Oddly enough, though, Dick Williams never visited him, and Conigliaro was never able to forgive him for that.

A cyst reduced Conigliaro's vision in his right eye to 20/100; his right eye was 20/15. He tried to come back that season, but he couldn't hit the ball out of the infield against the Red Sox bat boy. His depression was compounded by the fact that he could actually see Fenway Park's right field from the window of his apartment. While all the other Red Sox celebrated madly in the clubhouse when the Angels beat the Tigers on the last day of the season, Conigliaro sat in front of his locker, crying.

In 1968 Dick Williams actually said, "We did it without his butt last year, and we'll do it without his butt this year." But the Red Sox didn't do it in '68, as Conigliaro sat idle, contemplating retirement. He decided to go to the Instructional League as a pitcher, and the Red Sox humored him. But minor league manager Billy Gardner kept insisting that Tony take batting practice, and soon he began to hit. When Conigliaro went to the ophthalmologist that winter, the doctor told him the "hole" in his left eye was gone, and on Opening Day in 1969 in Baltimore, Conigliaro was in the lineup.

In the tenth inning, he hit Pete Richert's fastball over the left-field fence to win the game. When he got to the dugout, "the guys were all reaching for me at one time, Reggie [Smith] and Rico [Petrocelli], Yaz and everybody. They were pounding my back and I was being hugged to death. Then Dick Williams came over and kissed me on the cheek. At that moment I could have bit him in the neck."

Ken Harrelson was larger than life—larger, maybe, even than Belinsky. He was nicknamed The Hawk by his minor league teammate Dick Howser for his outstanding nose, a feature that attained its uncommon prominence by being broken five times. In his 1969 autobiography, *The Hawk,* he put it this way: "Nosewise, the Hawk is the noblest Roman of them all. You can talk about Caesar, Cyrano, Durante or any of those other jokers, but they're pikers compared to me."

Harrelson arrived in Boston on the heels of his misadventures in Kansas City. As related by a young Chicago sportswriter named Brent Musberger, the trouble began on TWA flight 85 on the night of August 3, 1967. Some of the A's acted up on the trip and started annoying broadcaster Monte Moore, generally known to the players as "Monte the Ripper," who reported them to traveling secretary Ed Hurley, who in turn told Moore it was none of his business. That should have been the end of it, but two weeks after the flight owner Charles O. Finley decided to fine pitcher Lew Krausse $500 and suspend him indefinitely, and also to ban alcoholic beverages on future flights. When manager Alvin Dark refused to fine and suspend Krausse, Finley called Dark to his Chicago hotel room to fire him. Dark told him, "Before I go I want to tell you a few things about your organization. You've got great young talent. By 1971 this team could be a pennant winner."

Finley was so touched by Dark's speech that he rehired him for two more years at a considerable raise in pay. But the players had already given a statement to the press that said, "If Mr. Finley would give his excellent manager and fine coaching staff the authority they deserve, these problems would not exist." Infuriated, Finley fired Dark again. That provoked the outspoken Harrelson to tell a reporter, "Finley is a menace to baseball." When the owner read that, he summarily released Harrelson, who had hit .305 in his 61 games for the A's. That set off an auction among four contenders in the league, and the Red Sox won the bidding. Although the winning offer of $75,000 seems paltry now, the Hawk was really the first of the modern free agents. "The first thing I'm going to do," said Harrelson at the time, "is send Charlie Finley some money I owe him, a thank-you note, and a dozen roses."

Harrelson was a pioneer in other ways. He was the first to use a batting glove—actually, a golf glove that he pressed into use after playing 36 holes on the day before a game he hadn't expected to start. In Boston, where he would become a folk hero during an MVP-quality season in '68, he won renown as a clothes horse of epic proportions, spending $10,000 annually on his wardrobe. "I must have thrown away 19 Nehru jackets," the Hawk once recalled. "I remember parties where people would just walk away with my stuff, half a dozen glasses, a dozen sweaters, 20 pairs of pants, all because I had my name on them. I used to go to sleep in the middle of my own parties, and when I'd wake up, Wendell would be so angry because all this stuff was gone." Wendell, incidentally, was Harrelson's Filipino houseboy, another accoutrement that set the Hawk apart.

In 1969, just before the start of the season, the Red Sox traded Harrelson and pitchers Juan Pizarro and Dick Ellsworth to Cleveland for catcher Joe Azcue and pitchers Sonny Siebert and Vicente Romo. Harrelson was so crushed he refused to go, and only after the intervention of newly named commissioner Bowie Kuhn did he assent.

But Harrelson quit the game soon thereafter, and became a professional golfer. The impression he left on baseball was much like the impression he left on Cleveland teammate Duke Sims. "I remember the time the Hawk entered the Northern Ohio Long-Driving Contest," Sims recalled. "Everybody's waiting for him, when all of a sudden this helicopter shows up. The Hawk gets out, takes one swing, wins the contest, and then takes off in the helicopter."

THE MIRACLE METS

In 1968 the New York Mets finished ninth, an encouraging sign for them, but with one week to go in the season their manager, Gil Hodges, had a heart attack. So the Mets and

Hodges were scrutinized a little more than usual during the spring of '69. Although they were given a 100-1 shot of winning the world championship, the Mets did impress one observer, Casey Stengel. "This team can go very far upward," he intoned.

The Mets did have some fine young arms: Tom Seaver, Jerry Koosman, Nolan Ryan, Tug McGraw, each of whom went on to a long, fruitful career. They had a catcher, Jerry Grote, who was so good defensively that Johnny Bench once said, "If we were on the same team, I'd play third." They had two life-long friends from Mobile, Ala., Tommie Agee and Cleon Jones, in the outfield. And they had an outstanding little shortstop, Bud Harrelson. But not many people thought they had sufficient offense to overtake the Cardinals or the Cubs.

Of course 1969 was also the year that man landed on the moon, and the winning entry in the Mets' annual Banner Day competition that year was "One Small Step for Hodges, One Giant Leap for Metkind." The Mets weren't really taken seriously until the night of July 9, when Seaver took a perfect game into the ninth against the Cubs, only to have an obscure player named Jimmy Qualls single with one out. Seaver called it his "imperfect game." But it pulled the Mets to within three games of the Cubs. Harrelson was on Army Reserve duty at the time and watched the game with some buddies in a restaurant in Watertown, N.Y. "It was the strangest thing," said Harrelson. "I began feeling more and more like a little kid watching that game and that great performance, and I wanted to turn to the others and say, 'I knew Tom Seaver. Tom Seaver is a friend of mine.'"

Seaver was the embodiment of the Miracle Mets. He was an incredible success on the mound, but his greatest contribution to the club may have been his attitude—he didn't think losing was so funny. And the Mets began to play better behind him.

The son of a Walker Cup golfer, Seaver grew up in comfortable surroundings in California's San Joaquin Valley. Yet after high school, he elected to go into the Marines, where he matured physically. He signed out of the University of Southern California with the Braves, but the signing was voided on a technicality and the Mets won him by a lottery. In 1967, his first season, he won 16 games and was dubbed Tom Terrific. In the Miracle Year of '69, he won 25 and the Cy Young Award. By the time he retired seventeen years later, he'd won 311 games.

Seaver was also a study in contrasts, not unlike Mark Harris's fictional Henry Wiggen. He was a clubhouse cutup with a distinctive, high-pitched laugh—"When Seaver laughs," said broadcaster Lindsay Nelson, "he makes dogs whine"—who chewed tobacco and swore with the best. But he also favored preppie clothing and such high-toned pursuits as squash, jazz, wine, and bridge.

And he did not easily forget slights. Seaver and his wife Nancy were so miffed that he didn't win the Cy Young Award in 1971 that they named their cat after the pitcher who did, Ferguson Jenkins, just so they would always be reminded.

The Mets' chief competitors in the summer of '69 were the Chicago Cubs, managed by Leo Durocher. Durocher still had some of his once-brilliant faculties, and he had retained all of his famous bile. He was particularly brutal on non-regulars. Once he sent Lee Thomas up to pinch-hit, then gave his own running commentary on the bench: "Look at the bleep bleep bleep. He can't run, he can't hit, I don't know why the bleep bleep bleep I got him. Look at him! He's going to pop up." And sure enough, Thomas popped up. Durocher then turned to Ted Savage and told him to pinch hit. "Why should I go up there," Savage said, "and subject myself to abuse?"

Durocher's Cubs were a pretty good club—the best Cubs in three decades, in fact. Ernie Banks was finishing out his career at first base, but third baseman Ron Santo and left-fielder Billy Williams were in their prime, and Jenkins was a marvelous pitcher. Santo and Williams had come up together in the Cubs' system, and Santo once recalled the time Rogers Hornsby was the organization's minor league hitting instructor. Hornsby called all the minor leaguers together and sat them down on a row of bleachers. One by one, he went down the line, dismissing players with such crude comments as "You better go back to shining shoes because you can't hit." He eliminated one prospect after another, and Santo whispered to Williams, "If he says that to me, I'm going to cry."

Hornsby came up to Williams and said, "You can hit in the big leagues right now." Then he turned to Santo and said, "So can you."

But the Cubs, even anchored by such talents as Williams, Santo, and a still-powerful Banks, couldn't stop the phenomenon that was the Mets. Joan Whitney Payson, the Mets' matriarchal owner, became so enchanted that she arranged for the radio station nearest her summer home in Maine to pick up the club's broadcasts. Celebrities such as Jacqueline and Aristotle Onassis began showing up at Shea Stadium.

At 10:13 p.m., Eastern Daylight Time, on September 10 the Cubs slipped into second, the Mets into first. Things were going so well for the Mets that when Steve Carlton of the Cards struck out nineteen of them on September 16, New York still won, 4-3, on a pair of two-run homers by Ron Swoboda. The Mets clinched the division title on September 24, and after the game Hodges tried to explain the season to the still-disbelieving reporters. As his players celebrated next door, Hodges patiently talked about good pitching, good defense, confidence, momentum, self-reliance. Then someone said, "Gil, how did it all happen? Tell us what it all proves." Hodges leaned back in his chair and said, "Can't be done." Then he laughed.

The Mets swept the Braves in three games in the first NLCS, while over in the American League, the Orioles swept the Twins. By this time, America had adopted the Mets, and so the Orioles were a little resentful of the attention New York's team was getting. In the clubhouse after Baltimore won their third playoff game, Oriole outfielder Frank Robinson shouted, "bring on Ron Gaspar!"—referring to the Mets' light-hitting outfielder, Rod Gaspar.

A teammate corrected Robinson. "Not Ron—Rod, stupid!"
"Okay," said Robinson. "Bring on Rod Stupid."

In Game 1 of the World Series in Baltimore, the Mets brought on Rod Gaspar, trailing 4-1 with two on and two out in the top of the seventh, but all he could do was tap the ball weakly off Mike Cuellar, and Brooks Robinson made a spectacular bare-handed scoop to throw him out. The Orioles won the first game, 3-1, beating Seaver and taking a little euphoria out of Metmania.

The next day, though, Koosman and Dave McNally dueled into the ninth, each allowing only one run. In the top of the ninth, the Mets rallied for a run with two outs on successive singles by Ed Charles, Grote, and Al Weis, an infielder not known for his hitting, or for much of anything else. In the bottom of the inning, Koosman retired the first two O's, but gave way to relief pitcher Ron Taylor after walking Frank Robinson and Boog Powell. Taylor induced Brooks Robinson to ground to third, giving the Mets a 2-1 victory and evening the Series.

Shifting to New York, the Orioles seemed to have an edge, with Jim Palmer going against Gary Gentry. But Agee hit a lead-off homer in the first and made two spectacular catches later in the game as the Mets went on to win 5-0 behind Gary Gentry and Nolan Ryan. The stage was set for one of the most exciting and controversial games in Series history.

Again, it was Seaver versus Cuellar, but this time, Seaver nursed a 1-0 lead into the ninth, thanks to Donn Clendenon's solo homer in the second. With one out in the ninth, Frank Robinson singled to left, and Powell singled him to third. Brooks Robinson then lined what appeared to be a certain single to right center. But Swoboda dove—fully extended, glove hand outstretched—and caught the ball as his head smacked the ground. Even though the tying run scored, Swoboda had saved the day with what some people still describe as the greatest catch in post-season play.

Seaver pitched on through the tenth. With none out in the bottom of the inning Baltimore left fielder Don Buford lost Grote's short fly in the sun, and the ball fell in for a double. Gaspar came in to run for Grote, and Harrelson was walked. Then Orioles coach Billy Hunter, who was managing because

Earl Weaver had been thrown out back in the third, brought
Pete Richert in to pitch to J. C. Martin, who was hitting for
Seaver. The managerial wheels were turning, and so was the
wheel of fortune. Martin laid down a standard sacrifice, and
Richert reached it before the catcher. He threw to first, too
close to the runner, and hit Martin on the shoulder. As the
ball bounced into short right field, Gaspar—Rod Stupid—
jumped on the plate with the winning run.

The Orioles took a 3-0 lead off Koosman in the fifth game
on a two-run homer by McNally and a solo blast by Frank
Robinson. But then the Mets received two big breaks involving hit batsmen. In the sixth, a ball hit Robinson's thigh, but
plate umpire Lou DiMuro maintained it had hit his bat handle first, and Robinson ended up striking out. In the bottom
of the same inning, a pitch hit Cleon Jones in the foot, and
again DiMuro didn't believe it. But then Hodges came out of
the dugout, and borrowing a scene from a popular TV commercial of the time, he asked the umpire to look at the ball
for shoe polish. There was, in fact, a smudge of polish, and
DiMuro awarded Jones first base. Clendenon followed with a
home run that brought the Mets within one, and in the seventh, Weis, with two homers all season, led off with a game-
tying home run.

The Orioles fell apart in the eighth, and the Mets went ahead,
5-3. Koosman walked Frank Robinson to start off the ninth.
Then Powell grounded into a force, Brooks Robinson flied to
right, and Davey Johnson, who seventeen years later would
preside over a Mets World Series victory, flied out to Cleon
Jones in left.

At 3:14 p.m., EDT, October 16, 1969, the Mets were world
champions. The fans tore up the Shea Stadium turf, Casey
Stengel came down from his box to hug Hodges, Mrs. Payson
cried. And one rooter held up a sign that read: "There are no
words."

WEAVER'S ORIOLES

Frank Robinson once called Earl Weaver "the most patient impatient man I've ever met." By that he meant that Weaver would stay with a player an entire year, as he did with outfielder Don Buford one horrendous season, desperately hoping all the while that the player would snap out of his slump, eating his liver when he didn't. Weaver's teams didn't steal, or bunt, or hit and run much; he believed in "Dr. Longball" and the big inning because he knew that in most games the winning team scored more runs in one inning than the losing team would score in the entire game. He was one of history's greatest managers—only once in his seventeen seasons did a Weaver team finish below .500, and his clubs won at least 90 games in ten different seasons.

Weaver never gave his players the green light to steal. The year Reggie Jackson played for the Orioles, he wanted to run on his own. So one day, with right-handed slugger Lee May at the plate against a left-hander, Jackson stole second easily. After May walked and a pinch hitter ended the inning, Jackson came back to the dugout, beaming. Weaver scowled. "Yeah, you stole," he said. "That opens first base. The lefthander walks May. Then I've got to bring in a right-handed pinch hitter. I had the gun loaded with May. You take the bat out of his hands and make me waste another player. That's what the stolen base got us." Jackson never ran on his own again.

Pat Kelly, an outfielder and born-again Christian, once told Weaver, "You got to walk with the Lord, Skip." "Hell," Weaver replied, "I'd rather you walk with the bases loaded."

During an Oriole tour of Japan, a Sumo wrestler happened by the clubhouse, and to demonstrate his strength, he hoisted Weaver above his shoulders with one hand. Whereupon the Orioles shouted as one, "Drop him! Drop him!"

He may not have been entirely likeable, but Weaver was full of surprises. He could play the ukelele, and he knew almost every Nelson Eddy and Jeanette Macdonald song by heart. He loved growing vegetables, playing golf, and drinking. One day in spring training, Weaver was getting on retired umpire Ron Luciano about some of the inaccuracies in Luciano's book. Luciano pleaded poetic license. And Weaver told him, "Like it says in *Hamlet,* Ron, 'This above all: to thine own self be true.'"

Weaver quoting Shakespare is remarkable enough, but the kicker to the story came after Weaver's literary allusion appeared the next day in a column by Edwin Pope in the *Miami Herald.* An editor decided to improve on it by having Weaver say, "Like Horatio said in *Hamlet . . .*" The next time Weaver saw Pope, he yelled, "Edwin, if Polonius didn't fucking say it, I've lived the last 35 years of my life backwards."

There have been many superstitious players, but few could match Baltimore pitcher Mike Cuellar. When Cuellar and the team arrived in Milwaukee once, he solemnly informed Weaver that he had left his lucky baseball cap behind in Baltimore, and that even though he was on a nine-game winning streak, he would surely lose the next night if he pitched with a replacement cap. Weaver ordered the Baltimore traveling secretary to send for Cuellar's cap, and with the help of one Oriole front-office executive, two airline representatives, two pilots, and a series of hand deliveries involving a change of planes in Chicago, the cap was presented to Cuellar just before game time. Cuellar opened the envelope containing the cap and cried out, "It's not my GAME cap! They sent my PRACTICE cap!"

Milwaukee hitters sent Cuellar to the showers in the third inning, but before he reached the dugout, he threw the cap down and stomped on it.

Jim Palmer won at least 20 games eight times, and 268 games in all for the Orioles from 1965 until 1984. He had a habit of positioning his fielders just so, and the Orioles liked to tell of the time Palmer moved the right-fielder over just a notch in a crucial situation, then threw a pitch that the batter lined directly to the stationary right-fielder.

Hollywood handsome, Palmer was an underwear model and

TV commentator in his spare time. He was also Prince Hal to Weaver's Falstaff, and although the two respected each other, they were constantly engaged in verbal conflict over Palmer's endless series of minor injuries. Once Weaver was pulled over for driving while intoxicated and the police officer asked him if he had any physical infirmities. Weaver replied, "Yeah, Jim Palmer."

One of their most spectacular skirmishes occurred when Palmer threw a fastball to a weak-hitting opponent, who proceeded to hit a damaging bloop double off the bat handle. When Palmer got back to the dugout, Weaver said out off the corner of his mouth, "The rest of the bloody league is throwing sliders to bloody .167 hitters."

Palmer stomped off toward the clubhouse, with the diminutive manager in hot pursuit. Weaver was jumping up and down, yelling at Palmer, when the pitcher turned around and said, "Why, Earl, I've never seen you so tall."

Another Oriole who used to drive Weaver crazy was second baseman Davey Johnson. Johnson, a math major in college, was always coming to him with lineup ideas based on the statistics he assiduously kept. Johnson once went to the mound to counsel pitcher Dave McNally, who was uncharacteristically wild on this particular day. "Don't you know about the unfavorable chance deviation theory?" Johnson asked McNally. "When you're wild, aim for the middle of the plate because, since you're wild, it won't go where you want it. The ball will hit the corners, which is what you really want."

It was once written that while Baltimore belonged to Brooks Robinson, the Orioles were the property of Frank Robinson. He came over to the Orioles from the Reds before the '66 season in one of the more lopsided trades of the era; the Reds got pitchers Milt Pappas and Jack Baldschun and outfielder Dick Simpson. "We feel he's an old 30," said Reds president Bill DeWitt, explaining why his club had given up on Robinson. But Frank immediately led the Orioles to a world championship with a Triple Crown year (.316, 49 homers, 122 RBIs), becoming the first player to win MVP awards in both leagues. In 1969, '70, and '71, he carried the O's into the Series, not only as their right-fielder and cleanup hitter, but also as the chief justice of their clubhouse kangaroo court.

Although he got into some scraps early in his career, Robinson was a natural leader. His former Reds teammate Vada Pinson, a fellow alumnus of McClymonds High in Oakland, Calif., recalled a game against the Braves. "Frank slid into third base hard—like he always does, no matter what the score may be—into Eddie Mathews. Mathews jumped on top of Frank and punched him in the eye. It swelled out to here and nobody thought Frank could possibly play the second game of a double header that day. But when the game started, there was Frank in the lineup. Not only did he hit a home run to win the game, but he also made a catch and fell into the left field stands—on a ball that Mathews hit, incidentally—that saved the game. He got a standing ovation, and I guess that's one of the biggest thrills I've ever felt in baseball."

CHARLIE FINLEY AND THE A'S

Charles O. Finley had an ass named Charley O. that he designated his team's mascot, and the two were often confused. After Finley suffered a mild heart attack, some fans in Oakland displayed a banner that summarized their feelings about him: "Finley Couldn't Have Had a Heart Attack—He Has No Heart."

A former batboy for the Birmingham Barons, Finley made his fortune in insurance, and for years he hung around the baseball meetings, trying to find a team to buy. When Kansas City owner Arnold Johnson died early in 1960, Finley acquired controlling interest from the estate, and one of his first acts was to try to move the club to Dallas. Then he cast his sights on Atlanta. Finally, after the '67 season, he succeeded in shifting the franchise to Oakland. Said Missouri Senator Stuart Symington at the time, "Charles O. Finley is one of the most disreputable characters ever to enter the American sports scene. . . . The loss of the A's is more than recompensed by the pleasure of getting rid of Mr. Finley."

As the A's owner, Finley tried to foist upon the public such monstrosities as orange baseballs and color-coded bases (red, yellow, and blue). He pioneered garishly colored uniforms, and even managed to dress Joe DiMaggio (whom he'd hired as a coach) in hideous green and gold for two years. Finley also thought up the designated hitter, the night World Series game, and the pinch-running specialist. One of his infamous pinch-runners, Allen Lewis, called "The Panamanian Express," once tried to score from second by way of the pitcher's mound.

None of those monstrosities could compare, though, to his treatment of players, managers, and coaches; in retrospect, he makes George Steinbrenner look like Eleanor Roosevelt. He was always putting his stars through painful and unnecessarily protracted contract negotiations, and once made a big deal out of lending Catfish Hunter $150,000 for his farm—then he almost immediately called in the loan, pestering Hunter for the money on the day of his starts.

Still, Finley knew talent. He assembled an excellent band of players, then hired Dick Williams to mold them. United in their enmity for Finley, they became the only team besides the 1936–39 Yankees and the 1949–53 Yankees to win three world championships in a row.

The A's first began to attract attention in 1971, in large part thanks to Vida Blue, their sensational rookie pitcher. With Blue winning 24 games and Hunter 21, and Reggie Jackson hitting 32 homers, the A's finished the regular season with 101 victories. But they lost the playoffs to the Orioles in five games. To show his gratitude for a Cy Young season, Finley offered Blue a contract for $45,000, only $70,000 short of what Blue's agent was asking. Blue announced that he was taking a PR job with a plumbing fixtures firm, and Finley countered by trading for the washed-up Denny McLain. The 1972 season, already delayed by a players' strike, started without Blue in uniform. Blue finally capitulated on May 1, signing for close to Finley's original offer, but he was bitter and out of shape, and he would win only six games all year.

But the 1972 season would establish the Oakland reputation for excellence, and also for facial hair. Jackson started the unshaven look over the winter, and Rollie Fingers, Bob Locker, and Darold Knowles picked up on it during the spring. Whereas any other owner would have demanded they shave, Finley, to his credit, decided to offer a $300 bonus to any of his men who grew a mustache by Father's Day. On June 18, a special Mustache Day was held, and every member of the team collected a bonus.

In 1973 the A's won their second straight World Series, and Reggie Jackson (who had been injured the previous year) got his first real shot at being Mr. October. It took the A's seven games to defeat the underdog Mets in the Series, but when it was over, Jackson was the MVP with a .310 average, six RBIs, and a crucial two-run homer in the deciding game. He did all that under a death threat: for the entire Series he was followed around by a huge bodyguard named Tony Del Rio. After the last out of the last game, Del Rio carried Jackson off the field in his arms as if he were a baby.

Jackson's heroics were nearly overshadowed by the villainy of Finley, who outdid himself after the second game of the Series. In the twelfth inning of that game, second baseman Mike Andrews made two errors that helped the Mets win. While Andrews accepted the blame manfully, Finley decided to concoct a shoulder injury for the second baseman so that he could activate rookie Manny Trillo in his place. The owner enlisted the help of Dr. Harry Walker, the team's orthopedist, who stated that Andrews "is unable to play his position because of a biceps groove tenosynovitis of the right shoulder." Andrews at first refused to sign a statement that he was hurt, but Finley threatened to blackball him from baseball if he didn't, and Andrews relented.

The A's became mutinous when Andrews was not on the plane ride to New York, and Finley further infuriated the team by forbidding the showing of the in-flight movie, *1776,* because he did not like it. The players held a clandestine vote whether or not to throw Finley out the emergency door, but someone argued that such an ejection would depressurize the cabin, thus disrupting their card games. Finley was spared.

Finley continued his petty ways. He had promised the players better World Series rings the second time around, but they were instead given cheap rings with little artificial emeralds in them. Finley had a shoe contract with Adidas, but some of his players had individual deals with other shoe companies. He threatened to fine or fire them if they wore anything but Adidases, and the players openly defied him. This time he gave in.

Despite such distractions, or perhaps because of them, the A's went on to win their third straight championship in '74. But Finley got his comeuppance in the offseason at the hands of Hunter, the Cy Young Award winner. In the contract Hunter signed for 1974 he had asked that half of his $100,000 salary be set aside for an insurance annuity. Finley agreed, unaware that he would have to pay the taxes on the $50,000. After Finley refused to pay up, the pitcher was declared a free agent because the A's had breached his contract. After hearing offers from all but two clubs, Hunter signed with the Yankees for a package of $2.85 million, a then-unheard-of sum.

Asked what his signing would mean for the future of baseball, Hunter said, "I think the owners will start reading their contracts better."

The A's won another division title in '75, but Boston swept them in three games, and that was the beginning of the end. After the season, Jackson and Ken Holtzman were traded. In June of 1976, faced with the prospect of losing some of his stars to the new system of free agency, Finley sold Blue to the Yankees for $1.5 million and Joe Rudi and Rollie Fingers to the Red Sox for $1 million apiece. Bowie Kuhn voided the sales "in the best interest of baseball." But Rudi and Fingers were gone soon enough, as were several other key players. By 1977 the A's were a last-place team and Finley was running a ghost ship.

BIG GUYS

The first baseman for Weaver's Orioles was the gargantuan Boog Powell, a power hitter with a pretty good glove and stupendous appetite. "Sometimes when you're driving," Powell once said, "the car just seems to turn by itself into a McDonald's, and while you're there, you might as well get a large order of fries."

Another ballplayer with a weight problem was Tigers lefthander Mickey Lolich. His paunch, though, didn't stop Lolich from pitching an amazing 376 innings in 1971, a year in which he won 25 games. "I think I'll just keep the tools I've got," said Lolich. "And remember my watchword for this year: there are a lot of skinny guys with bad arms." Lolich, in fact, had a skinny cousin in the majors, Ron Lolich, an outfielder for the Indians. "The last couple of months Ronnie has been hitting .050," Lolich said in '73. "He's just got to fatten up and you'll see that average climb."

Lolich thought of himself as a role model. "When I'm out there pitching a Saturday game that is nationally televised, there is some fat guy in front of the set at home in his T shirt and shorts. He looks at me and says, 'Mabel, that guy's fat just like me. Now get me another beer, will ya?'" When Lolich retired, he opened a doughnut shop.

Ron Luciano, a former professional football offensive lineman with a fondness for bird-watching and Shakespeare, was one of the more unusual umpires baseball has ever known. Luciano was a showman, and it often got him in trouble with his superiors. In 1972 he was working first base in Boston when a bat slipped out of the hands of Yankee Bobby Murcer. The bat came spinning down the first base line toward Luciano, and when it came to rest in foul territory, he gave it a rather emphatic foul call. The replays of the call were shown over and over, and Luciano was fined $200 for "conduct unbecoming an Umpire."

During a spring training game once, Luciano was kidding third baseman Buddy Bell about what a bad day he was having in the field, and when Bell made yet another error, he flipped his glove to Luciano and said, "Here, you play third, I'll umpire." And Luciano did—for an inning. On one play, he took a throw from the outfield and tried to throw runner Mike Epstein out at second. The throw was too high and too late, but second base umpire Joe Brinkman called Epstein out anyway. When Epstein started to argue, Brinkman cut him off and said, "Who do you think threw it?," pointing to Luciano. Epstein just said "Oh," and walked off the field.

Luciano was a longtime nemesis of Earl Weaver, dating back to their common time in the Eastern League. Weaver was ejected frequently in his career, and Luciano was probably the leading ejector. But Weaver finally got his revenge in 1975, when Luciano had to change a call on a ball hit by California's Tommy Harper in Baltimore. The ball landed near the left-field foul pole, but Luciano lost it in the sun. "I looked at the Orioles' left-fielder, Don Buford, and he was looking into the seats. I listened to the Baltimore crowd. The fans were quiet, as if something terrible had happened to their team. I figured it had to be a home run.

"But because I wasn't positive, and I knew it was a close call, I decided to give it the full Luciano special. I was going to sell it so hard, no one could possibly doubt I knew what I was doing. I leaped high into the air, I twirled my hand, I spun around. I shouted at the top of my lungs. I blew up a small sandstorm." From the reaction of the Orioles, though, Luciano knew immediately that he had made a mistake. As Weaver came toward him, Luciano shouted, "Don't get yourself thrown out of the game, I'm gonna get help." With Weaver running interference for him, Luciano walked toward home plate, then realized the plate umpire was Armando Rodriguez, a Mexican umpire who knew little English. Luciano then headed toward first base, where crew chief Bill Haller was working. "I blew it, huh?" said Luciano.

Haller shrugged and said, "Oh, I don't know. What's 40 or 50 feet?"

"I gotta change it, right?"

Haller agreed.

"But if I do, [California manager Dick] Williams is going nuts and I'm gonna have to run him out, right?"

"Right," said Haller.

Luciano did change the call, Williams did go nuts, and

Luciano did eject him from the game. Weaver, of course, was merely thrilled by it all.

WILLIAMS RETURNS

No one thought it possible, but in 1969 Washington Senators owner Bob Short lured Ted Williams out of retirement to become his manager. Williams inspired the sad-sack club to an 86-76 record—far above expectations—and was voted the AL Manager of the Year. Williams got the news while on safari in Africa when Bob Addie of the *Washington Post* somehow managed to reach him by phone. "Are you sure?" asked an excited Williams. When Addie confirmed it, Williams said, "I'll tell you something. It was just another case of the writers being wrong again. Weaver and Martin deserved it more."

On that same safari, a Rhodesian hunter named Mike Cameron saw right through Williams's assertion that he loved hunting more than baseball. "He is pleased, but he will not dream of the buffalo," said Cameron. "He will relax with the problems of adding 50 percentage points to Mr. [Paul] Casanova's batting figure. Or how to make Mr. [Joe] Coleman a better pitcher. Because he is a magnificent fraud, your Ted. He is genuinely enthusiastic about everything. He argues about the strength of fishing line and ballistics, and he is very positive in his arguments, but I suspect he has only one true love, and he denies her."

BOUTON'S BESTSELLER

Jim Bouton was a decent enough pitcher; he won 21 games for the 1963 Yankees, and the next year won two World Series starts on top of his eighteen regular season victories. But Bouton's greatest contribution to the game came with the publication, in 1970, of *Ball Four*.

The book, written with Leonard Shecter, was like no other

baseball book that had ever been published—a remarkable string of stories about drunkenness, infidelity, and other aspect of boorish and irresponsible behavior among ballplayers. Breaking the long-standing code of discretion that emanated from the game's clubhouses (said his critics), revealing as had no one before the true nature of the baseball life (said his supporters), Bouton and his book caused shockwaves. He was called on the carpet by Commissioner Kuhn and ostracized by many of his former (and current) teammates. But he was resented especially by those players' wives who, wrote Nancy Marshall (wife of pitcher Mike Marshall), "didn't want to think about the times when their husbands were on the road, let alone read a story that confirmed their worst suspicions."

THE EMANCIPATOR

Curt Flood was an uncommonly good center-fielder for the St. Louis Cardinals, a mainstay of their three World Series teams in the 1960s. But he criticized the front office in '69, infuriating owner August Busch, Jr. On October 7 he received a phone call from Jim Toomey, a functionary for general manager Bing Devine. "Curt, you've been traded to Philadelphia." Flood didn't say anything at the time. Later, though, he said, "There ain't no way I'm going to pack up and move twelve years of my life away from here. No way at all."

Flood decided to challenge baseball's reserve clause. To do that, he had to sit out the 1970 season. He escaped to Copenhagen. "I bought a sketch pad and beret and grew a goatee. I played artist on street corners and in the happy hunting grounds known as Tivoli Gardens. 'Little do these beautiful Danish pastries realize,' I mused, 'that the esthetic black in the beret is actually Curt Flood, the famous St. Louis business tycoon and athlete, vacationing between triumphs."

Triumphs? The case, which made it to the Supreme Court, was never fully resolved, and in fact became moot when Flood signed with the Washington Senators for the '71 season. In the meantime, his businesses went into bankruptcy, and he lost most of his money. He played only a handful of games for the Senators before he quit for good.

Still, Flood made the public aware of the players' situation, showing how the individual had no control over his contractual destiny. His efforts paved the way for free agency in baseball, and the game's millionaires owe him a debt of gratitude. In explaining his decision to fight, Flood quoted the ex-slave Frederick Douglass: "If there is not struggle, there is not progress. Those who profess to favor freedom, and yet deprecate agitation, are men who want crops without plowing up the ground. . . . Power concedes nothing without a demand. It never did and never will."

THE TRAGEDY OF CLEMENTE

For 18 seasons, Roberto Clemente had been the magnetic heart of his Pittsburgh teams, as charismatic as he was gifted. More than any player of his time, his very presence on the field could determine the shape of the game. In the 1971 World Series, wrote Roger Angell, he played "a kind of baseball that none of us had even seen before—throwing and running and hitting at something close to the level of absolute perfection." That year, Pittsburgh beat Baltimore four games to three.

After the '72 season in which the Pirates again won the NL East yet could not advance past Cincinnati, Clemente had exactly 3,000 hits, a .317 lifetime average, and several years still ahead of him; although he was thirty-eight, he was still a .300 hitter and a spectacular fielder. But on the night of December 31, 1972, while on a mission of mercy to earthquake victims in Nicaragua, Clemente went down in a DC-7 overloaded with supplies. He had gone because he had heard that soldiers were stealing relief aid. "If I go to Nicaragua, the stealing will stop," he said, beating a palm against his chest. "They would not dare steal from Roberto Clemente."

Clemente was in such a hurry that the plane took off without out a certified flight engineer who might have detected engine trouble. And when the engines did sputter, and the pilot banked to turn back, sixteen 60-pound bags of sugar which had not been tied down suddenly shifted, and the plane crashed into the heavy seas off Puerto Rico.

Manny Sanguillen, who had to replace Clemente in right field the next season, said, "When he die it was so big in Puerto Rico people stop everything. Nobody have any more parties for New Year's. Everybody go to the beach to try to find him. Try to find the body or at least something. I was really hurt for his wife. She went down to the beach every day, too, to pray or see what she could do. I think she is still going down there.

"Clemente is still on the ballclub. His spirit belong here. You know how great he was in the outfield. And he gives his life for somebody he don't know."

STEVE BLASS

It came to be known as Steve Blass disease: a sudden inability to throw the ball where you're supposed to. But that wasn't really fair because Blass had some fine years with the Pirates and won two games for them in the 1971 World Series. He was one of the best control pitchers in baseball at one time, but in 1973, he suddenly lost it. He could not get the ball over the plate. That he was an especially thoughtful man made his plight even more poignant. "I never struggled at pitching before," he said during his last comeback attempt in '74. "I mean, I was never uncertain about whether or not I wanted to walk out to the mound. Now, it scares me. Scares hell out of me. You have no idea how frustrating it is. You don't know where you're going to throw the ball. You're afraid you might hurt someone. You know you're embarrassing yourself, but you can't do anything about it. You're helpless. Totally afraid and helpless."

In his last spring training with the Pirates, Blass worked 20 innings, giving up 17 hits, 33 walks, and 22 runs, while hitting 10 batters. Through it all, though, he kept his sense of humor. Asked if he thought he was being punished for his transgressions, Blass said, "No, if God wanted to punish me for my sins He would have zapped me four years ago."

LUIS TIANT

Luis Tiant was one of the more delightful characters and puzzling pitchers of the modern era. A Cuban who smoked his fat $1 cigars even in the shower, Tiant could throw a fastball, curveball, slider, or knuckler with three different deliveries, effectively giving him 12 different pitches. He would pivot so dramatically in mid-motion that his back would be turned toward the plate. The Red Sox pulled him off the scrap heap in 1971, and he became their most consistent pitcher over the next few years, leading them to the World Series in '75.

Tiant was so cagey a competitor that he once stepped off the mound, ostensibly to look at the runner on second. But in the very act of doing so he fired a strike past the startled batter. After some reflection, umpire Nestor Chylak charged Tiant with a balk for deceiving the hitter.

AARON'S RECORD

For years, Hank Aaron had been practicing his particular brand of excellence, but usually in the shadow of flashier talents—men like Mays and Mantle and Frank Robinson. He stuck to his work, relying on ferocious powers of concentration as well as his physical gifts.

Pitcher Claude Osteen once said of him, "Slapping a rattlesnake across the face with the back of your hand is safer than trying to fool Hank Aaron." He had an odd habit while sitting in the dugout of looking through one of the holes in his cap at the pitcher, to isolate his adversary and study him. And, strangely enough, he never saw any of his 755 homers—he always kept his head down until he reached first base to make sure he touched the bag, figuring that "looking at the ball going over the fence isn't going to help."

What helped was his remarkable conditioning. Between the ages of thirty-five and forty, he hit at least 34 home runs a year. When he hit 40 in his fortieth year, it became clear that Babe Ruth's record of 714 lifetime homers was about to be obliterated.

As Aaron approached Ruth's record in '73 and '74, he wasn't sure if he was chasing Ruth or vice versa. "Babe. Babe. Babe Ruth," he said. "I never made a study of the man, but I know an awful lot about him. It seems that everybody I talk to tells me a little bit more." Aaron also received a lot of hate mail, much if it racially motivated. But he kept his cool, and in April of '74, baseball geared up for the big night. Baseballs thrown to Aaron were specially marked with numbers that could be seen under a fluorescent lamp so that there would be no question as to the identity of the ball. On his first swing of the season, Aaron tied Ruth at 714. He then sat out a few games to make sure he broke the record at home in Atlanta.

The victim of the historic home run was Al Downing of the Dodgers, who threw a 1-and-0 fastball a little higher and a little more over the plate than he wanted. Aaron shot it right back out, on a nice arc into the Braves bullpen in left. There it was caught by relief pitcher Tom House, who ran the ball in to give to Aaron. Aaron recalled the moment this way: "I don't remember the noise or the two kids that I'm told ran the bases with me. My teammates at home plate, I remember seeing them. I remember my mother out there, and she hugging me. That's what I'll remember more than anything about the home run when I think back on it. I don't know where she came from, but she was there."

Actually, House may have had the best perspective on the scene: "I've got my master's degree in marketing, and I don't suppose my professors would give me high marks for opportunism, with so much being offered for the ball. But I'm not at all sorry. What made it worthwhile was what I saw when I ran in with the ball holding it in my gloved hand, running really fast—in fact my teammates joked afterward that it was the fastest I'd run in a couple of years—really just wanting to get rid of it, to put it in Henry's hand. In that great crowd around home plate I found him looking over his mother's shoulder, hugging her to him, and suddenly I saw what many people have never been able to see in him—deep emotion . . . I looked and he had tears hanging on his lids. I could hardly believe it. 'Hammer, here it is,' I said. I put the ball in his hand. He said, 'Thanks, kid,' and touched me on the shoulder. I kept staring at him. And it was then that it was brought home to me what this home run meant, not only to him, but to all of us."

MALCONTENTS

Dick—also called Richie—Allen carried his fearsome bat and his difficult personality from Philadelphia to St. Louis to Los Angeles to Chicago and Philadelphia again, then finally to Oakland in his 15-year career. He was a tremendously gifted player who preferred horse racing to baseball, a student of hitting who eschewed batting practice, a man who inspired tremendous respect from teammates yet showed up drunk for ballgames. George Myatt, interim manager of the '60 Phillies, said of Allen, "I don't think God Almighty could completely handle Richie Allen, so all I can do is try."

Allen, who came from Wampum, Pa., and carried a huge, 42-ounce bat to the plate, won the MVP Award with the White Sox in 1972 when he hit .308 with 37 homers and 118 RBIs. Most of his career, though, was promise unfulfilled. He left many tales behind, stories of how he once got a hit while carrying on a conversation with the other team's bench, of his punchout of teammate Frank Thomas, of the time he put his fist through the headlight of his vintage car, severing tendons in his hand.

But perhaps Allen's most telling legacy was his form of protest during his first stint with the Phillies. Playing first base, he took to writing messages in the dirt. Commissioner Bowie Kuhn finally told the Phillies to make him stop, and when Allen was given the order, he responded with three more messages: *No, why,* and *mom.* Why *mom?* "To say she tells me what to do, not the man up there," said Allen.

Like Allen, Alex Johnson was a gifted hitter with a troubled spirit. He won the AL batting crown in 1970, but in 1971 the Angels suspended him for ten days "for failure to give his best efforts to winning of games." He played hard only when the spirit moved him, and the spirit did not move him often. Trying to explain the reason for his disenchantment with the Angels, Johnson said, "Ever get sick of a thing? I mean sick, sick, sick? I mean really sick, sick, sick? That's the way it is with me and this club. I didn't consciously decide to do this. But things are just so disgusting, it drills on my mind, drills on my mind."

Things got so bad that Johnson accused his only friend on the team, Chico Ruiz, of pointing a gun at him in the clubhouse. The accusation made the Angels the butt of some bad firearm jokes. Opposing players, for instance, would ask Angels if they would prefer to take batting or target practice. Johnson survived the season without getting fired upon, and in fact had several more productive years with other teams.

But he would ever be remembered for his truculence, not his physical skills. One season early in his career, he had hit more home runs by the all-star break than he had the entire previous season. In Philadelphia, a writer asked, "Alex, what's the difference between your home runs this year and last year?" Johnson stared at his inquisitor malevolently and said, "Four, you motherfucker, four."

EX-CONS

Gates Brown was a sensational and sensationally rounded pinch-hitter for the Detroit Tigers with a most unusual background. He was discovered while serving time in the Mansfield State Reformatory in Ohio for breaking and entering. The coach of the team, Chuck Yarman, wrote letters to several clubs, and the teams loved what they saw. The Tigers won a bidding war with the Indians, and he rewarded them with 107 career pinch hits. In 1968 Brown hit .370 off the bench and helped the Tigers get into the World Series.

Years later, when Brown returned to his Crestline, Ohio, high school to give a talk, the principal of the school asked him during an assembly, "Gates, I'm sure some of our students would be interested to know—what did you take when you were in school?"

"Overcoats, mostly," said Brown.

Brown's success in Detroit paved the way for another ex-convict. Ron LeFlore was a nineteen-year-old drug addict when he suggested to his friends that they rob a little neighborhood bar called Dee's on Detroit's east side in January of 1970. The three of them got away with nearly $35,000, but the driver didn't notice the lights were out on the getaway car, and a passing police car did. LeFlore was sentenced to five to fifteen years in the State Prison of Southern Michigan in Jackson. He was hardly penitent. He goaded guards and found himself in and out of solitary confinement. But while in solitary, he started getting in shape doing pushups and situps. He was invited to try out for the baseball team, and although he had never shown any real interest in the sport, he turned out to be a natural. Another inmate at Jackson started writing letters to a friend named Jimmy Butsicaris, who was both the co-owner of a popular Detroit bar and the best man at one of Billy Martin's weddings.

Martin, who was managing the Tigers at the time, invited LeFlore to come down to Tiger Stadium for a tryout when he was released in 1972. Although LeFlore wasn't due out until August, he was granted a weekend furlough and worked out at Tiger Stadium in front of the other players. "I was crazy about him," said Martin. "Mickey Stanley, Norm Cash, Al Kaline—all the guys liked him, too. But one guy in the organization, and I don't want to name him, said, 'But Billy, he's in jail.' And I asked the guy. 'Where do you think you got Gates Brown from—kindergarten?' "

The Tigers did sign LeFlore, for $5,000, and with the promise of a job, he was released from prison a month early. He broke into the majors the next year as a twenty-six-year-old rookie center-fielder, and his specialty was still theft: he stole 23 bases in 59 games. By 1978 he was so explosive on offense that he scored a league-leading 126 runs, and in 1980 for the

Montreal Expos, he stole 97 bases. After his retirement, Le-Flore tried to come back to the game as, of all things, an umpire.

HERO

Rick Monday made thousands of catches in his nineteen years as a major league outfielder, but is most remembered for one shoestring grab he made for the Cubs in Dodger Stadium on April 25, 1976. In the fourth inning of that game, Monday, the left-fielder, noticed two spectators climb out of the stands and go to a spot in left-center. "One of them had the American flag tucked under his arm," Monday recalled. "The next thing I saw was the glint of the can. They were sprinkling its contents on the flag. I figured it wasn't holy water. I said to myself, 'My God, they're trying to burn the sucker.' That's when I took off. They couldn't see me coming from behind but I could see one had lit a match. The wind blew it out, and just as they lit another and were about to touch it to the flag, I grabbed it. They threw the can of lighter fluid at me, just missing my head."

Monday deposited the flag in the bullpen. The culprits, William Thomas and his eleven-year-old son, were protesting the treatment of American Indians during the Bicentennial year, and they were arrested for trespassing. As what had happened dawned on the Dodgers fans, they gave Monday a standing ovation. In the days and weeks that followed, Monday was widely honored. Said his teammate, Jose Cardenal, "Now we have three great patriots: Lincoln, Washington, and Monday."

Following the '76 season, Monday was traded to the Dodgers. When his six-year-old son Michael went to games in Dodger Stadium, he would point to the flag flapping in center and say, "Look, Mommy! There's Daddy's flag."

BROADCASTER

Harry Caray was a broadcaster of immense popularity in St. Louis and later Chicago. Born Harry Carabina in St. Louis, his trademarks were a shouted "Holy Cow," a rousing rendition of "Take Me Out to the Ballgame" delivered during the seventh-inning stretch, a biting wit, and a capacity for drink matched by few men.

Caray reportedly left the employ of the Cardinals after he became involved with a young woman who had married into the Busch clan. "I'd rather have people believing the rumor and have my middle-aged ego inflated than deny it and keep my job," he said.

Years earlier, in 1968, Caray was crossing the street in front of the Chase-Park Plaza Hotel when he was struck by a speeding auto, suffering broken legs, a broken shoulder, and a broken nose. On Opening Day of the next season, sensing the dramatic possibilities, he stepped out of the St. Louis dugout after his introduction, hobbling on two canes. As he crossed the foul line, he tossed one cane aside. Approaching the field mike, he threw the other cane away. As the crowd stood and chanted his name, Caray limped unaided the rest of the way. "Well, it's all show business," he said. "I hadn't needed those canes in weeks."

TWO PITCHERS

When he first broke into the majors in 1966 with the New York Mets, Nolan Ryan could throw the ball harder than anyone else. Remarkably he could make the same claim twenty years later. The all-time leader in no-hitters (5) and strike-outs (and it should be mentioned, in walks as well), Ryan proved his grit with the Astros during the 1986 National League Championship Series when he shut down the Mets while pitching on a broken ankle.

Ryan was fiercely proud of his pitching ability. Once, while pitching for the California Angels, he went up to catcher Ellie Rodriguez and asked if he would be catching that day. When Rodriguez confirmed that he was, Ryan said, "Well, I'll be throwing these," and handed him a tiny rubber ball. He then went out and beat Baltimore 1-0 in the fourth no-hitter of his career.

The Mets had traded away Ryan in an effort to fill their long-gaping hole at third base. But Jim Fregosi, the player they acquired, became only one more victim of what came to be known as the Bermuda Triangle of Baseball. From 1962 through 1987, 86 different men tried to play third for the Mets, and only three of them (Wayne Garrett, Hubie Brooks, and Howard Johnson) lasted more than 250 games.

Chronologically, the first Mets third baseman is also the last one alphabetically—Don Zimmer. Number one in the alphabet is Bill Almon, and in between come such memorable names as Cliff Cook, Joe Foy (whom they got from KC for Amos Otis), Pumpsie Green, Rick Herrscher, Rod Kanehl, Phil Linz, Phil Mankowski, Joe Moock, Danny Napoleon, Bobby Pfeil, Al Puig, Amado Samuel, Ted Schreiber, and Roy Staiger. In 1980, when Elliott Maddox took over third, he looked like he might be there for a while. But then he said, "I don't know why nothing's happened to me yet," and several days later he pulled a hamstring. He was gone at season's end.

Steve Carlton won an unprecedented four Cy Young Awards for the Phillies with a slider so hard to hit that Willie Stargell once compared the effort to "trying to eat soup with a fork." He finished his career ranked second in strikeouts, ninth in wins, and seventh in innings pitched.

Lefty, as he was universally known, was a mysterious fellow who maintained a nearly 15-year silence with the press. Even on the night he won his 300th game, he said not a word. It was only when Carlton started going from team to team at the end of his career that he went public, bringing to mind the old line, "He was learning to say hello when he should have been learning to say goodbye." His last stop was in Minnesota, and Carlton-watchers weren't surprised to note that in a picture of the 1987 world champion Twins on the White House lawn that appeared in the *St. Paul Pioneer-Press,* the man in the sunglasses identified as an "unnamed Secret Service agent" was actually Lefty.

BASEBALL BECOMES INTERNATIONAL

It was in the sixties that Japanese baseball began to become an alternative for over-the-hill or not-up-to-par American players, and though the Japanese paid well, their cultural traditions presented all sorts of problems for foreigners. One of the first Americans to make the migration was former Giants third baseman Daryl Spencer. Spencer insisted on following his own training routine while with the Hankyu Braves, and that did not sit well with the manager. One night as Spencer rather lackadaisically worked out before a game, the manager told him, "You don't look sharp. You need a rest."

"What do you mean, I need a rest?" Spencer replied. "Who's leading this team in home runs, anyway?"

"I don't think you can hit this pitcher."

"I can't hit him? I'm batting .340 against that guy."

"Not tonight. That's my feeling. You're out."

Spencer angrily stormed into the clubhouse to change into street clothes. But while he was changing, he heard his name announced in the starting lineup. The manager had put him down for third in the order, but only because he was going to fool the opposition by pinch-hitting for Spencer.

Now Spencer was furious. When the game began, and he heard the name of the second batter announced over the loudspeaker, he walked out to the on-deck circle in his underwear and shower clogs and took a few practice swings. The manager fined him $200, but Spencer said, "It was worth every penny."

One player who seemed perfectly suited for Japan was former Dodgers outfielder Willie Davis. Davis was a devout member of the Soka Gakkai, a Nichiren Buddhist sect. When he signed to play for the Chunichi Dragons, he naturally assumed he would feel right at home.

Unfortunately, Davis was too Buddhist for his teammates. He faithfully pulled out his beads and chanted before every game, which annoyed the other Dragons immeasurably. "It gave the others the feeling they were at a Buddhist funeral," said the manager, Wally Yonamine. Davis played beautifully, but the team's *wa*—the Japanese ideal of unity—was out of whack. After Davis, who was batting .306 with 25 homers that season, broke his wrist, the Dragons immediately went on a winning streak. When the season ended, they traded him away.

On the day he turned forty-five, becoming eligible for his major league pension, George Brunet of Aguila de Veracruz in the Mexican League pitched a three-hitter to defeat Leon 3-0. After the game, the ballclub threw a surprise party for *El Viejo,* the Old Man. Brunet, genuinely touched, blew out the candles and with a tear in his eye, said, "Muchas gracias. Nadie nunca a hecho esto para mi"—nobody had ever done that for him. After 28 years in professional baseball, 30 different uniforms, and 4,719 innings, George Brunet was finally honored.

Brunet was a baseball mercenary with a strong left arm who had begun his career in 1953 in Class D, in Shelby, N.C. He first reached the majors in 1956, with Kansas City. The first batter he faced was Ted Williams, who hit into a double play. "The next day Williams comes over to me before the game and says, 'Kid, if you keep that fastball down, you've got a long career ahead of you.' "

Alas, most of that career was spent in the minors. Although Brunet was one of the better left-handers in the American League from 1965 to 1968, his career won-lost record in the majors was only 69-93. He wasn't much for staying in shape, and he had a few problems with management. But the most amazing thing about Brunet's career was that he never wore a protective cup or anything else under his uniform pants. "Getting out of the way of ground balls up the middle has cost me a few singles over the years," he said.

As part of a cultural exchange program in the early '80s, some Japanese minor leaguers were sent to Miami to play Class A ball. Pitcher Masahito Watanabe knew very little English when he arrived, but he began picking up the language in bits and pieces. Whenever he spotted an attractive woman in the stands, he would say, "Oooh, looking sweet!" When asked what other English phrases he had learned, he once replied, "Muy bien."

But Watanabe outdid himself when he was sitting in the

dugout next to the water cooler and the home-plate umpire came over for a drink. "How's it going?" the umpire asked, making small talk. "Kiss my black ass," said the smiling Watanabe.

THE BIRD

In June of 1976, a Detroit Tigers rookie named Mark Fidrych pitched a one-hitter on national television. In the process he charmed a nation with his enthusiasm, his Harpo-like hair, and his habit of talking to the baseball before he threw it. He became known as The Bird because he resembled Big Bird on Sesame Street (a pitcher named Doug Bird consequently became known as The Fidrych). Opposing teams would spread bird seed on the mound. One Royal went to the plate talking to his bat. At the height of Fidrych's popularity, his home was jammed with bird mascots of every description. As Ron Fimrite wrote, "They peer out at him from every cranny of the small apartment, monsters his celebrity has created. Nevermore. Nevermore."

Fidrych was the AL Rookie of the Year that season, winning 19 games and leading major league starting pitchers in ERA at 2.34. In the off-season, Tiger owner John Fetzer took him to the baseball meetings in Los Angeles to show him off. "He wanted to educate me. So all I see there is guys, and all they're doin' is talkin' about baseball. Baseball. Baseball. Night and day. That ain't for me . . . Me, I just wanna goof around. But these guys are askin' me, what d'ya think of this and that? Hey, I say, I don't know. I'm just playin'. I've met Elton John and the Beach Boys. That was a thrill to me. Out in L.A. I got to meet Cary Grant, Monty Hall, Don Rickles, and Frank Sinatra. That's more for my folks. I mean, what am I supposed to say to Frank Sinatra: 'Hi, there, Old Blue Eyes'?"

He didn't really talk to the ball, Fidrych explained. "What I'm really doing is talking out loud to myself, not the ball. I'll tell myself to bring my arm down, things like that. Haven't you ever talked to yourself walking down the street?" The Bird was really just Fid, a good-natured townie from Northboro,

Mass., who had celebrated the spring training news that he was going north with the Tigers by making love to a girl-friend on the pitcher's mound in Lakeland.

"I don't like this Bird thing at all," said his mother. "Markie's not a bird. He's a human being. He's my only son." He also was not long in the limelight. Knee and arm troubles limited Fidrych to just ten more major league victories over the next three seasons, and he ended his baseball career as a minor leaguer in the Red Sox farm system.

PETE ROSE AND THE REDS

It's doubtful anybody ever played the game with more zest and zeal than Pete Rose. "Charlie Hustle" was a force from the very first time he ran down to first base on a walk in his rookie season of 1963 to the night be broke Ty Cobb's record of 4,191 hits in August of 1985. He won three batting titles and retired with a lifetime average of .303, but more than that, he led the Cincinnati Reds into the World Series four times, the Philadelphia Phillies twice. He played in the All-Star Game at five different positions: second base, right field, left field, third base, and first base. Once when his young daughter Fawn asked his then-manager Sparky Anderson why her daddy didn't have a summer vacation like all the other daddies, Sparky replied, "Because I need him, dear."

Rose would go on to win three batting titles, lead six teams into the World Series, and play in more games (and get more hits) than anyone in history. "Pete Rose," Anderson once said, "is the best thing to happen to the game since, well, the game." Rose lived and breathed baseball, and not only could he recite each and every one of his own statistics, but he knew the strike zones of every umpire, the tendencies of every pitcher, the length of every blade of infield grass.

As for his looks—well, Dave Parker once said, "If I had his head, I'd make a butcher-block coffee table out of it." When Rose heard that, he said, "Your face would look old, too, if you'd been sliding on it for 23 years."

In 1979, when he was thirty-eight, Rose was asked if he thought he could match Cobb's record of 4,191 hits. He shook his head no. But he hit .331 that year, helped the Phillies to a world championship in 1980, and batted .325 at the age of 40. Sensing that he was nearing Cobb, he named his infant son Tyler, and he started asking the Reds' ancient broadcaster Waite Hoyt all about Cobb.

Just before Rose set the hit record in 1985, a reporter asked him, "Do you think Ty Cobb is up there looking down at you as you chase the record?"

Rose replied, "From what I know about the guy, he may not be up there. He may be down there."

Johnny Bench may have been the finest catcher who ever lived. He revolutionized the position by catching with one hand. He had a rifle arm and a remarkable ability to control the pace and tenor of a game. He could also hit 45 homers a year. After his first full season, the twenty-one-year-old Bench approached Ted Williams in spring training with a baseball in his hand. "Would you please autograph this for me, sir?" Bench asked deferentially. And Williams did, inscribing it, "To a Hall of Famer, for sure."

Bench was as confident as he was talented. When he was a rookie, he was catching a journeyman pitcher named Jerry Arrigo. "He thought he had a fastball," Bench recalled. "He was pitching against a hitter I knew he couldn't possibly throw it by. I called for a curve, and he shook it off, a curve again and he shook it off, a curve one more time and he shook it off. He finally threw a fastball outside." Bench displayed his disdain by reaching out and catching the ball barehanded.

THE '75 SERIES

The 1975 World Series between the Reds and the Red Sox was one of the most memorable ever, and the best of the contests was the sixth game, in which the Red Sox prevailed in 12 innings to tie the Series at three games apiece. Boston took the early lead in the game on Fred Lynn's three-run homer, but the Reds tied it up in the fifth, an inning in which Lynn, chasing a shot by Ken Griffey, crashed into the center-field wall with a thump audible at home plate.

The Reds took a 6-3 lead in the eighth, but in the bottom of the inning, Lynn singled, Rico Petrocelli walked, and pinch-hitter Bernie Carbo, a part-time hairdresser and full-time flake, hit a game-tying home run. The Red Sox might have won the game in the ninth, but Denny Doyle tried to score from third on a short fly ball hit to George Foster in left. "I was yelling, 'No! No!' " said third-base coach Don Zimmer. "I thought he was saying 'Go! Go!' " said Doyle. In any case, Doyle was thrown out, and the game went into extra innings. At one point, Pete Rose came to the plate and said to Boston catcher Carlton Fisk, "This is some kind of game."

The Red Sox loaded the bases in the tenth with no outs, but failed to score. In the top of the eleventh, with a man on, Cincinnati's Joe Morgan hit a ball deep to right field, but Dwight Evans speared it just before it went into the seats, turned around, and threw the ball in to double the runner off first—thus turning a two-run homer into a double play.

Finally, in the bottom of the twelfth, Fisk hit Pat Darcy's second pitch into the night toward the left-field foul pole. The videotape of Fisk urging the ball fair with body english became the most repeated baseball image of the era.

The next night, the Red Sox took a 3-0 lead, but the Reds came back to win 4-3 on Morgan's two-out single in the ninth. Still the game was an anticlimax; the sixth game couldn't possibly be topped.

Bill Lee, who started the seventh game of the '75 Series, won 17 games three times for the Red Sox, a pretty good record for a lefthander in Fenway Park. But his popularity in Boston was based on more than pitching. The "Spaceman" was a free spirit whose espousal of everyone from the mystic philosopher Gurdjieff to the crazed songwriter Warren Zevon, and everything from marijuana to beer, endeared him to the hip-liberal population in Boston and Cambridge. He called his manager, Don Zimmer, a "gerbil," said the owners of his team, Haywood Sullivan and Buddy LeRoux, were "gutless," and described Boston hero and American League president Joe Cronin as an "idiot." The Oakland A's championship clubs of 1972, '73, and '74, said Lee, "are emotionally mediocre. They remind me of Gates Brown lying on a rug." Cincinnati's Big Red Machine "is about the third-best team in fundamentals I've ever seen—behind the Taiwan Little Leaguers and the USC NCAA champions of 1968." The California Angels "couldn't break a chandelier if they held batting practice in a hotel lobby." And the New York Yankees were "a bunch of vagabonds with bad wheels" who were "a fine sociological study of human frailties." Another time, he described the Yankees as "a bunch of hookers swinging their purses."

Lee was always retiring from baseball, usually when the Red Sox, or later the Expos, would trade one of his pals. When Bernie Carbo, a kindred spirit who would buy an extra plane ticket so he could take his stuffed gorilla with him on road trips, was sold to the Indians, Lee walked out for a day and was fined $533. He asked management to make it $1,500 "so I could take another couple of days off."

Lee's peculiarities flowered early. In college at Southern California he justified his lateness for a doubleheader by explaining that the early dew on the ground combined with the acorns in the outfield gave off an unpleasant odor. "I always understood everything Casey Stengel said," said USC coach Rod Dedeaux. "But I knew that all my hours with Casey helped prepare me for Bill Lee."

Lee pitched well in the '75 Series, and when he departed the seventh game in the sixth inning, the Red Sox had a 3-2 lead. But after the Reds won, Lee said "[Cincinnati pitcher Don] Gullett is going to the Hall of Fame, and I'm going to the Eliot Lounge"—a popular Boston bar.

MIKE SCHMIDT

Selected by the Phillies in the second round of the 1971 draft (behind pitcher Roy Thomas), Mike Schmidt started out as a bust, batting .211 as a shortstop in Double-A Reading. But after a fine triple-A year in 1972, where he was converted to a third baseman, Schmidt got a major league shot in '73. He proceeded to hit 18 home runs, but batted only .196 with an amazing 136 strikeouts in only 367 at bats.

Soon, though, Schmidt became the premier third baseman and the leading slugger in the National League, and probably the best third baseman ever. He led the league in homers eight times, won ten Gold Gloves, and joined Stan Musial and Roy Campanella as the only three-time MVPs in NL history. In 1974 he hit a ball that might have traveled 600 feet had it not hit a speaker descending from the ceiling of the Astrodome; it turned out to be the longest single in history. In 1976 he joined the tiny group of hitters with four homers in a game, performing the feat in an 18-16 win over the Cubs in ten innings. Schmidt maintained his place at the top of the game with a sense of pride bordering on arrogance, and a strong work ethic that gave him a physique like no other in baseball. Said Pete Rose, "Just to have his body, I'd trade mine and my wife's and throw in some cash."

As most sluggers do, Schmidt had a love/hate relationship with his team's fans—which is saying quite a lot, since Phillie fans mostly love to hate. Some time after the team lost the World Series to the Orioles in '83, Schmidt pulled up alongside a school bus to see if his daughter Jessica was on board. As he casually chatted with the bus driver, the kids on the bus began chanting, "Choke! Choke! Choke!" Said Schmidt, "That's your Philadelphia fan in the making." As for the vituperative Philadelphia sportswriters, Schmidt once said, "Philadelphia is the only city in the world where you can experience the thrill of victory and the agony of reading about it the next day."

But it was after the Phillies won their first World Series in 1980 that Schmidt uttered his best line. At a sports banquet in Wilmington, Del., Phillies owner Ruly Carpenter rhetorically asked the audience. "What can I say about Mike Schmidt after his being named MVP for both the National League and the World Series?" Whereupon Schmidt shouted from his seat, "Renegotiate!"

TOM SEAVER'S LAST HURRAHS

In June of 1977 the Mets did the unthinkable and traded Tom Seaver to Cincinnati. Seaver was embroiled in a contract dispute with Chairman of the Board M. Donald Grant, and the issue for Seaver was not so much money as it was loyalty. "Tom wanted to live and die at the Mets' stadium," said his wife, Nancy. But when columnist Dick Young, who fed the feud at the behest of Mets management, dragged Nancy into the fray, Seaver literally ran to a phone, screaming into it at a Mets official, "That's it! Get me outta here!"

And all the Mets got for him were pitcher Pat Zachry, infielder Doug Flynn, and outfielders Dan Norman and Steve Henderson. It was a disastrous trade from almost every standpoint, and it began a long depression for the Mets. Seaver pitched a three-hit shutout in his first game as a Red, and he went 14-3 for Cincinnati that season. "Everybody knew it would happen," said Mets catcher Jerry Grote. "But even then it floored the hell out of us. It was like knowing that an elderly person is going to die, but when it finally happens, you're still surprised."

Seaver returned to the Mets for the '83 season, but then they let him go again, when he was left unprotected before the major league draft and was grabbed by the Chicago White Sox. So he ended up winning his 300th game at Yankee Stadium for the White Sox in 1985.

In that game, he demonstrated yet again that he was a thinking man's pitcher. Actually, he had been thinking about the game for days beforehand. "I knew I wanted to keep [Rickey] Henderson off base and [Dave] Winfield and [Don] Mattingly in the ballpark, and somewhere in there I knew Winfield would be coming up as the tying run or winning run in the last three innings. And sure enough, Winfield came up in the eighth with runners on first and third and two out." The White Sox were leading 4-1 at the time. "What I wanted to do was get the count to 3-2 and use Winfield's aggressiveness against him." Seaver did work the count to 3-2. Then he came to a stretch position, looked toward first base, and stepped off the rubber. "I'm sure people were thinking, 'Why would he be concerned with the runner at first?' I was priming the pump. I was getting [Winfield] anxious." Seaver threw a changeup, and Winfield, way out in front, struck out.

THE BRONX ZOO

While the Mets were in their decline, the Yankees returned to their imperial status under the ownership of George Steinbrenner III, a shipbuilder from Cleveland. When Steinbrenner purchased the club on January 3, 1973, from CBS for $10 million, he said that he would be an absentee, silent owner.

He turned out instead to be a meddling, boorish buffoon who thought money could buy not only championships, but loyalty. His most foolish moment came during the 1981 New York–Los Angeles World Series, in the so-called "elevator incident." Here is the basic version that Steinbrenner gave reporters: At 8 o'clock that night, he left his suite on the 11th floor to meet his wife and some Yankee offficials for dinner. He got on an empty elevator and pressed the button for the lobby. On the way down, the elevator stopped, the doors opened, and in came two drunken young men in their twenties. One of them had a Dodgers cap on and was holding a beer bottle.

"Steinbrenner, right?" said one of them.

"Yes," said George.

"You're going back to the fucking animals in New York, and you're taking your choke-ass ballplayers with you," said the man.

"Go fuck yourself," said George.

Then one of his elevator companions swung at Steinbrenner with a beer bottle, whereupon George dispatched both young men with two rights and a left. They fled and vanished before George could report them.

Naturally, the story was subject to some doubt. Why hadn't anyone seen this incident? A caller to a Los Angeles radio talk show claimed to have been one of the men in the elevator and said that although it was true he and his friend had traded

obscenities with Steinbrenner, what had actually happened
was that the Yankees owner had punched the elevator door
in anger, and they had punched him. Even Edward Bennett
Williams, the lawyer who owned the Orioles, had to wonder.
"If the fight really took place the way George says it did, this
is the first time a millionaire has ever hit someone and not
been sued."

Three days after Steinbrenner's phantom adventure in the
elevator, the Dodgers won the series—and Steinbrenner issued a public apology for his team's play. By then, no lapse in
judgment, taste, or wisdom was beyond Steinbrenner, and his
players came to resent him a great deal. During one of his
more frantic periods, when he was flying from city to city to
inspect his troops on the road, one Yankee said hopefully, "The
more we lose, the more often Steinbrenner will fly in. And the
more he flies in, the better chance there is of a plane crash-
ing."

Steinbrenner's most annoying habit, of course, became the
perpetual hiring and firing of Billy Martin as his manager.
At least Martin's first axing, which began with a missed bunt,
made for good theatre.

Once upon a time, Martin was a pretty good manager. He
took his beloved Yankees to the World Series in 1976 and
1977, winning the latter on Reggie Jackson's three homers in
the sixth game against the Dodgers. But the two men with
the Hall of Fame egos were in a constant state of combat
readiness, and in July of 1978, Martin began resting the
slumping Jackson against left-handers. The Yankees were also
slumping. In extra innings one night against the Royals, Martin gave Jackson the bunt sign with Thurman Munson on first
and no outs. Jackson missed the bunt, and Martin gave him
the hit sign. But Jackson squared around once again, and fouled
the pitch. This time, third base coach Dick Howser delivered
the message personally: Hit away. Disobeying orders, Jackson
again attempted a sacrifice, and struck out. The Yankees ended
up losing the game. Martin, who was understandably furious,
suspended Jackson for five days. The player sniped back at

his manager through reporters, and his every word infuriated Martin. Then Martin found out that Steinbrenner had talked to the White Sox about trading managers, Martin for Bob Lemon. At Chicago's O'Hare Airport, Martin told reporters that Reggie and George deserved each other. "One's a born liar, and the other's convicted," he said, referring to Steinbrenner's 1974 guilty plea for illegal campaign contributions.

Martin was fired and replaced by Lemon, who had just been dismissed by the White Sox. A few days later Billy reappeared at the Yankees' Old-Timers Game, where a new Steinbrenner fetish first became clear with the announcement that Martin would again manage the team in 1980. He would return (and be fired again) three more times in all, at various times engaging in fights with bar-room denizens, his own players, and (most famously) a traveling marshmallow salesman.

With Lemon at the helm in 1978, the Yankees made a ferocious charge at the pennant, coming from 14 games back to overtake the Red Sox with two weeks to go. The Red Sox trailed the Yankees by a game going into the last day of the season, but when Luis Tiant beat the Blue Jays 5-0 and the Indians beat the Yankees 9-2, the pennant came down to a playoff game in Boston. The Red Sox took a 2-0 lead early on, but in the seventh inning Mike Torrez of the Red Sox gave up a three-run homer to little Bucky Dent, a shot that landed in the netting above the left-field wall. The Yankees went on to win 5-4.

Dent had borrowed the bat of teammate Mickey Rivers to hit that home run, and years later Rivers announced that the bat had been corked. It was a characteristic Rivers assertion—he was a true original who moved to the beat of an entirely different orchestra. He played much dumber than he was, and spoke in a language all his own. He called most everyone "Gozzlehead," except when he called them "Mailbox-head" or "Warplehead." His philosophy of life, he once explained, was: "Ain't no sense in worrying about things you got control over, 'cause if you got control over them, ain't no sense worrying. And there ain't no sense worrying about things you got no control over, 'cause if you got no control over them, ain't no sense in worrying about them."

Rivers liked to play the horses too much. He was always asking the Yankees for salary advances and in 1977 threatened to sit out the last game of the American League playoffs unless the club came up with some dough. He also liked women too much. He brought both his wives on the road with him once, and when they discovered each other, they had a nasty fight.

But the Yankees liked having Rivers around. Even George Steinbrenner liked him. "He's just a sweet kid," the owner once said. "You know, when he played for us, a lot of times I'd come into my office at the Stadium in the afternoon, and he'd come in and visit. He'd just sit there, across the desk from me. I'd ask him 'any problems?' and almost always, he'd say, 'no problems, no complaints,' and he'd just sit there." Such was Rivers's demeanor that his teammate Graig Nettles called him "The Chancellor"—because, Nettles explained, Rivers was the one person he knew who was "least likely to be chancellor of anything."

In his last season—with Texas, in 1984—Rivers hit .300 and then all but disappeared. When he surfaced a few years later, he was a professional bingo player, and called himself Miguel Rivera.

Thurman Munson, who died in the crash of his private airplane in August of 1979, was a great catcher, a pretty good hitter, and a team leader. He was also something of a mule, as this story told by former Yankees PR man Marty Appel attests:

Munson did not like being compared with Boston's handsomer, more stately catcher, Carlton Fisk. One day Appel quite innocently listed in his press notes, AL ASSIST LEADERS, CATCHERS: FISK, Boston 27; MUNSON, New York 25. Players rarely read the press notes, but on this day, Munson did. "What's the idea of showing me up like this?" he demanded of Appel. "You think for one minute he's got a better arm than me? What a stupid statistic!"

Munson stormed off. Then, during the game, he dropped a third strike, recovered, and threw to first base to get the batter. The same thing happened in the next inning, and it began to dawn on Appel what Munson was doing. A short time later, Munson dropped another third strike, thereby passing Fisk as the league's leader in assists by catchers.

Reggie Jackson arrived in New York in the fall of '76, the recipient of a then-unprecedented five-year, $2.9 million contract. He had said if he played in New York he would have a candy bar named after him, and the "Reggie Bar" debuted soon after. During the spring of his first New York season, he wrote an article with Robert Ward of *Sport* magazine in which he said, among other things, "It all comes back to me. Maybe I should say me and Munson, but really he doesn't enter into it . . . Munson thinks he can be the straw that stirs the drink, but he can only stir it bad."

The interview naturally caused an uproar among the Yankees. Munson walked around the clubhouse, holding the magazine in his hand, saying, "Can you believe this? Can you believe this?" Fran Healy, the backup catcher, tried to calm Munson down by pointing that some of the quotes had likely been taken out of context. "For four pages?" said Munson.

Jackson became estranged from his new teammates because of the article, and then he and Martin nearly came to blows on national TV when the manager pulled Reggie out of a game in the middle of an inning for loafing. That summer Jackson nearly suffered a nervous breakdown. But eventually things blew over, and in the 1977 World Series Jackson indelibly became "Mr. October." In the sixth game of the Series, he tied Babe Ruth's record of three home runs in one World Series game, each one on a first pitch.

This was just the moment Jackson had long been waiting for, and he milked it beautifully. For hours after the game he entertained and enlightened battalions of newsmen while sipping champagne and exchanging congratulations with teammates. He partied long into the night, and the next day appeared on the *Today Show*, participated in the ticker-tape parade for the Yankees, shopped at Cartier's, picked up his Rolls, and read about himself in the newspapers. The next day, at his Fifth Avenue apartment, he hosted waves of friends and wellwishers. "To me I'm just another person," he said. "It confuses me when people get all hyped up over what I do."

The leading prankster among the Yankees was Sparky Lyle, a reliever who won the Cy Young Award in 1978 and gave Yankee Stadium its most famous modern nickname—"The Bronx Zoo" (it was the title of Lyle's book, published in 1979). One of his favorite practical jokes was inspired by a coffin which shortstop Fred Stanley had ordered so that he could make a bar out of it. The casket was delivered to the Yankee clubhouse, where it sat for a while. Bill Virdon was the manager at the time, and during a clubhouse meeting before a series against the Orioles, the door to the coffin creaked open. Lyle, wearing a surgical mask and sporting lamp back around his eyes, rose up and asked in his best Bela Lugosi imitation, "How do you pitch to Brooks Robinson?" Virdon then ordered that Lyle be tied down.

The peasants revolted against George III, which is what Red Smith called Steinbrenner, one May evening in 1982. On that night, Reggie Jackson, who had not been re-signed by the Yankees, returned to New York with the California Angels and hit a titanic homer off Ron Guidry. At first the fans began chanting, "Reg-gie, Reg-gie," but then they realized who had really beaten them, and they started chanting, "Steinbrenner sucks, Steinbrenner sucks." As the crowd left the ballpark, Steinbrenner had his second elevator incident. As Jackson told it, he was standing in the street-level lobby of the Yankees offices when the elevator doors opened. There was George. Their eyes met. George let the doors close without getting off the elevator. A few moments passed, and the doors opened once again. And again their eyes met. Just before the doors closed again, Jackson heard Steinbrenner mutter something about the elevator not working. Rather than embarrass him any more, Jackson simply left the lobby.

There is one story about Reggie Jackson in an elevator that is definitely not true but gained such wide popularity that it became part of his legend. According to the teller, two older women are visiting New York City, and when they get into the elevator at the Waldorf or the Plaza or an apartment house on Fifth Avenue, there is a black man with a big dog on a leash. The man says, "Lady, sit," whereupon the two matrons drop to the floor of the elevator. It turns out that the man is none other than Reggie Jackson addressing his dog; he chuckles at their reaction, and if the incident has happened in a hotel, later that night Reggie picks up their dinner tab with a note reading, "Thanks for the best laugh I've had in ten years—Reggie Jackson."

N. Brooks Clark of *Sports Illustrated* traced the story to an old episode of the *Bob Newhart Show,* in which a black man with a shaved head and dashiki comes into the reception area with his dog and says, "Sit, Whitey," at which point Jerry the dentist sits down on a desk. It never happened to Jackson. Besides, Reggie's own dog, a Golden Retriever, was named Miss October.

CHAWS

Chewing tobacco has always been as much part of baseball as the seventh-inning stretch. Images of the chipmunk-cheeked Nellie Fox or Harvey Kuenn are indelibly etched in the minds of most baseball fans. But Rocky Bridges was probably the inspiration for more chaw stories than any other player. Once when he was coaching third base for El Paso, one of his players, Ethan Blackaby, hit a home run. As Blackaby rounded third, Bridges, extending his hand in congratulations, pressed a wad of wet tobacco in Blackaby's hand. Blackaby, much to his credit, took the chaw in stride and passed it on to the next batter, Tom Egan, waiting to congratulate him at home. It was Egan who nearly fainted.

Among other legendary chewers was Johnny Sain. When Sain was pitching for the Boston Braves, he would reply to writers' questions in squirts. If he spit straight downward, it meant "Yes," and if he spit outward, it meant "No." But the most disgusting practitioner of all was a pitcher for the Phillies named John Boozer. "You have to have a strong stomach for this story," said catcher Clay Dalrymple. "Boozer used to go into the clubhouse and spit on the ceiling. When it dropped back down he would catch it in his mouth. He was a breed all of his own. He would try to turn guys' stomachs. He had no scruples. He was a beaut, and a real nice guy."

Former Reds, Brewers, and Braves manager Dave Bristol had this to say about tobacco: "Only trouble I ever had with chewing tobacco was that the orthodontist said my daughter was going to have to give it up because of her braces."

In the '70s, following the lead of Reggie Jackson, ballplayers began moving away from tobacco on toward sunflower seeds. Jackson once gave Roy Blount, Jr., instructions on how to chew the seeds properly. Wrote Blount:

"In the Yankee dressing room, Jackson indicates the bulge caused by a cache of 20 seeds in his right cheek. With his tongue—the same one that leads the majors in quotes—he selects a seed and slides it between his bicuspids. He opens his mouth, points to the chosen seed and says, "There!" Then he raises an index finger as a sign to pay close attention and deftly cracks—but does not yet demeat—the seed. He reopens his mouth, and now the seed is held firmly, but not too firmly, between his incisors. It's important, Jackson notes, to have the ends of the teardrop-shaped seed against the points of the teeth. His mouth closes. Inside, something deft is done. His mouth opens again. The shell is now halved and the nut is on the middle of his tongue. He clenches his teeth, spits out the shell and chews the meat."

But seeds are a bother to traditionalists such as Bridges. "We had an onslaught of those things the last few years," said Bridges in 1977. "Most of those dugouts looked like bird cages. I had a couple of players that I had to watch pretty carefully—I was afraid they were going to start moulting."

PHIL NIEKRO

One day in 1949 a coal miner in Lansing, Ohio, taught his ten-year-old son how to throw a knuckleball. Phil Niekro's knuckler would dance every summer for the next 38 years. From 1964 to 1983 he pitched for the Braves in Milwaukee and Atlanta, winning 268 games for them and conducting himself with great dignity. "When people ask me my greatest thrill in baseball," Dale Murphy once said, "I tell them, 'knowing Phil Niekro.' "

But after the '83 season, the Braves decided to let the forty-three-year-old Niekro go. He signed with the Yankees, and in February of '84, he headed south for spring training. "I've done it so many times," he said, "I could've put the truck on automatic pilot and it would've ended up in the parking lot of Municipal Stadium in West Palm. I was driving along, thinking maybe I'd stop by the Braves' clubhouse anyway, have a cup of coffee, say hello to some of the guys. Then I told myself, 'Hey, you don't work there anymore.' "

Niekro won 32 games for the Yankees over the next two seasons and another 18 in two years with the Indians, and he finished, aged forty-eight, with 318 career victories. The Braves brought him back for one last game, and now a statue of Niekro stands outside Atlanta-Fulton County Stadium.

GEORGE BRETT

As George Brett went, so went the Kansas City Royals. They came to prominence just as he did, and when he won his first batting title in 1976, the Royals won their first division title. That title was subject to some controversy because on the last day of the season Brett got three hits to edge teammate Hal McRae, and one of those hits was a flyball that fell in front of Minnesota outfielder Steve Brye. McRae, bitter over losing the title, accused Brye of letting the ball drop so that a white man could win. Brett and McRae later joked about it, but Brett said, "It took a lot of fun out of winning the title."

Four years later, Brett went after bigger fish: a season average of .400, accomplished last by Ted Williams in 1941. With two weeks to go in the season, after 400 official at bats, Brett was hitting precisely .400. But then he tailed off and ended up hitting .390, just five hits short of .400. It was the highest batting average by any third baseman since John McGraw. Brett drove in 118 runs in 117 games, the first time a player averaged more than an RBI a game since 1950, and his slugging percentage of .664 was the highest in the majors since Mickey Mantle's .687 in 1961. He also hit 24 homers while striking out only 22 times.

Brett was a batting disciple of Charlie Lau, a hitting instructor whose precepts included using the whole field, keeping the head down, rocking back before moving forward in the swing, and hitting through the ball. Brett would go over the litany of Lau instructions in the on-deck circle before every at bat. But more important than such rote was Brett's work ethic and love of the game—he would routinely show up at the ballpark at 2:30 for night games. And his competitive desire was forged in a family that also produced Ken Brett, an older brother who first made a name for himself pitching for the Red Sox in the '67 World Series.

Ken was the golden boy of the family, and although he never quite lived up to his potential, his three brothers suffered in comparison in the eyes of their father, Jack. When George was just starting out with the Royals, he phoned home, and his dad asked, "Get any hits today?" When George said no, his father started screaming at him on the phone, saying, "George, your brother's a pitcher and he's outhitting you." As it happened, Ken, pitching for the Pirates that day, had gotten a hit in the first game of a doubleheader and pinch-hit a triple in the second game. George hung up the phone, threw it against the wall, ripped it out of its mounting, then slugged a full-length mirror, shattering it. "Buck Martinez was my roommate then," said George later, "and poor Buck didn't know what to say."

Brett's infamous temper got the best of him on July 24, 1983. On that day he hit a two-run home run off Goose Gossage with two outs in the ninth to give the Royals a 5-4 lead over the Yankees. But Billy Martin complained that Brett had too much pine tar on the handle of his bat—the rules say it can't be more than 18 inches up the handle—and when umpire Tim McClelland found that Martin was right, he disallowed the homer. Brett flew into a wild rage. He and manager Dick Howser, coach Rocky Colavito, and pitcher Gaylord Perry, who had tried to hide the bat, were thrown out of the game, and the Yankees won 4-3.

But AL president Lee MacPhail overruled his umpires, saying that the homer stood and the game should be resumed; the rule was not on the books to prevent cheating, but merely to keep balls clean, and the umpires should simply have told Brett not to use the bat. So on August 18, an off-day for both teams, the Royals flew back to New York to resume the game with two outs in the top of the ninth. The Yankees fought MacPhail's edict in court, played the game under protest, and made an appeal play on Brett's homer. But the AL had affidavits from the original umpiring crew asserting that Brett had touched first, and the Yankees went down in order the last of the ninth before 1,245 curious fans and almost as many media representatives.

TWO IMPROBABLE MANAGERS

There are good managers and there are bad managers, and Maury Wills was a *bad* manager. As a player Wills had brought the stolen base back as an offensive weapon, and he'd fielded his shortstop position well, but he was a disaster running the Seattle Mariners in the early '80s. At the press conference announcing his hiring, Wills was asked who his center-fielder would be. "I wouldn't be a bit surprised if it was Leon Roberts," said Wills, who was more than a bit surprised when he was told that Roberts had been traded five weeks earlier.

During one game, Wills waved for the relief pitcher to come in even though he had nobody warming up. Another time he called Dave Edler into his office to tell the third baseman he was sending him down, but upon seeing catcher Brad Gulden walk by, Wills changed his mind and demoted Gulden.

The situation deteriorated so badly that the Mariners didn't care if they lost, figuring that each loss would speed Wills's departure. Said Edler, "Some players were sitting around after we beat Detroit, and one of them said, 'Hell, we screwed up. We won.'"

When he first took over the ownership of the Atlanta Braves, media mogul and yachtsman Ted Turner couldn't keep his hands off the club. On his very first night as owner, he went out to home plate to congratulate Ken Henderson on a homer. He would dance with the ball girls, and help them sweep the bases between innings. Once, after the Padres scored six runs in an inning, he grabbed the microphone and announced, "No-body is going to leave here a loser. If the Braves don't win tonight, I want you all here as my guests tomorrow. We're going to be in big league baseball for a long time, and one of these days we're gonna start beating hell out of those guys who've been beating hell out of us." Some 1,140 fans returned the next night to watch the Braves win 9-1.

Turner also went in big for promotions—bathtub races, mattress-stacking, ostrich races—all of which he participated in personally. When he discovered that most teams had their players' names on the backs of their uniforms, and the Braves did not, he ordered the names sewn on. Pitcher Andy Messersmith came to him with another idea, since his own last name was too big to fit properly on the uniform. Why not put nicknames on the back? So, for a time, the Braves wore such sobriquets as "Prof," "Heavy" and "Wimpy" over their numbers. Messersmith wore "Channel," not because it was his nickname, but because his number was 17. Thus did his uniform read "Channel 17", which happened to be the number of the Turner Broadcasting System's SuperStation.

One night in 1977, Turner decided to give his beleaguered manager, Dave Bristol, some time off. The Braves had lost 16 straight games. Bristol's replacement was Turner himself. Wearing number 27 and consulting with third-base coach Vern Benson, Turner led the Braves to a 2-1 defeat, extending the losing streak to 17. National League president Chub Feeney ordered him out of the dugout the next night, and the Braves finally won. Still, Turner appealed to Commissioner Bowie Kuhn, who sent a telegram: "Given Mr. Turner's lack of familiarity with the game operations, I do not think it is in the best interest of baseball for Mr. Turner to serve in the requested capacity." Turner quickly phoned the commissioner.

"How am I supposed to get the experience?" he asked.

"In the stands, like the other owners," said Kuhn. "Why can't you be like everybody else?"

"Because I'm in last place," said Turner.

Perhaps the best example of why Turner, who skippered *Courageous* to victory in the America's Cup, is called Captain Outrageous was his performance in front of the Commissioner after Turner tried to tamper with another team's player. Turner, who had probably just seen one of TBS's westerns, threw himself at Kuhn's feet with his speech:

"Give us a way out of this thing if you can as the guy who is supposed to be the Big Chief of Baseball. . . . I am like the little Indians out in the West. You hear about the Big Chief back in Washington, the Great White Father, who says, 'You've got to move off the reservation.' We kept moving the Indians back and back until they had to fight. A few of them had to fight. I do not want to fight. . . .

"Please go back to the Great White Father, soldier man, and tell him to please help us. I am very contrite. I am very humble. I am sorry. I would get down on the floor and let you jump up and down on me if it would help. I would let you hit me three times in the face without lifting a hand to protect myself. I would bend over and let you paddle my behind, hit me over the head with a Fresca bottle, something like that. Physical pain, I can stand."

Unmoved, Kuhn suspended Turner anyway. Not very contrite, Turner took the Commissioner to court, and under cross-examination, he told Kuhn's attorney, "Keep that up, and when this is over, you'll get a knuckle sandwich."

When Turner first took over the Braves, his front office people came to him with a problem. Their catching prospect, Dale

Murphy, had just converted to the Church of Jesus Christ of Latter-Day Saints, and he wanted to serve a two-year mission, as most Mormons do. Turner said he would call Murphy, but he was warned to be very careful because "the next Johnny Bench" was very serious about this. So Turner called Murphy in Portland, Ore., and said, "What's all this Mormon stuff? If you need to make converts, I'll let you work on me and my five kids."

Murphy turned out to be the stuff of John R. Tunis novels. After he won his first National League MVP award in '82, he went to the Instructional League to work on his hitting, and then won it again in '83. The only time he ever got a speeding ticket was when he was going 35 mph in a 25-mph zone because he was late to a speech before a church group. He might be late to the clubhouse before a game, but the manager would only know because Murphy left his fine money on the desk for him. But there was a point in his career when the Braves and Murphy thought he would never make it. As a catcher, he had developed a mental block about throwing the ball to second base. He would either hit the pitcher in the back or throw the ball over second into center field. But he was fast enough that the Braves decided to make him an outfielder—"to get me as far away from the plate as possible"—and he became the best center-fielder in the majors.

If Murphy had one weakness, it was his appetite. Not that he was fat, but he never met a doughnut he didn't like. Teammate Jerry Royster once said, "Dale will look at a menu and order everything on it but 'Thank you for dining with us.'"

THROWBACKS

Calvin Griffith was the last of the old-time owners, and certainly the last to earn a living from a baseball team. Adopted by Clark Griffith at the age of ten, he grew up around the Washington Senators and inherited most of his stepfather's penurious ways. Even though Calvin pledged in 1958 to keep the Senators in Washington "forever," he moved them to Minnesota in 1961. Shirley Povich of the *Washington Post* called the Capital's sense of loss "overwhelmingly small."

Calvin was always given to blundering statements, but he outdid himself in remarks he made to the Waseca, Minn., Lions Club in 1978. "I'll tell you why we came to Minnesota. It was when I found out you only had 15,000 blacks here. Black people don't go to ball games, but they'll fill up a rassling ring and put up such a chant it'll scare you to death . . . . We came here because you've got good, hard-working white people." At the banquet, Griffith also said his best player, Rod Carew, was a "damn fool" for signing a $170,000 contract when he was worth much more, and that catcher Butch Wynegar was having a bad year because he was too busy running around the bedroom with his new wife rather than running in the outfield. When the remarks were made public, a big advertiser on Twins broadcasts threatened to pull out; Carew said, "I'm not going to be another nigger on his plantation"; and Wynegar broke his finger punching a garbage can.

But Griffith knew his baseball, and he kept the Twins in contention with a never-ending string of prospects found by his able scouting department. He also could be generous. After Carew hit .388 and drove in 100 runs in 1977, Griffith gave him an extra $100,000. When 1965 American League MVP Zoilo Versalles ran into financial problems later in life, Griffith bailed him out. And he restored such veterans as Julio Becquer, Shorty Pleis, and Carroll Hardy to the roster after their careers were effectively over so they could qualify for pensions.

In 1988 a one-man play based on Griffith's life opened in Minneapolis. Calvin attended the premier, and as the curtain went up, a fat man was onstage, sleeping in a chair with a half-eaten hot dog in his hand and mustard all over his rumpled suit. Griffith turned to a companion and whispered with obvious pride, "That's me!"

A throwback of a different sort was Jimmie Reese, the Picasso of fungo hitting. Reese was a coach for the Angels who

hit 'em where they were well into his 70s. He was so adept
with a fungo bat that he could hit a flagpole 100 feet away on
the first swing. In the minors he even "pitched" batting practice with a fungo bat, and on a golf course he once shot an 82
for 18 holes using only his fungo bat and a putter. Reese's bat
was unlike other fungo bats; it was flat on one side so that he
could scoop up balls as fielders threw them back to him.

Reese, whose real name was James Herman Solomon, hit
.346 in a part-time role for the Yankees in 1930, but more
significantly, he was Babe Ruth's roommate that year. "He
had one of those unusual constitutions," said Reese, whose own
constitution was pretty unusual. "He could stay up all night
and still hit a ball 500 feet."

TWO FLAKES

Joaquin Andujar was a handful. Self-described as "one tough
Dominican," he once said, "My favorite word in English, and
I love this word, is 'youneverknow.'" Capable of winning 20
games a year, he was just as capable of spending most of the
season on the disabled list with a wide variety of ailments.
He lived in a house in the Dominican Republic that had 21
rocking chairs and a huge tin cutout in the ceiling because he
liked to go to bed hearing the sound of rain on the tin; it
reminded him of his childhood. Andujar was also a switch-
hitter unlike any which baseball had ever seen. He batted
right-handed against all southpaws, but also against right-
handers he did not know or trust—he didn't want to get hit
on his pitching arm. And if he needed to bunt, he would bat
righthanded.

Andujar came to center stage in the '82 World Series, pitching for the Cardinals against the Brewers. In the seventh inning of Game 3, he was coasting along on a two-hit shutout
when Ted Simmons hit a smash off his right knee. Andujar,
in deep pain, writhed on the ground, and his career flashed
before everybody's eyes. He had to be carried off the field, and
for the next few days he hobbled around on crutches. But, five

days later, he beat the Brewers again to clinch the Series for the Cards. This time he left in the seventh kicking and screaming in the embrace of umpire Lee Weyer and pitching coach Hub Kittle. It seemed that Jim Gantner, upset that Andujar had held his ground ball until the last instant before firing to first base, called him a hot dog. In a post-game press conference that was broadcast to the milling fans in Busch Stadium, Andujar said, "He tells me, 'You're a hot dog mother fucker.' I tell him, 'Fuck you, mother fucker. Fuck you. I'm going to kick your ass.' But we're friends. That's baseball. That's me. I don't take no guff from nobody."

As Gorman Thomas of the Brewers said, "Joaquin is missing all of the face cards."

Another Dominican pitcher, Pascual Perez, made a name for himself by getting lost. Perez, who had a habit of blowing on his forefinger as if it were a gun every time he struck out a hitter, was supposed to start a game for the Atlanta Braves in 1983. But he was unfamiliar with the Atlanta freeway system, so he kept going around and around the city until 7:10 p.m., when he pulled over for gas. He didn't even have a wallet with him, but, with minimal English and many gestures, he talked the attendant into giving him $10 worth of gas and directions. Perez didn't arrive at the stadium until the second inning of his scheduled start, so Phil Niekro pitched for him that night—and won.

STEVE GARVEY

Steve Garvey, who played first base for the Dodgers and Padres, was a Southern California icon; a junior high school in Lindsay, Calif., was even named after him. His father, Joe, had driven a bus for the Dodgers in spring training, and Steve was the team batboy for a while, so his career was storybook stuff from the start. A consistent .300 hitter with power, Garvey was the backbone of the Dodgers in the '70s and early '80s. He was also unerringly polite and cordial, and he never cussed an umpire. The angriest he ever got at an ump was in the first game of the '77 World Series, when Nestor Chylak called him out at the plate. Garvey thought that Chylak was out of position and couldn't possibly have seen Thurman Munson's tag. Garvey leapt up and screamed, "Oh, no, Nestor! That was an injustice."

Garvey was enormously popular with the media, the fans, the advertisers. He had married his college sweetheart, and for a while, Cyndy and Steve seemed to lead a Barbie and Ken existence. But his teammates often resented him; some thought he was insincere. Then his marriage broke up, and the Dodgers elected to let him become a free agent.

His baseball story did have a happy ending. Garvey signed with the Padres and led them to the NL championship in 1984, as the hero of their dramatic victories over the Cubs in Games 4 and 5 of the championship series. Afterward, on a plane flight from San Diego to Detroit for the start of the World Series, the inflight movie was *The Natural,* and at the climactic scene in which Robert Redford hit his big homer, Padres fans stood up and chanted, "Gar-vey, Gar-vey."

BALL DOCTORS

One of Garvey's occasional antagonists on the Dodgers was pitcher Don Sutton. After he and Garvey got into a fight in the clubhouse over a personal matter, Sutton commented, "I know you won't believe this. We had a slight disagreement. I couldn't convince Garvey that the Southeastern Conference is as good as the Big Ten."

Sutton was often accused of doctoring baseballs to his liking. Asked if it was true he used a "foreign substance," Sutton said, "Not true at all. Vaseline is manufactured right here in the United States of America." An umpire searching Sutton's person for incriminating evidence once came across this note in his glove: *You're getting warm but it is not there.*

The master of doctored baseballs, of course, was Gaylord Perry. Over a career which saw him win 314 games, Perry progressed from Slippery Elm throat lozenges, which produced a ready supply of saliva, to K-Y Jelly (for "greaseballs") to Pillsbury flour (which he mixed with rosin, to create a "puffball"). When Billy Martin was managing the Tigers, he once brought a bloodhound to the ballpark just to sniff out the Indians' ball bag before Perry pitched.

Occasionally, an amateur would try his hand at doctoring a baseball. On September 30, 1980, Rick Honeycutt of the Seattle Mariners, pitching against the Royals, was apprehended by umpire Bill Kunkel trying to scratch baseballs with a thumbtack hidden under a Band-Aid on the forefinger of his glove hand. "It was the third inning," Kunkel recalled. "I wasn't looking for anything in particular, but Willie Wilson had complained about some of the pitches. I saw the Band-Aid on his finger and asked him what happened. When I grabbed his hand I got stuck. I was shocked."

Honeycutt was just plain embarrassed. "I thought the thumbtack trick up all by myself. Pretty smart, huh? Look, I was desperate at that point in the season"—he was 10-17 after a 6-0 start. "I figured, 'What did I have to lose?' Well, as soon as I see Kunkel come out to the mound, I tried to get rid of the tack. But I had done too good a job of taping it on. I felt like I was being pulled over for speeding. All I wanted to do after that was plead my case. I wanted to tell everybody I was really sorry, that what I did was stupid and that I'd never do it again. I never wanted this to happen, I didn't know the consequences. Besides, I'd only scratched three balls that night, and none of them did anything."

For his crime, Honeycutt was expelled from the game, fined $250, and suspended for 10 days—the first pitcher since Nels Potter of the 1944 Browns to be suspended for cheating.

MORE FLAKES

In 1982 the Orioles employed a productive left-field platoon of John Lowenstein, Benny Ayala, and Gary Roenicke. The three men accounted for over 30 homers and 125 RBIs, and the first two of them also created more than their share of local legends.

Lowenstein, called Brother Lo, was an anthropology major in college who favored such pursuits as snake hunting and casino management. One night in 1980 he was trying to stretch a single into a double when a throw by first baseman Jeff Newman of the A's hit him in the head. Lowenstein lay motionless at second, as the trainer and team doctor ran out to examine him. Then Lowenstein was placed on a stretcher and carried off the field in front of a hushed Memorial Stadium crowd. As the stretcher neared the dugout, he rose to a sitting position and gave a two-fisted salute.

Ayala, for his part, was something of a Puerto Rican mystic. He said he sometimes thought about pitchers he would face three weeks in advance. A few Orioles were talking about a desert movie once when Ayala, who had shown no prior interest in the discussion, interrupted to ask, "What is the minimum number of men it takes to safely cross the Sahara Desert?" After a few moments of silence, Ayala answered his own question. "One hundred," he said.

Once, as Ayala was about to hit, Lowenstein asked him what he was looking for in the particular situation. "Something white," said Ayala, "coming through."

Dan Quisenberry, who learned his underhand delivery from Kent Tekulve of the Pirates, had a remarkable six-year run as the Royals' stopper, averaging 35 saves a year from 1980 to 1985, including back-to-back seasons of 45 and 44 saves. "The Australian" (as he was called, for pitching from "down under") had a delightful, off-the-wall sense of humor. "I have seen the future," he once said, "and it is much like the present. Only longer." He said his pitching success began when "They found a delivery in my flaw." In the bullpen, he would pass the time by playing teammate Renie Martin's protuberant teeth as if they were xylophone keys while Martin sang about the game in progress. When he first came up, he had only one pitch, a sinker, and when he finished a game, his catcher John Wathan would say, "Way to mix 'em up," and Quisenberry would say, "Way to call 'em."

The Quiz liked to confound reporters when they questioned him. After he gave up a game-winning pinch-hit to Angels rookie Daryl Sconiers, someone asked if that was the worst possible way to lose a game. He proceeded to rattle off 20 worse ways, including balking a runner all the way from first and an earthquake causing the center-fielder to miss the last out.

The following exchange between a writer and Quisenberry is transcribed verbatim:
Reporter: Did you know your records this year are actually better than they were last year?
Quisenberry: How do you know? I'm into classical this year instead of pop.
Reporter: Are you trying to disguise your knuckleball?
Quisenberry: No, actually I want to give it away. If the hitters know it's coming, I'm hoping they'll change the swings that got them to the big leagues.
Reporter: Did the weather affect your performance?
Quisenberry: Actually, I think my problem is that I haven't been clipping my toenails properly. The club is after me to change that.

There was a serious side to Quisenberry that came out in a story in *Sports Illustrated* which he himself finished up for the writer, just as he did baseball games. "It's not that easy anymore," he wrote. "I feel more guilty if things don't go right. I think about the starting pitcher and the fans and the owner and the general manager and the friends and relatives who are going to read the paper the next morning, and the guys who built the lead. Everybody expects me to close up shop nicely, and I feel guilty when I don't.

"I don't want to sound depressing, and I'm only talking about maybe 10% of the games I'm in that I don't do the job. It's just that I've come to expect a lot more out of myself. So when everything goes right, and I get the save, I'm the one who's saved."

Quisenberry concluded, "It's funny. The bullpen is a closed environment, but I get a sense of freedom there that I don't get in the dugout or the clubhouse. I guess I just like being locked in a closet, taking verbal abuse from a lot of hostile people."

When he was at the top of his pitching form, Quisenberry received a complicated contract from the Royals that was tied to real estate investments and valued at more than $2 million a year. But he fell into disfavor and subsequently disuse. Quisenberry casually asked Donald Fehr, the director of the Players' Association, if he had any recourse if the Royals refused to pitch him. "Well," said Fehr, "you could always buy them."

ONE-YEAR WONDERS

The winner of the 1980 American League Cy Young Award was a sometime poet, part-time restaurateur, and former Kent State batterymate of Thurman Munson named Steve Stone. Stone, who went 25-7 for the Orioles that year, won the award by using his curveball 60 percent of the time. "I knew it would ruin my arm," he said, "but one year of 25 and 7 is worth five of 15 and 15."

Ben Oglivie, a Brewers outfielder who hit 41 homers in 1980 to share the AL home-run title with Reggie Jackson, was a rather unusual player. Only one player as light as the 170-pound Oglivie, Mel Ott, had ever hit as many as 41 home runs before, but Oglivie took one of the most vicious cuts in the game. And the swing was preceded by a rhythmic bat waving that resembled a puppy wagging its tail.

Oglivie, raised in Panama, became enamored of books when he came to this country, and his quest for learning took him into some unusual areas. He studied philosophy at Wayne State when he played for Detroit, and he was probably the first home run champion since Lou Gehrig to carry around a volume of

Plutarch. Oglivie professed that his own favorite philosophers were Rousseau, Thoreau, and Bruce Lee, and he often quoted them.

In an interview with a writer once, Oglivie said, "One of the best quotes I know comes from Augustine. He said, 'The body manifests what the mind harbors.' " Ah yes, said the writer, St. Augustine.

"Actually," said Oglivie, "it was Jerry Augustine, our relief pitcher."

SUPER JOE

The 1980 American League rookie of the year was an out-fielder with the Indians named Joe Charbonneau. Cleveland beat writer Terry Pluto first encountered Charbonneau that spring and, said Pluto, "I thought I'd found Shoeless Joe from Hannibal, Mo.—you know, Joe Hardy from *Damn Yankees*." Pluto's first impression was remarkably accurate in at least one way—Charbonneau's career lasted about as long as Hardy's. After batting .289 with 23 homers and 87 RBIs for Cleveland in '80, Charbonneau played just 48 more games in the majors. It really seemed as if he had made his pact with the Devil.

But it was fun while it lasted. Charbonneau, the biggest thing to hit Cleveland since Rocky Colavito, inspired a song, a poster, and a book. His legend was filled with tales—some real—of his prodigious strength, his imperviousness to pain, and the wonderful things he could do with a beer bottle. A direct descendant of Toussaint Charbonneau, the guide for Lewis and Clark, Joe grew up on the wrong side of the tracks in Santa Clara, Calif. He earned money by boxing bare-knuckled in boxcars—$20 for winning, $10 for losing. He had his nose broken three times, and once he tried to fix it himself with a pair of pliers. Another time a doctor had to remove all the cartilage in his nose, which enabled Charbonneau to drink beer through his nose, either by direct pour or with strong sniffs through a straw.

Charbonneau was also stabbed a lot. After being knifed by a migrant farm worker, he closed the wound himself with fishing line. While in Mexico City for an exhibition game, Charbonneau was approached by a man who suddenly plunged his pen into Joe's left side; unfazed, Charbonneau merely wondered if the Bic could still write. While in the minors, he had a toothache but no money, so he cut around the tooth with a razor and pulled it out with a vise grip.

After his talents mysteriously disappeared, Charbonneau drifted through the minors. While playing for Buffalo, he landed a small part in the *The Natural,* which was the last the baseball world saw of him.

STRIKE BASEBALL

The 1981 strike season might have been a total washout but for the arrival of a rotund Dodgers lefthander named Fernando Valenzuela. He came from a small farm in Etchohuaquila, Mexico, and he was discovered quite by accident by scout Mike Brito, who had gone down to Mexico to take a look at a shortstop on the team Valenzuela was pitching against. While in the minors, Valenzuela was taught the *lanzamiento de tornillo,* or screwball, by another pitcher, Bobby Castillo, and it was that pitch that brought him to the majors in a hurry.

Valenzuela won his first 10 games and quickly became a nation-wide sensation. He was also wildly popular among Los Angeles's large Mexican population. Dodgers pitching coach Red Adams said, "My only worry is that somebody will decide Fernando should lose weight, and then he'll become the best-conditioned pitcher at Lodi this year." In the strike-shortened season, Valenzuela won 13 games and the Cy Young Award, as well as the Rookie of the Year award.

During the strike, major leaguers suddenly found themselves with time on their hands. Some of them did have skills to turn to. Texas pitcher George Medich became Dr. George Medich, making the rounds at John Peter Smith Hospital in

Fort Worth with other orthopedic residents. Richie Hebner of the Tigers helped his father dig graves in West Roxbury, Mass. ("Whenever I see Hebner," said Medich, "he'll say, 'If you ever screw up, keep me in mind.'") Cincinnati second baseman Ron Oester helped his wife run her day-care center for forty kids, Cardinals outfielder Tito Landrum did some modeling, Brewers second baseman Jim Gantner worked as a plumber, Mike Lum of the Chicago Cubs worked on his magic act, and Dave Stewart of the Dodgers earned $6 an hour in the storeroom of a hardware store.

PSYCHOLOGISTS

Jim Frey, who managed the Kansas City Royals and Chicago Cubs in the '80s, had a wonderful, almost Socratic, method of getting his point across. When the Cubs were playing the Mets once, Frey's ace reliever Lee Smith had to face pinch-hitter Rusty Staub in a crucial situation. Smith quickly fell behind 2-and-0, and the 5′9″ Frey trotted out to the mound to talk to the 6′6″ pitcher.

"Rusty Staub is at the plate," said Frey.

"Uh huh," said Smith.

"One of the best pinch-hitters this game has ever seen, right?" Smith nodded.

"Helluva hitter. He's .280 lifetime with close to 3,000 hits." Nod.

"You know what that means?" said Frey, sticking his finger in Smith's chest. "It means he's made 8,000 damn outs. So just throw the damn ball over the damn plate."

Which Smith did, and Staub struck out.

Steve Boros was fired as the manager of the Oakland A's in 1984, in part because he supposedly wasn't "tough enough." But John Garrity, a writer for *Sports Illustrated,* knew differently. Six years before, Garrity had watched Boros during an ordinary batting practice with the Kansas City Royals, for whom Boros was a coach. "He just stood up the third-base line, hitting infield grounders but watching the cage, too," wrote Garrity. "Whitey Herzog, the manager, had ordered the Royals to practice their bunting, which had been poor. Every player who stepped into the cage dropped two bunts—one down each baseline—to a teammate standing a few yards away. Every player, that is, before Amos Otis. . . ."

Otis, the Kansas City center-fielder, didn't want to bunt, for some reason. He waved away the player waiting to field his bunts and started swinging away at pitches. Boros intervened. He stepped inside the third-base line, 10 feet from the plate, and put his bat on the dirt at his feet as a target for Otis. "Come on, Otis, regulars got to do it, too," said Boros. Otis ignored him, and when the pitch came, he lashed a line drive to right field. "Jesus!" said someone behind the cage. But Boros did not flinch. He calmly picked up the bat and put it down in front of the plate. This time Boros bent over, hands on knees, head up.

"Get out of the way," Otis said.

"Throw it!" Boros called to the mound, still staring at Otis.

"Throw the ball," Otis yelled to the young pitcher.

"Throw it!" Boros repeated.

So the pitcher threw it. The ball whistled past Boros's left ear, and to the alarm of everyone watching, Otis swung. The ball rocketed up, bouncing off the overhead rail of the cage. Boros didn't even blink.

First baseman Pete LaCock pleaded with Otis to bunt. Someone ran into the clubhouse to find Herzog. "Throw it!" Boros shouted once again. Otis took his stance, drew back his bat, and . . . laid a perfect bunt down at Boros's feet. As observers breathed sighs of relief, Boros took up the same position along the first base line. Otis dropped down another perfect bunt.

"How's that, Steve?" Otis asked.

"They'll do," said Boros.

The next day, with Boros throwing BP, Otis laid the first pitch down the third-base line and the second down the first-base line. Boros did not gloat; he just continued to throw.

ERROR OF THE CENTURY

The sixth game of the 1986 World Series between the Mets and the Red Sox will go down as one of the most exciting ever, although it really was a badly played game, with both managers, John McNamara of the Sox and Davey Johnson of the Mets, making poor strategic decisions. McNamara was particularly criticized for 1) not sending the right-handed-hitting Don Baylor up to pinch-hit for the lefty-swinging Bill Buckner against Jesse Orosco with two outs and the bases loaded in the eighth inning and the Red Sox holding a 3-2 lead; and 2) not replacing the hobbling Buckner with a defensive substitute late in the game. Actually, McNamara was all set to take Buckner out of the game, but the veteran first baseman talked him out of it.

The game went into extra innings, but in the top of the tenth, the Red Sox scored twice, on a solo homer by Dave Henderson, a double by Wade Boggs, and a single by Marty Barrett. In the bottom of the inning, trying to protect a 5-3 lead, Boston's Calvin Schiraldi retired the first two Mets in order. In the Boston clubhouse, the champagne was laid out for the Red Sox's first world championship in 68 years. An NBC crew set up a platform as announcer Bob Costas, commissioner Peter Ueberroth, and Red Sox owners Haywood Sullivan and Jean Yawkey were placed in position. Keith Hernandez, who had made the second out for New York, went back into the clubhouse and grabbed a beer. His teammate, Kevin Mitchell, was already on the phone, his pants off, making plane reservations back to his home in San Diego. Writers furiously typed their historic leads.

But then Gary Carter singled to left. Called upon to pinch-hit, Mitchell pulled on his pants—he had nothing on underneath them—went out onto the field, and lined a single himself. Ray Knight singled, scoring Carter and sending Mitchell to third. McNamara brought Bob Stanley in to face Mookie Wilson. It was a magnificent at-bat. With the count at 2-and-2, Wilson fouled off two superb pitches. Then Stanley threw an inside pitch that catcher Rich Gedman couldn't handle, and the ball rolled to the screen as Mitchell scored to tie the game, Knight proceeding to second. With eerie efficiency, the platform was removed from the Boston clubhouse, and Costas, Ueberroth, Sullivan, Yawkey, and the champagne were all whisked away. Finally, on the tenth pitch of his at-bat, Wilson topped a ground ball toward first base. Buckner, playing deep behind the bag, reached down to snare the ball . . . and it went through his legs. Knight scored, and the Mets won 6-5.

The Mets also won Game 7, of course, and Red Sox fans had yet another patch for their perennial hair shirt. What the rest of the nation had was a joke that was still circulating twelve months later: What do Michael Jackson and Bill Buckner have in common? They both wear a glove on one hand for no apparent reason.

ENVOI

As baseball prepared to enter the last decade of the twentieth century, it was vastly different from what it once had been. In many places plastic turf had replaced real grass, polyester had replaced flannel, and a more conventional character type had by and large supplanted the rough-and-ready, outside-the-mainstream sort who had seemed to embody the game just half a century earlier.

There were far more button-down personalities than there were Paul Waners or Pepper Martins, Babe Hermans or Leo Durochers. Players were better educated, more articulate, mindful of public relations and off-the-field responsibilities.

But there was no reason to think that the game's color would fade entirely. Three closing stories illustrate the reasons why:

First, there was the persistence of improbability, of the game's incredible ability to present something new on the fan's every visit to the ballpark. Take the September, 1986, game in which Bob Brenly, playing third base for the Giants, made four errors in the fourth inning, allowing four runs to score.

Then, in the fifth, Brenly hit a solo home run. In the seventh he singled in two more runs. And in the bottom of the ninth, he hit a game-winning homer. Said his manager, Roger Craig, "This man deserves the Comeback Player of the Year for this game alone."

Second, there was the rich irony that inevitably flourishes wherever people pursue the same task day after day. Take the reaction of Oakland catcher Ron Hassey on meeting pitcher Todd Burns during the 1987 season. Burns has been called up from the minors to the A's on short notice, and only a few hours after he arrived he found himself pitching in a crucial situation. Hassey, his catcher, approached the mound. Ah, thought Burns, he's coming out to give me some encouragement; Hassey, however, had something else in mind.

"Who," asked Hassey, "are you?"

And finally, baseball retained its special character because of those blessedly rare individuals who somehow found their way into the game's embrace. Who better to take as our final character than Yogi Berra, in the late '80s still a coach with Houston? One day he climbed into the whirlpool in the Astros' clubhouse, and yelped in mock pain. "What's the matter?" the trainer asked. "Is the water too hot?"

"I don't know," Berra replied. "How hot is it supposed to be?"

INDEX